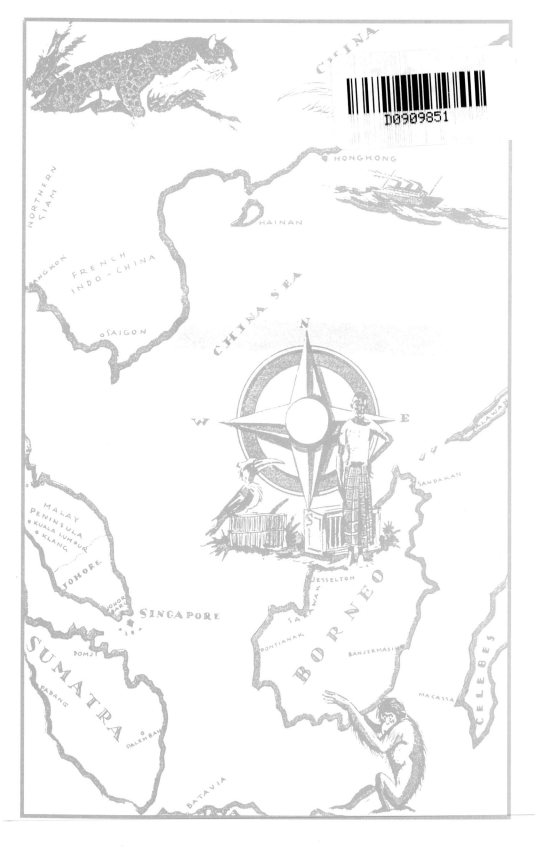

BRING 'EM BACK ALIVE

BRING 'EM

BACK ALIVE

The Best of
Frank Buck

Introduced and Edited by Steven Lehrer

Texas Tech University Press

This book was set in New Century Schoolbook and Letter Gothic. The paper used in this book meets the minimum requirements of ANSI/NISO Z39.48-1992 (R1997).∞

Unless otherwise specified, all photos belong to the Buck family private collection and are provided courtesy of Barbara Buck.

Design by Tamara Kruciak

Printed in the United States of America

Library of Congress Cataloging-in-Publication Data
  Buck, Frank, 1884–1950.
      Bring 'em back alive: the best of Frank Buck / introduced
  and edited by Steven Lehrer.
          p. cm.
      ISBN 0-89672-430-1 (cloth : alk. paper)
          1. Wild animal collecting. 2. Animal behavior. I. Lehrer, Steven,
      1944–   II. title.

  QL61 .B782000
  591.5—dc21
                                        99-086898

00 01 02 03 04 05 06 07 08 / 9 8 7 6 5 4 3 2

Texas Tech University Press
Box 41037
Lubbock, Texas 79409-1037 USA

800-832-4042

ttup@ttu.edu

Http://www.ttup.ttu.edu

CONTENTS

Chapters I–XI are from *Bring 'Em Back Alive* (1930); chapters XII– XIX are from *Wild Cargo* (1932). Chapter II contains an excerpt from *Fang and Claw* (1935). Chapter XVII contains an excerpt from *All in a Lifetime* (1941). Chapters XVII and XIX contain excerpts from *Animals Are Like That!* (1940).

INTRODUCTION

In 1930, the publication of *Bring 'Em Back Alive,* an instant best-seller, made its author, Frank Buck, an international celebrity. The stories of animal behavior told by this intrepid animal collector and jungle adventurer enraptured generations of readers.

Bring 'Em Back Alive "is vivid and lively, and the book can be recommended to anybody who likes being made to sit on the edge of his chair and gasp for breath as his eyes eat up the print to see what happens next," wrote the *New York Times Book Review* in 1930.

Although attitudes toward animals have changed, a good deal of the writing in *Bring 'Em Back Alive* is still timely and of considerable interest to a modern reader. Where else, for example, can one find out how a tiger becomes a man-eater or how to catch and tame a wild elephant? Frank Buck learned these lessons and more over a long and spectacular career.

Early Years

Frank Howard Buck was born in Gainesville, Texas, on March 17, 1884. As a child he was fascinated by all kinds of animals and by his school geography books filled with the exotic names of far-off places.

The young Frank Buck was an inveterate collector and trapper of small animals, birds, and snakes. He relates in his autobiography, *All in a Lifetime*, the story of his mother finding him with a poisonous snake:

She came into the barn one day when I was experimentally holding by the neck a two-foot copperhead that I had caught alive very neatly with a forked stick. Having heard of the deeds of the snake charmers of India I was attempting to extract the poison fangs of my copperhead with father's pliers, which I had borrowed from his tool chest. Mother took one look at the snake, then cried:

"Frank! Hold onto it! . . . Now drop it!"

I was so startled by her sudden appearance that I obeyed her orders. On her second command the snake slithered to the barn floor. My mild little mother, fear and fury in her eyes, snatched up a pitchfork. And she dispatched that copperhead as efficiently as if she had been killing reptiles all her life.

With the snake dead, I thought she might faint. She didn't. Instead she advanced on me, told me to "turn over," and fear gone with the copperhead dead, she used what remained of her fury on my well-padded behind.

"And never again let me see you with a snake!" she cried.

Buck quit school after the seventh grade with an acute case of wanderlust. He worked at a series of jobs, notably as a cowpuncher on a Chicago-bound train. In Chicago, he fell in with an unsavory character named Al Romero. In Sedalia, Missouri, Frank Buck suddenly got wise:

One black night I found myself in the basement of a Sedalia hardware store, Al with a bottle of "soup" (nitroglycerin) in his pocket, a steel drill in his hand, and an old-fashioned iron safe before us in the light of matches, which I constantly lit and held. The whole picture was just a little too much. I realized this was not the place for me. The lighted match in my fingers suddenly showed nothing but Al's tight, hard face, his knotted hands clasping the drill, and the black, forbidding front of the safe.

"Al," I said suddenly, "I'm getting out of this."

He stared at me, his eyes narrow and cold.

"What do you mean?" he asked.

"I'm quitting, right here and now."

The match went out and I couldn't see him very well, only his gray shadow in the almost-dark of the basement.

I heard a faint tinkle of glass on the cement floor, and I realized he had put down the bottle of soup. In the next instant he was at me, the steel drill flailing in his hands. I ducked, heard it whir above my head, then closed with him. I think he had expected to knock me out with the heavy drill. He certainly hadn't expected the short, stiff punches I clouted to his middle. I heard his "Ouff-ouff" with each one of them, and I heard the drill clatter to the floor.

Then I saw his cigar-cutter's knife. Gray as a streak of dawn it flickered in that dim cellar and I leaped away from its straight-edged blade.

We were both afraid of the bottle of soup, which was invisible on the dark floor. A hefty kick from our shuffling feet would have set it off, and it would have blown us through the cellar wall of the building. But that flashing knife was even more terrifying to me. My heart was so high in my throat that Al surely would have missed it had he stabbed me in the chest.

I let go at him with a long baseball slide. It took me under the knife. I hit Al, and Al hit the floor. In an instant I was on top of him with both fists swinging. They were good, hard Texas fists, and after a second or two Al didn't move any longer.

Frank Buck returned to Chicago, was bitten by the show business bug, and worked as a "music man," selling songs to vaudeville singers for a local music publisher. Meanwhile, he persuaded a down-and-out preacher to teach him to read and write. In return he kept the whiskey-soaked parson in booze for a year and a half. Buck was, by then, a craggy-looking, medium-sized, rawboned young man who loved a good fight so much that, in his own words, he enjoyed even the swollen eyes, sore noses, and scraped knuckles that came along with barroom brawling.

At age seventeen, while working as a bellboy at the Virginia Hotel in Chicago, Buck married a forty-one-year-old Chicago *Daily News* drama critic, Amy Leslie (pen name of Lillie West Brown [1860–1939]).[1] But for Frank Buck, the lure of the jungle was stronger than the lure of domestic life; in 1916 he and Amy Leslie were divorced.

The Animal Collector

In 1911, Buck won $4,500 in a poker game and headed for Brazil to buy exotic birds, which he sold for a profit in New York. Hooked on the animal business, he decamped for the jungles of India, Borneo, Sumatra, and the Philippines. The first large animal he caught was a twenty-eight-foot python, which he lassoed, just as he had steers in his native Texas.

The First World War gave Buck his golden opportunity. Before the war, a single German company, Hagenbeck,[2] controlled the jungle animal business. German consuls in the smallest ports of Asia and Africa had been Hagenbeck agents on the side. From the natives these consuls had bought up mammals, birds, and reptiles, which Hagenbeck distributed to American and European zoos. But the war hurt Hagenbeck, which could operate only in the neutral Dutch territories. The Germans quickly lost their African colonies, and the British naval blockade prevented Hagenbeck animals from reaching Europe. A few got to America on German ships, but as American public opinion turned increasingly against Germany, Hagenbeck was shut out, whereas Buck's business grew exponentially.

Buck spent the rest of his life capturing alive every species of animal, from birds to snakes to elephants. There being no tranquilizer darts in those days, he learned to build traps and snares in ways that prevented injury to the animals when he caught them. He housed his growing menagerie in his compound at Singapore and periodically shipped the animals to the United States and finally throughout the world.

Buck always accompanied his animals on shipboard trips to America to be sure they were well treated. And he refused to sell to anyone who did not have an impeccable reputation for giving their animals the best possible care.

By the early 1920s, Frank Buck was the worldwide king of wild animal suppliers. So eminent in his profession was he that in 1922 he received an order to create an entire zoo for the city of Dallas.

In 1928, a fierce typhoon killed almost every animal that Buck had aboard a ship bound for San Francisco, costing him a small fortune in lost revenue. When the storm-damaged ship arrived in San Francisco, Buck discovered that all his life savings had been wiped out in a "secure" investment he had made on the East Coast.

Undaunted as ever, Buck fell in love with a girl named Muriel Reilly, married her, borrowed $6,000 from some friends, headed back to the jungles of the Far East and Africa, and in two years had turned the $6,000 into a $110,000 profit.

Frank Buck's Books

An author friend, war correspondent Frank Gibbons, persuaded Buck to write a book about his experiences. This book, *Bring 'Em Back Alive* (1930), was followed by seven others. Three writers collaborated with Buck on these books.

Bring 'Em Back Alive and a second book, *Wild Cargo* (1932), were written with Edward Anthony, an eminent figure in New York literary circles. Of the three coauthors, Anthony was most talented at imparting immediacy and freshness to Buck's narrative. Anthony wrote the stories in a modest, matter-of-fact, all-in-a-day's-work fashion; yet almost every one has its own breath-catching spice of danger. With his knack for eliciting telling details, Anthony created a real sense of drama, and as a result, Frank Buck's first two books are his best.

In 1933, Anthony filed suit in Brooklyn Supreme Court to recover two percent of the motion picture profits that Buck had earned on the adaptation of *Bring 'Em Back Alive*, effectively ending their collaboration.

Anthony wrote or cowrote many other books, among them *The Big Cage* with the wild animal trainer Clyde Beatty. He also served as publisher of two magazines, *Woman's Home Companion* (1942–52) and *Collier's* (1949–54). Edward Anthony died August 17, 1971, age seventy-six.

Ferrin Fraser, a radio and short story writer, was coauthor of five books with Frank Buck: *Fang and Claw* (1935); a novel, *Tim Thompson in the Jungle* (1935); *On Jungle Trails* (1937), for many years a sixth-grade reader in the Texas public schools; Buck's autobiography, *All in a Lifetime* (1941); and a lavishly illustrated children's book, *Jungle Animals* (1945). Fraser also wrote scripts for the *Little Orphan Annie, Lights Out,* and *Nick Carter* radio series. Ferrin Fraser died April 1, 1969, age sixty-five.

Carol Weld, a journalist, was coauthor of *Animals Are Like That!* (1940), Buck's sixth book. Ms. Weld had worked as a foreign correspondent for news organizations in Paris, including the United Press. She had also been on the local staffs of the old *New York American* and *New York Herald*. Carol Weld died March 31, 1979, age sixty-five.

Similarities with Stories in Kipling's *Jungle Books*

"Both the substance and the dramatic unfolding of Mr. Buck's stories suggest comparison with the early work of Mr. Kipling," wrote the London *Times* literary supplement in a 1935 review of *Fang and Claw*. Indeed, it is interesting to compare *Bring 'Em Back Alive* to *The Jungle Books* of Rudyard Kipling. Kipling was writing only a few years before Buck about the same animals in the same place.

Born in Bombay, India, Kipling (1865–1936) was brought up by *ayahs* (native nurses), who taught him Hindustani and the folklore that continued to haunt his imagination. In 1907 he won the Nobel Prize for literature.

Though much of Kipling's work glorifying the British Empire and the white man's burden is not widely read today, *The Jungle Books* (1894 and 1895) are enduring favorites. Kipling, of course, did not invent the animal fable in *The Jungle Books*. He was preceded by Aesop, Jean de la Fontaine, and the *Uncle Remus* stories of Joel Chandler Harris, which Kipling particularly admired.

In some stories in *The Jungle Books,* Kipling follows the older mode of Aesop by treating the animal in question as a disguised human. In others, Kipling actually assumes the persona of his animal protagonist, as in *Rikki-tikki-tavi,* the story of a mongoose who saves an English family from two evil cobras, Nag and his wife Nagaina. In the introduction to Book I of *The Jungle Books,* Kipling attributes his knowledge of snakes to "one of the leading herpetologists of Upper India," who apparently died of snake bite.

Kipling probably never got too close to most of the animals he portrays, other than during visits to the zoo, and he uses dialogue to establish animal characteristics. His animals speak with human voices, often in biblical cadences. We learn that Nag is dangerous when he addresses Rikki-tikki-tavi:

> "Who is Nag?" said he. "I am Nag. The great God Brahm put his mark upon all our people, when the first cobra spread his hood to keep the sun off Brahm as he slept. Look and be afraid!"

In *Bring 'Em Back Alive,* a cobra also confronts Frank Buck:

> I hesitated long enough to give the snake a chance to right itself. It reared its head three feet and spread its greenish brown hood. Then it saw me.

Instinctively I jumped backward. There wasn't far to go. Another four or five feet, and I'd hit the back of the shed. As I made my brief retreat the snake struck, missing my leg by only an inch or two.

I was trapped. I suffered more from plain ordinary fright at that moment, and I'm not ashamed to admit it, than at any time in all my career. Through my mind flashed a quick picture of what had happened to the Sakai [native] that this terrible reptile had bitten. It made me pretty sick.

I flattened myself against the back of the shed, grimly eyeing the killer that lay almost at my feet. The expressionless eyes calmly looking back at me gave me a cold and clammy feeling. I didn't want to die this way. It was not my notion of a decent death. Surely there must be some way out. Desperately I ran my eyes around for something to bring down over the enemy's head. I wasn't particular. Anything would do, anything that could be converted into a club, a stick of wood, a . . .

The cobra was poising itself for a second strike. The hideous head rose slightly and stretched forward a bit. I got the impression of a calculating foe gauging its distance before launching another attack . . .

In *The Jungle Books,* when the villainous tiger Shere Khan wants to devour Mowgli the man's cub, protected by Father Wolf and Mother Wolf, dialogue establishes Shere Khan's character:

"The wolves are a free people," said Father Wolf. "They take orders from the head of the pack, and not from any striped cattle-killer. The man's cub is ours—to kill if we choose."

"Ye choose and ye do not choose! What talk is this of choosing? By the bull that I killed, am I to stand nosing into your dog's den for my fair dues? It is I, Shere Khan, who speak!"

The tiger's roar filled the cave with thunder. Mother Wolf shook herself clear of the cubs and sprang forward, her eyes, like two green moons in the darkness, facing the blazing eyes of Shere Khan . . .

In *Bring 'Em Back Alive,* Frank Buck sees the mutilated body of an unlucky native, mute witness to a tiger's lust for human flesh:

When we arrived we found a group of excited natives standing around the mangled remains. One leg had been eaten off to the thigh. The animal had also consumed the better part of one shoulder and, to give the job an added touch of thoroughness, had gouged deeply into the back of the neck.

Buck finally confronts the tiger, which he has trapped in a deep pit:

> Stretching out on my stomach, I took a look at the prisoner below, withdrawing without the loss of much time when the animal, an enormous creature, made a terrific lunge upward, missing my face with his paw by not more than a foot.

When Buck and his native helpers are able to raise the vicious animal from the pit with ropes in a driving rainstorm, the tiger's appearance is frightening:

> After working in this fashion for an hour till my shoulder ached from the awkward position I was in, I succeeded in looping a noose over the animal's head and through his mouth, using a fairly dry fresh rope that responded when I gave it a quick jerk. The noose accomplished my purpose, which was to draw the corners of his mouth inward so that his lips were stretched taut over his teeth, making it impossible for him to bite through the rope without biting through his lips. I yelled to the coolies who were standing by ready for action to tug away at the rope, which they did, pulling the crouching animal's head and forequarters clear of the bottom of the pit. This was the first good look at the foe I had had. The eyes hit me the hardest. Small for the enormous head, they glared an implacable hatred.

In *The Jungle Books* the image of an unnatural situation, the child Mowgli raised by Father Wolf and Mother Wolf, is an old one in literature, dating back at least to Romulus and Remus and the founding of Rome. But serpents, in stories since *Genesis,* have not usually been portrayed sympathetically. Thus Kipling's huge rock python, Kaa, the teacher and protector of Mowgli, is a surprising formulation, especially when he allows Mowgli to use him as a chair:

> That afternoon Mowgli was sitting in the circle of Kaa's great coils, fingering the flaked and broken old skin that lay all looped and twisted among the rocks just as Kaa had left it. Kaa had very courteously packed himself under Mowgli's broad bare shoulders, so that the boy was really resting in a living arm-chair.

The interaction of a python in the wild with a human being is frequently somewhat different. In *All in a Lifetime*, Buck describes how he caught his first python with Ali, his native assistant:

> We followed the trail for perhaps fifty yards. Then we saw the snake. It was in deep grass near a large durian tree, and my heart came up in my throat as I saw its size. It was far bigger than any of the five pythons I had bought. It looked as big around as a sewer pipe to me, and its eyes, small as they were, seemed as large as saucers as it glared at me. As a matter of fact, this python measured twenty-eight feet, which is considerable for a snake.
>
> Along the trail Ali had cut a long, thin stick. With this he touched the huge reptile's tail. The python reared around instantly, thrashing in the grass, and with its head raised charged us like a bolt of shining lightning. I dodged the charge and dropped the noose of my Texas lasso over the head and a foot or two along the gleaming throat. In dodging, I leaped for the nearby durian tree. It was lucky I did. The tree trunk made a perfect snub for the rope, and with Ali shouting directions at me it was an easy matter to lash the huge reptile's head fast to the tree by merely running in wide circles about it and letting the rope do the rest. When I had finished my exercise I had a well-bound head of a python against a tree.

Of course, there is no way to truly compare the charming animal fables in *The Jungle Books* with the realistic descriptions of the same animals in *Bring 'Em Back Alive*. Nevertheless, the child who has read Kipling might like to turn to Frank Buck to learn how jungle animals really behave.

Frank Buck's Use of Malay

Frank Buck spent much of his life in regions of the Far East where Malay is spoken, and by his own account he heard many Malay dialects. In all of his books, he uses Malay words and phrases.

The Malay language, a member of the Western or Indonesian branch of the Austronesian (Malayo-Polynesian) language family, is the native language of more than thirteen million persons distributed over the Malay Peninsula, Sumatra, Borneo, and the numerous smaller islands of the area. It is widely spoken in Malaysia and Indonesia as a second language.

Of the various dialects of Malay, the most important is that of the southern Malay Peninsula. This dialect is the basis of standard Malay and the official language of the Republic of Indonesia. A Malay pidgin called Bazaar Malay (*melayu pasar,* "market Malay") was widely spoken as a *lingua franca* in the East Indian archipelago during Frank Buck's time and was the basis of the colonial language used in Indonesia by the Dutch.

Modern Malay is written in two slightly differing forms of the Latin alphabet, one used in Indonesia and one in Malaysia, as well as in a form of the Arabic alphabet called *Jawi,* which is used in Malaya and in parts of Sumatra.

Of his command of Malay, Frank Buck writes in *Bring 'Em Back Alive,* "while I speak the language with difficulty, I have a sufficient knowledge of it to be able to understand the average conversation." But he probably did not read or study Malay. Thus when writing Malay in his books he simply sounded out the words as best he could, and he made frequent errors. A review of *Tim Thompson in the Jungle* in the London *Times* literary supplement (1935) noted: "Young readers may pick up some useful lessons in tracking and forest craft; but they are to be warned against the authors' very odd Malay."

In this edition of *Bring 'Em Back Alive,* all Malay has been emended to conform to modern, standard Indonesian usage.

Movies, Radio, and Later Life

Shortly after writing his first book, Buck arranged with RKO to make a movie of *Bring 'Em Back Alive.* In 1931, he traveled to the Far East with a movie crew and shot 125,000 feet of spectacular film. When released in 1932, the film version of *Bring 'Em Back Alive* was a blockbuster. A total of 82,660 persons saw *Bring 'Em Back Alive* during its first seven days, reported New York's Mayfair Theater—6,300 over the attendance mark for the first week of *Frankenstein,* which held the previous record for the theater.[3]

In 1934, Buck opened a wild animal exhibit, called Frank Buck's Jungle Camp, at the Chicago World's Fair. Over two million people thronged through the exhibit, and when the fair closed Buck moved the entire exhibit to a holding camp at Amityville, Long Island. For years afterward, people continued to visit Frank Buck's Jungle Camp.

Buck's popularity and fame were awesome. He replaced Amos and Andy with his own radio program during the famous duo's first vacation in five years.[4] With his pleasant tenor voice, inflected with only a hint of Texas, he was the most in-demand guest on every radio show in the United States, and for good reason.

The 1920s and 1930s were a period when Americans idolized heroes. Charles Lindbergh, Admiral Richard Byrd, Babe Ruth, Jack Dempsey, and Red Grange were celebrities. Frank Buck was a member of this illustrious group. A stocky, powerfully built man, Buck was incredibly brave, constantly exposing himself to the possibility of being mauled by a tiger or a leopard, bitten by a deadly snake, or stomped to death by an angry elephant. Yet he maintained that he was just as scared as anyone else might be in such situations.

Ringling Brothers, Barnum & Bailey made Buck such a lucrative offer that he ended up touring with the circus as its featured attraction, astride an elephant. But there were labor problems.

As the *New York Post* reported (May 5, 1938):

> Frank Buck today insisted that when he rides an elephant around the arenas of the Ringling Brothers Barnum & Bailey Circus, he is a scientist, not an actor. This was his reply to threats of new labor troubles for the big show unless Buck, chaperon for its star attraction, Gargantua the gorilla, joins the American Federation of Actors. The union insisted that all performers in the show, by terms of a contract with the management, must join the union. There was talk of a strike when the circus opened in Brooklyn, unless Buck joined. Buck said he might compromise on his principles and join the union if the circus actually faced a strike, but such an act would be against his wishes. Buck also said he had every sympathy for the common worker, yet he described many of them as sweepers, shovelers, and performers of other mundane functions for the comfort of elephants.
>
> "I've worked many years to get to my present position of a scientist, and that's all the work I perform in the circus," Buck said. What has riding an elephant around the ring to do with science? he was asked. "Well, that's how I got to be a scientist—riding an elephant. Don't get me wrong. I'm with the working man. I worked like a dog once myself. And my heart is with the fellow who works. But I don't want some—union delegate telling me when to get on and off an elephant. John Ringling North [head of the circus] has told me that his contract with the union does not compel me to join this union."

Threat of a strike was finally averted when the American Federation of Actors gave Buck a special dispensation to introduce Gargantua the gorilla without joining the union.[5]

After this victory, Buck couldn't resist an offer to put another wild animal exhibit in the New York Word's Fair in 1940. And he wore his jungle pith helmet practically everywhere. The helmet and the phrase "Bring 'Em Back Alive" became the symbols of his fame.

Wild Cargo[6] and *Fang and Claw*[7] were made into movies, starring, of course, Frank Buck. These were followed by another movie, *Jungle Cavalcade*,[8] a compilation of footage from the first three films; and a serial released by Columbia Pictures, *Jungle Menace*.[9] In 1949, Buck appeared as himself in the Abbott and Costello feature, *Africa Screams*. He was also the model for the jungle film director Carl Denham (played by Robert Armstrong), who brings Fay Wray to Skull Island in *King Kong*.

In his later films, Buck tried to avoid his early mistakes. In a famous sequence in *Bring 'Em Back Alive*, a tiger and a python lock in mortal combat. But after considerable intercutting, the two combatants simply walk (or slither) away from one another, leading some viewers to suspect that the outcome had been rigged. One wag suggested that the tiger had not torn the python to pieces because he had left his false teeth at home. Thus when Buck subsequently filmed a battle between a black leopard and a python for *Wild Cargo* (described in the chapter "Coiled Lightning") the scene is continuous, with no intercutting, and the python finally crushes the leopard to death.

The Second World War brought a temporary end to Frank Buck's visits to the jungles of the Far East, but his enormous popularity kept him busy on the lecture circuit, and he filmed another movie, *Jacare*, in 1942.[10] After the war ended, he was back in the jungles. "Same old stuff—no radar, no nothing," he told *The New Yorker*. "You dig the same old-fashioned pits and use the same old-fashioned knives and come back with the same old-fashioned tigers."

Mortally ill, in 1949 he made one last trip to Singapore, recorded *Tiger,* a children's album,[11] and then returned to his native Texas. After a lifetime of dealing face to face with the world's deadliest animals, often coming within a hair's breadth of being killed or horribly maimed, Frank Buck died in bed of lung cancer, March 25, 1950, in Houston, age sixty-six.

Frank Buck and Wildlife Conservation

Frank Buck's efforts to capture and preserve the world's animals no doubt played a large part in making us aware of how important it is to conserve the vast treasure that is our native wildlife. His writing clearly reveals the respect, intrigue, fascination, and awe he had for all animal life. Though he transferred some of the world's wildlife from native habitats to zoos, thereby depleting populations in the wild, he placed these animals into environments in which they could breed and propagate without the threat of extinction. Thus Frank Buck was one of the first wildlife conservationists, at a time when conservation was a sadly neglected matter.

Most important of all, Buck abhorred the senseless slaughter of animals. As he tells us in the introduction to *On Jungle Trails*, "I am proud of the fact that in my whole career of dealing with wild creatures I have never willfully or unnecessarily harmed or injured a single one. I have made it my business to bring them back alive, for I have only feelings of kindness for every creature that breathes on this Earth."

A final word may be in order regarding the zoo animals that Frank Buck spent his life collecting. After all, should zoos even exist? Bruce Weber, a *New York Times* reporter, gained an interesting insight into this question during a two-day visit to the International Wildlife Conservation Park (also known as the Bronx Zoo):

> Once again I found myself thinking about animals in captivity, their instincts on hold. It's a complicated issue, and I'm an amateur at it, but still: Who belongs where? I thought about Maggie and Lucille [a dog and cat], their apparent contentment with apartment living, inanimate food, me. What do they think, really? Is this a good life?
>
> And then I encountered the lion. It was the frigid afternoon after Christmas, and I heard him from some distance away. I'd been scrutinizing the gelada baboons, trying to figure out why a young female had apparently been banished from the family cave; she was sitting, unhappily, it seemed, her back to her relatives, shivering a bit, her tufted facial hair blowing in the nippy wind. (I was probably overpsychoanalyzing; the flat rock she was crouching on turned out to be heated.) In any case the lion's roar, an aching bellow with the piercing resonance of the bass notes from my neighbor's stereo system, beckoned me.
>
> I was not alone; perhaps a dozen other people also gathered round, in interested, still silence. All, I guessed, felt isolated enough and

cowed enough by the furious beastliness to contemplate themselves in awe. Unfenced in, separated from us by a wall and a moat, the lion disappeared behind a rock, then returned to view, maybe 30 feet from where I stood.

He shook his maned head and growled almost silently. Then he turned away; with his back to me, he began bellowing again; they were bleats of a monumental nature, and I noticed that his haunches and the muscles around his ribs clenched with each one. These were gut-wrenching cries, not a bellyache or any other specific complaint, but—or so I imagined—a lament of existential proportions.

Maggie and Lucille do not do this, I thought. But it hit me: I do.

Notes

1. "Amy Leslie Is Married to Chief of Bellboys." New York *Morning Telegraph,* July 16, 1901.

2. Carl Hagenbeck (1844–1913) was an internationally known German animal dealer and trainer. He was famous for controlling animals by befriending them, rather than by using the beatings and hot irons then *de rigueur.* In his best-known animal act, three lions pulled him around a cage in a chariot.

3. *New York Times,* July 3, 1932.

4. New York *World Telegram,* June 4, 1934.

5. New York *World Telegram,* May 9, 1938.

6. "Though not as sanguinary as Mr. Buck's previous *Bring 'Em Back Alive,* it is every bit as entertaining and a shade more instructive." Thornton Delahanty, review of *Wild Cargo,* New York *Evening Post,* March 30, 1934.

7. "The thing which distinguishes Mr. Buck's animal pictures from many others is the suspense and excellent story telling quality sustained in his films from the first moment to the last . . . Since Mr. Buck is never cruel in capturing his prey, one's sympathy is always with him." Marguerite Tazelaar, review of *Fang and Claw,* New York *Herald Tribune,* December 27, 1935.

8. "This omnibus of Mr. Buck's thrilling jungle adventures is well worth seeing because it contains the best and most exciting scenes he obtained in faraway places." William Boehnel, review of *Jungle Cavalcade,* New York *World Telegram,* July 5, 1941.

9. "Kids will love *Jungle Menace* for its harum-scarum adventure and for the presence of Frank Buck, with his Wild Animals Associates, Inc. Frank Buck plays the hero, Frank Hardy, when gangdom invades the rubber business and river pirates grab off plantation cargo. Plenty of old-time names are in the cast: Reginald Denny is a plantation foreman, Esther Ralston an owner, Charlotte Henry and William Bakewell play young lovers; also featured are Clarence Muse, Willie Fung, Leroy Mason, Richard Tucker, and Duncan Renaldo." *Variety,* October 27, 1937. Each of the fifteen episodes of this serial was twenty minutes long and contained lots of action: "One man defying a thousand deaths in a green hell of creeping horror! The fearless Frank Buck in his most hair-raising role! Merciless killers . . . a beautiful hostage . . . a cargo of wild animals run loose when the typhoon strikes! Terrifying adventures torn out of the heart of cruelest Asia!"

10. "Frank Buck's new animal hunting picture, *Jacare,* now at the Globe, was filmed in the Amazon jungle with a Buck protégé, James Dannaldson . . . Dannaldson's movie making, as evidenced in *Jacare,* isn't up to his master's, but as you can judge from his thrilling battle with jacare [the Brazilian name for a man-eating caiman or alligator, sometimes twenty feet long], his courage and resourcefulness fully justified Buck's confidence. 'The meanest, toughest, most malignant animal alive in the jungle today,' says Frank Buck, the film's narrator." *PM New York,* December 27, 1942. Miklós Rózsa, who composed the scores for *Spellbound, Ben Hur,* and *El Cid,* also scored *Jacare.*

11. In *Tiger,* Frank Buck tells how an escaped tiger is recaptured. He made the recording several months before his death, and Columbia Records released it April 18, 1950.

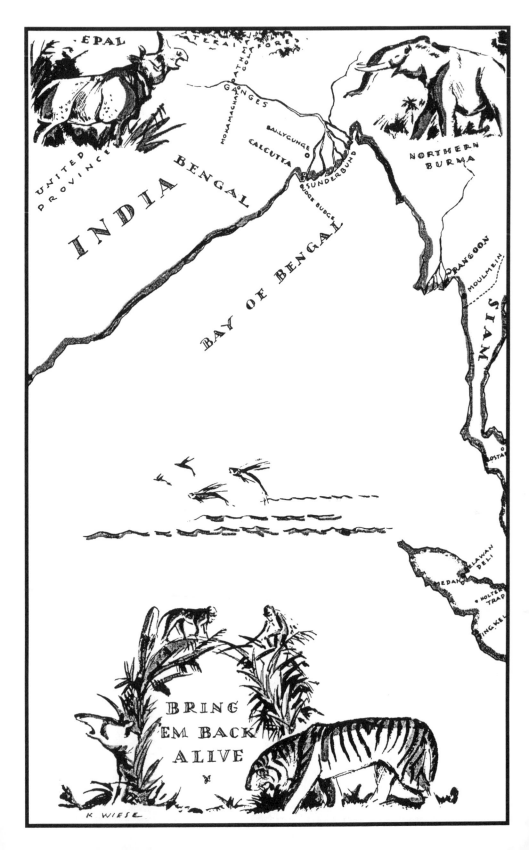

EPAL

TERAI FORES

GANGES

MOKAMAGHAT

CALCUTTA

BALLYGUNGE

SUNDERBUND

BUDGE BUDGE

UNITED PROVINCE

INDIA

BENGAL

NORTHERN BURMA

BAY OF BENGAL

RANGOON

MOULMEIN

SIAM

OSTA

ELAWAN

DELI

EDAN

MOLTER TRAP

ING.KEL

BRING
EM BACK
ALIVE

K WIESE

Life in the jungle is a free-for-all fight, no fouls recognized, and no weight limits. It is the greatest struggle in the world, the most stirring of all battles for existence.

Frank Buck

CHAPTER I

TAPIR ON A RAMPAGE

Almost any animal is dangerous when aroused. In 1926 I came close to being killed by a tapir, the meekest of animals.

I was in Sumatra assembling a group of specimens that included some pythons, Sumatra hornbills, langur monkeys, civet cats, porcupines, a siamang gibbon, and a tapir.

Normally it would have been safe to bet that the pythons would make more trouble for me than the rest of this collection put together. But this was not a normal situation. It was the tapir that won the Trouble Sweepstakes, breezing in with several lengths to spare.

The experience proved to me all over again how foolish it is to generalize about animals. I've seen two tigers, for instance, animals of the same sex and age and caught at the same time, display utterly different characteristics. One grew so tame that after a few weeks I was putting my hand inside its cage and stroking the back of its neck; the other became more and more vicious, until the process of feeding it involved real danger and required absolute caution.

It isn't much less intelligent to generalize about animals than it is to generalize about people. It's about as sensible to say, "elephants are kind," or "elephants are mean," or "tapirs can be trusted," or "tapirs can't be trusted," as it is to say flatly that all human beings are noble, or the opposite of that proposition. One finds almost as much variety in animal character as one does in human character.

Of course, there are certain basic things that are true of animals just as there are certain fundamentals that apply to most people, but this does not alter the fact that the minute a person starts generalizing about animals he displays his inexperience. Perhaps the nearest one can come to a generalization is to say that most animals are dangerous when they think they're in danger. And, after all, that is less a generalization about animals than it is a basic fact of life, involving human beings and the animal kingdom both.

The tiger that strikes at the person who is feeding him through the bars has decided that this person is an enemy with designs on his life; the gentler tiger has something in his makeup that resigns him to his captivity and tells him he has nothing to fear from the two-legged creature who is looking after him. Eventually the rougher specimen, when he discovers that his keeper is not someone he will one day have to fight for his life, tones down too and becomes manageable.

Of all the animals in the Malayan jungle the tapir is probably the least dangerous. He is much less formidable, for instance, than the wild boar, which has tusks that are capable of ripping open an unwary enemy in a fight.

The tapir in addition to having no tusks is also clawless. Each front foot has four hoof-like toes, each back foot three; and these are hardly weapons. He has huge powerful teeth, but since he is known to be a vegetarian these are feared by neither man nor beast. One is about as conscious of them as one is of the teeth, however capable, of the average horse, cow, or deer.

The tapir is a strange creature, in a class by itself. It is the only animal on Earth today that has come down the ages in its present form. Evolution has left it untouched. It was as it is today thousands and thousands of years ago when the camel was no bigger than a greyhound and the horse was a four-toed animal the size of a fox terrier. It has always been to my mind such a placid symbol of age and tradition, so perfect an embodiment of the quiet mellowness of the years, that I could have as easily imagined myself being suddenly attacked by the Sphinx as by a tapir.

I couldn't have given less thought to the troublesome possibilities of my specimen if he had been a jack rabbit. The only thing that made me at all conscious of him was the fact that he had a badly barked back.

He was a full-grown Malayan tapir, weighing about six hundred pounds. For the entire length of the back, along the spine, the skin of this animal was badly barked. He had walked into a trap that was a log-fenced enclosure with a gate that snapped to. (The inside of the trap and the approach to it had been baited with tapioca root, a favorite delicacy of the tapir tribe.) In his frantic efforts to escape he had plunged about blindly and succeeded in scraping whole patches of skin off his spine.

I had to do a job of healing on that back. I wanted to apply some ointment when I first noticed the animal's condition in Sumatra, but the conditions were not favorable there nor on the little Dutch boat on which I brought my collection back to Singapore.

On the outskirts of Singapore is the small town of Katong, where I maintained a compound. There I instructed Dahlam Ali, the Malay who served me on expeditions in and around the Malayan district (just as Lal Bahudar assisted me on collecting trips where a knowledge of Hindustani and Hindus was essential[†]) to build a small pen for the tapir. He and another man in my employ built one about twenty feet square. They drove posts into the ground and with two-by-four planks built an enclosure about five feet high, a height that the animal could not jump. When three sides were up I drove the animal in from his cramped native cage, and with Ali hastily nailed up the opening while the other man kept our captive cornered with a pole. Never had I seen a more harmless-looking tapir. It seemed as I regarded him that it had been wholly unnecessary to keep him cornered while we nailed him in. He was completely absorbed in the business of contorting himself so that he could scratch his irritated back, which was itching, against the planks of the enclosure.

No gate was made in the pen as this seemed unnecessary labor. The spaces between the planks (through which the animal was fed) provided a good foot-hold, and it was a simple matter to climb over. I did so, as casually as if I were entering a cow pasture. In my hand I carried a pound can of zinc ointment.

Ali was with the other man feeding a collection of birds that I had stored in a shelter two hundred feet away, a collection that included a cage of hill mynas. These are coal-black chattering birds with yellow wattles, some members of the species possessing the doubtful gift of gab even more prodigiously than parrots.

I scooped up a handful of the ointment, and, walking over to where this member of the animal kingdom's oldest family was

---

[†]   In *On Jungle Trails*, Frank Buck writes that Lal Bahudar, his wife, and their small children died tragically in a house fire.

scratching himself against a plank, slapped it over his back with as much detachment as if I were a bricklayer slapping some mortar on a brick. Bricks aren't very dangerous (unless heaved at one) and neither are tapirs . . . unless . . .

As I slapped that fistful of ointment over the tapir's spine he started running. I followed as best I could, with my hand over his back like a bareback rider preparing to leap aboard his charger. Suddenly the animal whirled around, dropped back a few feet and charged straight at me, burying his head in my stomach and knocking the wind out of me as his six hundred pounds sent me sprawling on my back. I had hardly hit the ground when the Meekest of Animals jumped on me, his front feet bearing down on my chest, his hind feet on the ground.

I started swinging over on one side in an effort to get up. This inspired the jungle's Prime Example of Humility to hoist his hind legs over my lower end, in the process dealing me a painful and weakening blow in a delicate region. It was a palpable foul, but as there was no referee present this pacifist proceeded to stomp up and down all over me, bruising me in a dozen places.

I didn't exactly enjoy what was happening to me, but neither did I become alarmed until the animal's six hundred pounds began to feel like a ton. It's hard to take a tapir seriously until something happens that forces you to do so. In all my previous dealings with the species it had lived up to its reputation for harmlessness, so it took me a few minutes to get it through my head that this tapir was more than nettled. The infuriated creature had murder in his heart.

It's hard to figure out what happened inside that animal's brain when I applied that first daub of ointment. The salve doubtless caused some irritation, but this hardly could have been enough to convince the beast that he was in the presence of an enemy.

The tapir had me painfully pinned down. I could feel his breath on my face. Not a sound came from him, except his heavy breathing. His eyes had a look that made my flesh creep. I had never seen such hate in a tapir's expression.

My first attempts to whirl around and free myself having failed, I poised myself for a desperate effort into which I put every ounce of strength I had. In swinging around I succeeded in partly freeing one shoulder, but accomplished nothing, for the enraged beast pounded me flat again, moving up a few inches closer to my head in the process.

And then I had a moment of horror. Opening his mouth, the animal bared his powerful teeth and reached to get hold of my face. It didn't take much computing to see that his awful mouth was capable of taking in the width of my head. Once he got my face between those jaws it would be an easy matter to pull the flesh off.

As I looked straight down the throat of this panting brute, I realized my danger, and the next thing I knew I was yelling—yelling for all I was worth. I'm not ashamed to admit it. I had no desire to have the meat ripped off my face by this vegetarian on a rampage.

With all the lung power I could summon, I fairly shrieked, "Ali! Ali!"—at the same time freeing one leg by a tremendous effort. As the animal strained forward, his teeth coming nearer and nearer, I got my right knee under his lower jaw, and reaching up, got hold of both his ears with my hands. He started furiously swinging his head right and left in an effort to shake me off, but I held on for dear life, my knee keeping his teeth and my face apart.

And then the creature started dragging me all over the enclosure, jumping off me to make it easier for him to take me for a ride. Every time I made an effort to get up he'd pound me flat against the turf with his front feet.

"Ali! Ali!" I yelled myself hoarse. Why didn't he come running over? Where was he? . . . And then I answered my own question. I had sent Ali to care for my birds. He was in the bird shelter, looking after them. . . . With a sudden vehemence, I found myself cursing my collection of hill mynas. These boisterous birds—all other birds seem quiet by comparison—were probably chattering away at such a rate that it was impossible for Ali to hear my cries.

I felt the power going out of my fingers, and in desperation I strove to tighten my hold on the crazed creature's ears. And, with one of those unnatural bursts of strength that come when destruction is staring one out of countenance, I stiffened my knee against the tapir's chin. With renewed fury he started dragging me all around the lot, adding new lacerations to my sore and battered body.

"Ali! Ali! Ali!" I put everything I had into this final cry.

I was beginning to wonder how long I could hang on. My back was aching as it had never ached in all my days, and my chest was sore from the pounding of those hoofs. I would have to scramble to my feet somehow and get over that fence. Having survived encounters with tigers and leopards I had no intention of being wiped out by a tapir.

My weakening fingers clutched the tapir's ears in a final frenzy of self-preservation. My knee, doing its best to seem a firm and determined knee, managed to maintain its wobbly intercession between me and the teeth of the four-legged lunatic that was trying to destroy me. Ali at last came running up, excitedly shouting, *"Apa ini, tuan? Apa ini?"* ["What is this, sir?"]

It wasn't necessary for me to answer Ali's question. Screaming for the other man to come over and help him, he grabbed a board, one of the pieces of lumber left over after the pen had been built, and started beating the animal over the head with it. The other man, who was at the far end of the compound, finally heard his screams and came tearing over.

This man had even more presence of mind than Ali, a real surprise to me, for over a period of years Ali had displayed more resourcefulness in emergencies than anyone I had ever employed anywhere in Asia. The newcomer grabbed a two-by-four scantling and shoved it into the open mouth of the would-be killer, the animal biting down on it. The surest way of saving my features was to put something besides my worn-out knee between me and those vicious teeth, and the scantling did the trick.

The animal, one piece of lumber between his teeth and another being brought down on his head, backed away a few paces. As he did, Ali reached through the fence and grabbed my arm, pulling me farther away from the maddened creature. At this point the other man jumped over the fence, and, while Ali beat the animal off with his board, lifted me to my feet. Almost falling against it in my weakened condition, I grabbed the top of the fence, putting one foot in an open space between the boards about a foot from the ground. Then this man who served as Ali's assistant—although in this stirring operation he was really the leader and Ali the assistant—gave me a boost, which, combined with my own efforts, sent me toppling over the fence onto the ground on the other side, where I landed in a limp heap. A mass of bruises, I lay there for half an hour before I could summon the strength to move.

When I stood up at last it was with the aid of Ali and the other Malay, who hustled me off to bed. The battering I had received left me black and blue from head to foot, and it was three days before I could get up.

The day after I was laid up for repairs, Ali, who was looking after me, sat beside the open window of my room chewing betel nut and using for his cuspidor that portion of Katong that lay beneath my window. Ali was hardly ever without a good gob of this Eastern equivalent for chewing tobacco, and he spat frequently. It seemed to help his thinking.

Ali was puzzled about that tapir. To him, as to me, the tapir was a perfect example of the peaceful attitude toward life. The normal role of the animal was running away from fights instead of getting into them.

Ali had more to say about tapirs that day than he usually has to say about everything in the course of a whole week. Under normal circumstances he did most of his talking through the medium of gestures—a shrug of the shoulders, a movement of the hand, a toss of the head. A few facial expressions rounded out his vocabulary.

Although he didn't bother selecting the right words, he spoke English understandably. But most of the time he was able to express himself without words.

Today, however, he needed words to unburden himself, words supplemented by a wrinkling up of his nose, his favorite method of expressing displeasure. Normally if I asked him what he thought, let us say, of some animal that I was thinking of taking off a trader's hands, he would wrinkle up his nose if he thought the creature a poor specimen. If he thought it a good buy, he would beam all over. No words.

That nose of his was as wrinkled as a prune as he started discussing the tapir. The animal had the devil in him, a whole tribe of devils. He spat vehemently to emphasize his point.

Ali seemed more picturesque to me than ever as he sat by the window speculating on how all those devils had got inside the tapir. He was dressed in an outfit that was standard for him unless he was at work on a dirty job. It consisted of an immaculate white starched *baju*, a shirt much like the top of a pajama jacket and worn over the *sarong* or skirt, which today was a red and blue affair, cut very full. On his head he wore a black velvet Mohammedan cap.

Ali wasn't in the habit of getting particularly excited about anything. His philosophy was the philosophy of *"Tidak apa?"* which in Malay means, "What does it matter?"

The soul of conscientiousness, he yet reserved the right to a resigned outlook. Things happened. That was life. Why examine anything too closely?

In considering the tapir that had tried to annihilate me, he made an exception to his *"Tidak apa?"* rule. It did matter. Tapirs had no business acting that way. One had enough problems in life with animals and people who were frankly one's enemies without having to face sudden attacks from what one had a right to regard as peaceful sources.

Over and over we discussed the whole race of tapirs, making many points, relevant and irrelevant.

The reader may be acquainted with the fact that tigers, leopards, and other carnivores regard the tapir as a very choice dish. The tapir, needless to say, is familiar with his popularity in these quarters as a table delicacy; and he uses every resource at his command to keep out of the way of his enemies. Nature has come to his assistance in making it possible for him to stay under water for several minutes at a stretch. Consequently his normal habitat is near a river. When pursued by some killer ambitious to dine off his chops, he calmly steps into his convenient river, walking along its bottom and passing the time in the gentle pursuit of pulling up the roots of water lilies and other aquatic plants. He is as fond of these morsels as the tiger is of tapir meat.

After nibbling away for a few minutes, he comes to the surface, swimming off to some other point where there are more tasty roots to eat.

But when the jungle fruits are ripe, the tapir, unable to resist these dainties, forsakes his river. He makes for the higher ground where rambutan, checo, jack fruit, and other jungle palate-ticklers fall to the ground.

Here in territory where he is easy prey for carnivores on the prowl, he vies with other herbivorous animals for his favorite delicacies. Cautiously emerging from the brush, he comes out into the more open spaces of the jungle where the fruit-bearing trees are found. In his movements is the accumulated timidity of thousands of generations of tapirs, all of them hunted animals.

Fear of attack is always uppermost in his mind. He isn't even free from it when he is near the water. More than one Dyak native has made a meal off the remains of a tapir he has found buried in the mud along the margin of a river or swamp, the victim of an assault by a bull crocodile that seized its prey in the water, held it under until it was drowned and then tore it to pieces.

Practically everything Ali and I said on the subject, and our experience with tapirs had been wide, contributed to the point that it was unusual for a tapir, one of the least courageous of the perpetually hunted animals, to make an attack such as the one to which I had been subjected.

This being so, didn't the *tuan* believe that the animal was full of devils? How could a tapir act that way otherwise?

I tried to tell Ali, in simple language, that the animal's conduct represented the aggressiveness born of perpetual fear. The creature had got it into his head that I was trying to destroy him, so he tried to destroy me. If there had been a river to run to, the tapir would have headed for that instead of me. It was as simple as all that. Ali wrinkled up his nose. He was displeased.

He kept after me until, to end the discussion, I told him that he was probably right. The creature must be full of devils.

Ali beamed. He knew all along that I would see his point. Of course the animal was full of devils! But he wasn't finished yet.

Did the *tuan* think it wise to ship to America an animal so full of devils? Would it not make trouble for me?

This was carrying a joke too far. I finally convinced Ali that an animal so full of devils should be shipped out of Asia, which was already overstocked with devils, with all possible haste.

For the good of my soul and that tapir's back, I was determined to resume my operations with the zinc ointment. This I did, but I confess that I ministered to his skinned back from the outside of the pen. I wrapped some rags around the end of a long stick and tied them securely in place. Then I put some ointment on the rags and with this homemade apparatus succeeded in giving him a thorough smearing. A series of these treatments proved effective and before long the tapir's back was healed. A few months later he went to a small mid-western zoo. There he proved as easy to handle as a kitten.

CHAPTER II

GIANT JUNGLE MAN

I had just returned to Singapore after a long and arduous collecting trip that took me to the wildest of the Borneo wilds. I was resting in my room in the Raffles Hotel when I heard a pounding on my door.

"Tuan! tuan!" The voice was Ali's.

"What do you want, Ali?"

"Open, *tuan!* Quick! Big news have happened." I let Ali in.

"What's it all about, Ali?" I asked. "Out with it!"

Then Ali informed me that "the grandfather of all orangs" had arrived in Singapore, the biggest animal of its kind he had ever heard of. If the reports were correct—and we had every reason to believe they were—we were on the trail of a gigantic "man of the forest" (*orang* being "man" in Malay and *utan* being "forest").

That was enough for me. If there was a record-breaking orang available, I wanted it. I hurriedly got into my clothes while Ali supplied further details.

A small boat had just arrived in the outer harbor from Jesselton on the north coast of Borneo with a party of Malays who had come to market a solitary possession that they owned jointly, an orangutan.

Someone on board had a gift for publicity for, according to Ali, within an hour of the time the boat arrived, he had heard from several people in the marketplace that the world's biggest orangutan was in town, for sale to the highest bidder.

At first Ali was inclined to pooh-pooh the story, but when he heard it from Chop Joo Soon, the Chinese animal dealer, he decided I ought to have the information. Ali reminded me that when I had told him that my next shipment for the United States was complete, I had added that if he heard of anything unusual he was to notify me.

Ali, as I finished dressing, told me he would never forgive himself if these Malays had nothing unusual to offer. He knew the *tuan* was tired and needed rest. He had no desire to be disturbful (Ali's command of English was growing by leaps and bounds, his mastery resulting in the addition of words not only to his vocabulary but to the language itself). But neither had he any desire to see those Japanese, in town collecting animals for the Tokyo Zoo, get anything that I wanted. He thought I'd prefer having my rest divided (he meant "interrupted") to taking the risk of losing an important specimen to the collectors from Tokyo. (Ali wrinkled up his nose so feelingly every time he mentioned the Japanese that I began to feel that perhaps he didn't like them.)

Ali had two rickshaws waiting in front of the hotel. *"Lekas!"* ["Hurry!"] It didn't take us long to get to the Tangon Pagar district, that part of Singapore where the docks and wharves are located. There we engaged a Malay dugout with three sturdy native paddlers, and we were quickly rowed out to the outer harbor where the boat from Borneo lay at anchor.

It didn't take us long to discover that the Malays had something really wonderful to sell. Ali's informants had not exaggerated. It was an amazing animal, by far the most enormous orangutan I had ever seen. It was also larger than any member of the species that Ali had ever encountered, and there probably wasn't anyone in all of Asia who had had as broad an experience with these creatures as he.

The beast weighed well over 250 pounds, a tremendous weight for an orangutan. It measured eight and a half feet from finger tip to finger tip. It was thirteen inches across the face. The bulging cheek growths, common to adult male orangs, the long shaggy hair about the face and chin, and the gaping wide mouth with the long, deadly canine teeth combined to give this ape as terrifying an appearance as I've ever seen in an animal.

The Malays had him imprisoned in a heavy cage made of a hard jungle wood and lashed together with rattan and other jungle fibers. It was one of those ingenious pieces of carpentry that one so frequently encounters in the East.

The animal was not enjoying his confinement. His cage was too small for him, and he expressed his opinion of his cramped quarters by alternately grunting and sucking in wind in the fashion characteristic of the species when angry. As I surveyed that tremendous chest and those prodigious arms with their bulging muscles, and reconsidered those murderous teeth, I had a feeling that in a rough-and-tumble fight this shaggy importation from Jesselton could have accounted for at least a dozen men, killing as many of them as he pleased. The orang's favorite method of doing damage in a fight is to pull the foe to him with his mighty arms and rip his victim to pieces with his teeth.

There were five Malays in the group that had come over from Jesselton with the giant jungle man. The fun began when I asked the headman how much he wanted for his hairy captive.

He and his associates put their heads together and went into conference. Then the headman, instead of naming a price, made a strange request. Would I mind dismissing my assistant? They hoped I would not misunderstand. The *tuan* must not regard this request as a reflection on the assistant. It simply meant that he (the headman) preferred doing business with me alone.

The headman, or *dato,* added that his English, while far from what he would have liked it to be, had proven adequate in transactions with *tuans* in the past, and that I would not need my interpreter. Time and again when Ali accompanied me to places where Malay was the language spoken, he would be regarded at once as an interpreter.

It soon became obvious that the reason why the *dato* requested Ali's dismissal was that he wanted to be able to talk freely with his comrades. Apparently it had not occurred to the spokesman that I might understand Malay. While I speak the language with difficulty, I have a sufficient knowledge of it to be able to understand the average conversation. I might miss the meaning of an occasional word, but I knew enough of the lingo to be able to comprehend, without much of a struggle, what most Malays were telling one another. I saw no reason why this group should be an exception. The confidential five would spill all their secrets in my presence, including the particular technique they employed in trying to put one over on a *tuan.* Unless all signs failed, I was due to have a thoroughly enjoyable time.

In the manner of one who is making a significant concession, I agreed to dismiss my "interpreter," insisting, however, that he be permitted to stay within calling distance so that in case we had any trouble understanding each other his services would be available.

My purpose in doing this, of course, was to lead the group further astray in their belief that I did not understand their tongue.

"That is well," said the headman, designating a place on the deck where Ali was to wait. "But we shall be possible to do business without him. My English language is not too big, but you will be able to understand what I mean to do." I understood fully what he meant to do. He meant to gyp me. His English, while flawed, was easy to comprehend, as was also his manner, which eloquently proclaimed his intention to stick me if possible.

"Let's get down to business," I said. "How much money do you want?"

"You realize, of course," he replied, "what it is, this that we make offering to sell?"

"Yes, an orangutan. How much?"

"Never before does the world see so big orangutan."

"Perhaps. How much?"

"In many years I have seen hundreds orangutans since I was *anak* [child]. I have not looked upon one so big as this we now offer to sell."

"I'm sure of that. You're not the kind that would fool me."

"I know you realize I am not like the *orang Chino* [Chinese man]. No, I am honest fellow."

"I knew that the minute I saw you. . . . How much?"

(Time out for the *dato* to address his comrades. He is telling them that all is well. "This *tuan* will not be hard to handle.")

"Tuan, I have been told by 'Merican gentlemen that in your country—you 'Merican, no?—[I nodded]—will be much excitement when news have arrived that big orangutan comes. Many will be happy to spend plenty money, he have told me, to see this orangutan *besar*." (The last word meaning "enormous.")

He was certainly building up a case for himself. His technique amused me, but after about two dozen of these digressions, all designed to impress me with the rareness of the animal he had for sale, I decided that I had had enough.

So I said: "I understand perfectly. This is a very unusual animal. [He nodded]. It's worth more than the average orangutan. [Another nod, accompanied by a beam of pleasure.] But it's not made of gold, and it isn't studded with rubies. [The *dato* stopped smiling.] So don't ask for a million dollars. Tell me what you want and be quick about it. I've got to get out of here."

Even this didn't accomplish the desired result. The *dato* launched into another speech, similarly calculated to make me feel what a favor he was doing me in permitting me to negotiate for his epoch-making catch, the most beautiful (it was wonderful but hardly beautiful) "piece of orangutan" that he had ever "experienced," that his family had ever "experienced," that his friends had ever "experienced," that the world had ever "experienced." At the height of this burst of oratory I found myself losing patience.

I turned heckler. Raising one hand, I fairly shouted, "I have a question to ask the speaker. How much does he want for his orangutan? Or doesn't he want to sell it?" I consulted my watch by way of emphasizing that if time wasn't a factor with the speaker, it was with his audience.

After three or four more assaults on the *dato*'s eloquence I managed to convince him that I wanted to hear his price, and nothing else.

He cleared his throat in preparation for the delivery of his answer. Finally it came. If it was anyone else he was dealing with (he had never seen me until I stepped aboard that little vessel) the price would be three thousand Straits dollars. Since it was I, however, the price would be only two thousand Straits dollars, little enough, he assured me, for the rajah of all orangs.

"You're crazy," I said. "I wouldn't pay that for a *gajah* [elephant]."

As I said this, the *dato* spoke hastily to one of his comrades in Malay. Without any difficulty, although I missed a few words, I understood this scheming headman to instruct his associate to go with all possible haste to see if he could find those representatives of the Tokyo Zoo, whose presence in Singapore he had heard about. The old rogue was trying to introduce a little competitive bidding.

The headman's plan was to keep stalling until the Japanese arrived. I didn't have to guess this; I heard him say so with a chuckle. Then he would start a sort of auction sale, with Japan and America bidding against each other until he had sent his price sky high.

I didn't want to lose this specimen. It was an amazing one. But neither did I want to pay a ridiculous price for it. Small monkeys are easy to handle and do not involve much of a risk, but great apes are a pure gamble. Not nearly so hardy in captivity as their smaller relatives, they present many real problems. For one thing, it is very difficult to transfer them from the food to which they are accustomed in their wild state to the substitutes that are available when they live in captivity. Sometimes one gets away with it without a hitch. The animal thrives and is healthy and happy once he's given sufficiently roomy quarters to exercise and amuse himself. But there are those trying exceptions when these great apes, unable to get used to the new diet, or suddenly stricken with lung trouble, die before anything can be done to save them.

I was in a ticklish position. If the Japanese arrived I would have to pay through the nose to get my orang. Obviously I would have to close the deal before they appeared on the scene. I made an offer of eight hundred Straits dollars, a good price. The *dato* pooh-poohed it. Turning to one of his comrades, he said in Malay, "This foolish *tuan* thinks he is going to get the better of me. But I will make him pay two thousand dollars. He cannot have the animal for less."

"Suppose the Japanese are not willing to pay that much?" (One of his comrades speaking.)

"Leave it to me. Two thousand dollars is our price."

An hour had elapsed since the time the *dato* had sent one of his cronies to find the Japanese.

I was willing to raise my bid in gold to a thousand Straits dollars ($570), but I saw no point in doing it yet. The rascally headman would not close for less than his original figure until he had heard from the Japanese. That was obvious. My one hope, it seemed, was that the gentlemen from Tokyo would not be willing to bid as high as the *dato* expected. After all, gold does not grow on trees in Japan any more than it does in America. Nevertheless, the prospect of competitive bidding did not appeal to me.

A half hour later the Malay who had been sent for the Japanese returned—alone. He had been unable to find them. The clerk at the Nikko Hotel in North Beach Road did not know where they were.

He had hardly finished his story, the whole meaning of which was perfectly plain, when the lying *dato* turned to me, and, without batting an eyelash, calmly announced that his comrade had just brought word that some Japanese animal buyers would be over in a little while. However, he was anxious to close the deal and get back to Jesselton. If I would pay him two thousand dollars, he would let me have the animal. He would rather deal with me, he said, confidentially adding that those Japanese are sometimes a tricky lot. But their money was as good as mine. If I would not meet his terms . . .

After more strenuous bargaining I landed the hulking orang for the thousand Straits dollars that I had fixed as my maximum. This was a fortune to the five Malays, a higher price than I had any right to pay. But I was delighted with my purchase just the same. The orang could be sold at a profit if I could get it across the Pacific in good condition.

Before leaving with my purchase, I wanted to hear the story of that animal's capture. The cleverest natives would have found it well-nigh impossible under normal circumstances to catch an orang of such prodigious proportions. Great apes do not go into traps like tigers, leopards, and other jungle animals. There are very few natives who would have risked a battle with so appalling an adversary, and it seemed a foregone conclusion that something must have happened to handicap the beast.

For this reason I wanted to hear the facts of the capture, curious to know in just what way the fates had set the odds against this tremendous orangutan that was capable of routing a couple of dozen natives and killing several in the process.

The *dato* told me the story, and since he had no money to gain by lying, I daresay he told the truth. At any rate it tallied with the story Ali heard in the Singapore marketplace shortly before he dashed off to drag me out of bed that I might become the owner of this orang of orangs.

Here is the *dato's* story (with much deletion of his own words, however, as his Malayan English resulted in a rambling narrative that took almost an hour to tell).

"Well, *tuan,* we played a mean trick on that orang. [Laughing.] If we hadn't, you wouldn't be his owner. He'd still be roaming the jungle.

"Abdul here [pointing to one of his men] found the brute's house in a big tree." (High up in some tall tree the orangutan builds a platform of branches over and around which he weaves more branches until he has a sort of nest or shelter of limbs and leaves.)

"Abdul discovered the big fellow's tree-house in the jungle *tiga makan sari* from our *kampung*. (Those Malay words mean "three eats [chews] of nut [juice] from our village." The Malay frequently figures time in such picturesque terms. It takes him about twenty-five minutes to polish off a mouthful of *sari,* or betel nut juice, so three chews would be about an hour and a quarter's walk, during which he would cover about three and one-half miles.)

"It was the dry season of the year in our section. That big orang had to go a long way for water or go thirsty, which he did for days at a time to save himself the long journey through the tree-tops.

"It was easy to watch his movements, a task to which Abdul was assigned. We knew the value of such an animal, and we made up our minds to capture him if we possibly could. Naturally we were in immense fear of this giant, having witnessed the terrible results when smaller specimens went on a rampage.

"It struck me that the thing to do first was to conduct an experiment at a safe distance. We filled a small tub with water, placed it near his tree and retired to await developments.

"From a clump of bushes a fair distance off we watched the big fellow's movements. For quite a while nothing happened. We were beginning to wonder how long we would have to wait before our friend (though he was hardly that, eh, *tuan?*) would decide to leave his house in the tree to see what was doing in the world below.

"He came down at length. For several minutes he devoted himself to studying the tub and its contents. He was obviously suspicious about something, though what actually went on in his head no one will ever know. He got close enough to the tub to take a drink and started bending over as if he were going to do so. Then, very suddenly, he righted himself. He had changed his mind. He took another hard look at the tub, his expression plainly indicating that he wasn't at all sure that he liked what he saw. By the time an orang gets to be as old as this one (my captive was probably twenty or twenty-five years old, and he might well have been more) he has had many tricks played on him, and he is nothing if not cautious.

"'He's not going to drink,' I said to one of my comrades. 'Not this time anyhow.' I had hardly uttered these words when the animal knocked over the tub and scrambled up his tree.

"The next day we refilled the tub and again awaited developments. One has to have patience in dealing with these wild creatures. One would never capture them otherwise.

"After a few hours, the big fellow came down, practically repeating his performance of the day before, the only difference being that this time, as he tipped the tub over with his foot, he jumped back as the contents splashed on the ground, as if expecting something to happen to him. Perhaps the fact that nothing did happen encouraged him to view the tub and its contents in a friendlier light. The third day he did not tip it over so vehemently, and the fourth day he drank—first a sample swallow, then another and another, finally drinking his fill.

"Each day we filled the tub, getting him used to the idea that he could depend upon it as a steady source. There were rambutans, banyan berries, and other fruits not far distant, so the big fellow need make only short trips out for food early mornings and late evenings, knowing that his water was near at hand. It made things quite convenient for this lazy giant.

"Then we started adding to the water a small amount of *arak,* our native gin. [Probably there is no drink in the world quite so powerful as the *arak* distilled by the Malays and the Dyaks, an innocent-appearing fluid that, like other gins, looks exactly like water. It was unnecessary for the *dato* to tell me about Bornean *arak.* I sampled it once, and though it went down smoothly enough, not long afterwards I thought I was on fire. Once a Malay said to me, in describing the concoction, "Why, *tuan,* three drops of this would make a rabbit walk right up and spit in a tiger's eye."]

Evidently the orang did not notice the taste of *arak* in the water, or did not mind it. After all, he had drunk plenty of water in his time that tasted worse. A thirsty animal in the jungle has learned not to be too particular, there being times when he is grateful for anything he can get, even muddy water seeming a luxury.

"However, the quantity of *arak* that we used at the start was so small that the water could not have tasted much differently. Each day we increased the dose, and the animal continued to drink. The *arak* taste did not seem to bother him at all. For all we knew, he might have developed a liking for it and the faint glow he must have experienced afterwards. The quantity we were giving him, *tuan,* was still not large and was so well diluted that it couldn't have had more than a mild effect on him. When we felt that this 'man of the forest' was ready for it, we filled the tub with straight *arak.* As soon as he was thirsty he slid down his tree for a drink, as was now his custom, the tub having become a regular part of his life. He took a mouthful, wasn't quite sure that this was the kind of water he wanted, retained it in his mouth for half a minute and then spat it out. He regarded the tub thoughtfully for a time, then decided to reconsider. He began to drink slowly and continued until he had drained the last drop.

"Then he sat down beside the tub, evidently feeling he needed a rest. After sitting there for about five minutes he started swaying to the right and then to the left like a mother rocking a baby to sleep by hand. Then he got up uncertainly and began to walk across the clearing, stumbling over something in the process and almost falling over. In the typical manner of a drunk who has stubbed his toe, he looked down angrily at the enemy that was trying to throw him, some matted underbrush, and decided to deal it a kick. In doing this he lost his balance and landed foolishly on his backside.

"He got up unsteadily, evidently concluding that something was wrong, in which event he had better go home to his tree-top hut. He turned around and looked doubtfully for his tree. Finally locating the tree with his eye, he made for it, in anything but a straight line.

"He managed to get part of the way up the trunk, but *arak* is *arak,* and when it starts asserting itself it's a serious handicap to man or beast in a tree-climbing mood. Down slid the bewildered animal, landing with a thud on its now-battered bottom.

"'I'll teach this drunken tree a lesson! Picking up a log, he wrathfully swung it against the trunk, the log snapping in half and its wielder, leaning over so far in dealing the blow that he became top-heavy, landing in a heap where he sat blinking in silly fashion at the part of the club that remained in his grasp. Again he rose uncertainly and started shakily across the clearing. Coming to a fallen tree, he put his hands on it to support himself, raised one leg to step over and fell down dead drunk. When he came to, some hours later, he found himself neatly crated at Jesselton awaiting shipment to Singapore."

Shortly after the *dato* had finished his story, Ali and I, with the aid of some boatmen, loaded the king of orangs onto a lighter, and we headed for Johnson's pier. There Ali got some coolies to help us lift our cage onto a bullock cart, which was sent on its way to my compound at Katong. A few days later I had the job of transferring my "man of the forest" from his cramped box, which I considered bad for his health and his disposition, to a fine new roomy one that Hin Mong, my Chinese carpenter, had built for the newcomer.

I've had much easier tasks in my time than the one of getting this savage beast out of his old box into the new. The two boxes were nailed and lashed together, with the openings, bars removed, facing each other. Some bananas were placed in the new box as an inducement to the beast to enter his new home.

The stubborn cuss refused to be tempted, for quite a while devoting himself to grunting and sucking in wind, his favorite method of expressing rage. When we pounded on his old cage in an effort to drive him into the new, he pounded back with powerful blows. If those cages had not been securely fastened together, we would have had to reckon with a terrible foeman.

After much effort, we got this great ape to go for the bananas, dropping the iron bars as soon as he entered. These bars, by the way, were spaced so close together that it was impossible for the animal to reach through. An orang as powerful as this one could have pulled a person to him, had he been able to reach through the bars, and killed him in a jiffy.

Although the giant jungle man's new cage was much more comfortable than the old one, giving him plenty of room, he showed no signs of taming down. He was in a rage most of the time. Every morning, when the keeper came to clean his cage, running an iron scraper through an opening at the bottom, he would take the implement in his powerful grip. The keeper's efforts to wrench it loose couldn't have been any less futile if he had been trying to yank a tree out by the roots. He would have to let go and wait until the animal tired of hanging on.

My orang was in fine condition when I got him ready for shipment to Hong Kong aboard the *West Sequana,* on the first leg of my journey to America. He was still a perfect example of sustained wrath, but he was eating regularly. His new diet consisted of carrots, sweet potatoes, bananas, sugar cane, boiled rice, raw eggs, and bread, and he was thriving on it.

At Hong Kong I transferred him to the *President Cleveland.* We stopped at Kobe, where I cabled my agent in San Francisco that I had a record-breaking full-grown male orang, the largest representative of this species in captivity. I included the creature's astonishing measurements in my message.

A reply was waiting for me at Yokohama. It was to the effect that the Ringling Brothers Circus was willing to accept delivery on the dock, which, of course, would relieve me of the risk involved in getting the animal to its ultimate destination in the United States. I accepted. I had sense enough to know that with the Ringling Brothers Circus, the finest in the world, the animal would receive excellent care. So far, so good.

The rest was not so good. About five days out of San Francisco my prize orang developed a bad case of dysentery, which is always serious in anthropoid apes. He had suddenly achieved one of those sunken stomachs that invariably spell disaster in his species. The ship's doctor had a serum that he thought would help if he could manage to inject it. Patiently we strove to make a quick injection, but we had no luck, two or three needles breaking off in the animal's fingers. That night the Rajah of All Orangs, as the *dato* had called him, died.

A few years later, Frank Buck was able to capture and bring back to America a large orangutan, as he relates in his book Fang and Claw *(1935):*

A male orang was what I wanted when I set out on my expedition —a male, and the largest orang ever caught. It was a tall order, and I knew it when I started to fill it.

There was difficulty even at the beginning. The Dutch own Sumatra, where many of the animals live, and the Dutch government is very strict where orangutans are concerned. Never very plentiful, many orangs have been shot for museum purposes and collected for zoos and menageries and other buyers, so that had the government not stepped in the orang might very easily in a few more years have become extinct. The Dutch also protect rare birds of their East Indian territories; the Victoria crown pigeon and the famously beautiful birds of paradise are likely to survive there.

I didn't expect much trouble when I left my compound at Singapore on a K.P.M. boat bound up the Straits of Malacca for Sumatra. All I wanted was permission to capture two orangs, and as I have always played fair with the government—and the Dutch know it—I knew I could get the necessary permit.

Because of the strict laws regarding orangs, there is occasional smuggling of these animals. Chinese boatmen in coastwise boats for a small sum will smuggle young orangs out of Sumatra whenever they can secure them at the little native ports where they call for jungle produce. Never having gone in for this sort of thing, I was able after landing at Belawan Deli, which is the port for the city of Medan, to get permission to capture and take out of the country the orangs I wanted. I might add that the permission was given me through the kindness and generosity of Dr. Dammermann, head of the Museum of Natural History of Buitenzorg [Bogor], which is just outside of Batavia [Jakarta], the capital of all the Dutch East Indies.

With permission obtained, I hired a motor at Medan, and Ali and I drove from the famous DeBour Hotel 250 kilometers north into Atchin. This route took us through one of the richest tobacco- and rubber-growing sections in the world. With typical Dutch thrift these plantations are as neat and well-ordered as the clean streets and clear canals of homeland Holland itself.

But the farther north we went, the wilder grew the country until we reached our final stopping place with the car—a rest house in Atchin on the border of the jungle. The governments of all Eastern provinces maintain these rest houses for the convenience of travelers in out-of-the-way places. They are the only fit roofs for a traveler to take shelter under.

From the rest house it was a matter of walking through jungle trails to a Batik village I knew and that I had visited before for orangs. We walked because Sumatran jungles are in places too dense to permit even a bullock cart to pass. Many of the trails were originally made by animals—thousands of animals over hundreds of years—taking the line of least resistance to the streams and water holes. And jungle man, like the animals, also takes the ready-made and easiest way to where he wants to go.

The jungles of Sumatra are as thick and dark and beautiful as any in the world. The trees are enormous. Towering durians rise a full two hundred feet into the air, with lesser tropical redwoods and jack fruit trees and marantis—the trunks of which the Batiks use to make their hollowed-out *perahus* (fishing boats) and canoes. The trees make a complete green roof over your head, matted with vines and creepers, and in places entirely blot out the sun, the sky, and the breeze. In their damp crotches outsized orchids and ferns grow, and I have seen the ground a mass of color from the petals of fallen flowers.

We finally reached the village I was headed for, and I got in touch with the *pangkulu,* the headman—who is about the same as a *pawang* in Malaya. He remembered me from former trips, and after giving me a delicious, cool drink of coconut milk, was ready to talk business. I told him I was in search of orangutans; that I wanted a full-grown male, and the biggest orang he had ever seen in his life. He immediately waxed eloquent.

"*Orangutan besar* [enormous orang] in this forest," he told me. "*Orangutan* so big trees shake when he climb. *Orangutan* so big he darken sky when he swing through tree tops."

Knowing typical exaggerations, I discounted sixty percent of what the *pangkulu* said. I knew he was anxious to get work for fifty or so of his villagers, and was laying the *besar* business on a bit thick. Yet he had worked for me before, and in general he was truthful. I had no doubt but what there was a genuinely enormous orang in the district, and I determined to have a look at it.

"All right, *pangkulu*," I said. "I'll make a camp here. Send out your scouts to find this *orangutan besar,* and I'll see what he looks like."

This "scouting" of a Sumatran jungle sounds much easier than it actually is. As I've said, it's as dense as any jungle anywhere, and to effectively cover thirty or forty square miles of it, on a search for an orangutan in the tree tops, is a business that wears out both feet and patience. An orang seldom makes a noise, and then merely a sucking-in of the lips that can be heard for only a short distance. So his presence cannot be easily spotted. And an orang seldom comes to the ground except for water, so his spoor cannot be followed like that of an elephant or tiger, as it is lost immediately when he takes to the trees again. It is necessary to see an orang in the trees, and then follow him as he swings from tree to tree, if you ever hope to capture him.

Consequently I was delighted one day when one of the *pangkulu's* scouts came running into the camp I had built with news that the *orangutan besar* had been found. He was eight miles away in the jungle, and men were on his trail and following every move he made.

Ali, the *pangkulu,* and I covered those eight miles as quickly as the dense growth of vines and creepers would permit. We came finally to the spot where the orang had been sighted and found that he had moved. Men, posted along the route, pointed continually south, and a mile farther into the jungle we caught up with him.

He was in a tree top ahead, high up, peering down at us from 150 feet above, and he really looked small up there against the sky.

As we watched him he launched his enormous brown body into the next tree, and with a tremendous rustling of branches swung away from us.

"Sorry," the *pangkulu* apologized. *"Orangutan besar* not *quite* so big as I say."

"Pangkulu," I said, "that's the biggest orangutan I ever saw in my life. You've done a grand job."

"Glad you pleased," he told me with a beaming face.

I was more than pleased. I knew that up in those Sumatran jungle trees ahead of me was an orang bigger than any that had ever been seen in captivity anywhere in the world. All that I had to do was capture him.

I presume that most of you have never captured a wild orangutan. Well, until you've seen one swinging through the tree tops, intent only on escaping from that queer animal called man on the ground below him, you've never realized how difficult a job can be.

I wanted that orang. We followed him for hours through that dark Sumatran jungle. At times he would hang high in a tree, looking down at us with his fierce, beady eyes; or he would swing swiftly from tree to tree, casting his weight from branch to branch so rapidly that it was difficult for us to keep up with him in the soft, dense going below.

But eventually I saw what I was looking for ahead. An immense durian tree loomed through the jungle. It rose high above the surrounding trees like an oak in a patch of scrub pine. And the orang was headed directly toward it.

"Pangkulu!" I called. "Get some men ahead of that durian tree, and on each side of it. When the *orangutan besar* swings into it I want to keep him there. Have your men pound on tree trunks and yell. I want to drive the *orangutan* to the top of that durian so he can't go any farther from tree to tree."

The *pangkulu* carried out his orders. As soon as the orang swung into the durian his men set up such an uproar that the astonished ape climbed high in the branches of the tall tree and peered down in amazement mixed with animal anger.

"Pangkulu!" I called. "Your men have got axes there. Start them chopping down all the trees around the durian. I want a whole circle cleared around that single tree so the *orangutan besar* can't escape by swinging to another limb."

The *pangkulu* was quick in getting the idea. We had chased that orang for a long way through the jungle, and the *pangkulu* was as tired of the job as I was. The headman saw the plan of segregating the great ape in a single tree, and he went to work on it. In a little while trees were crashing to the ground all around that circle of jungle, and the *orangutan besar* was looking down at us from his high perch with astonished and outraged eyes.

It wasn't until late that night when the last tree hit the soft earth that I heaved a sigh of relief. I had my jumbo orang a prisoner high in the air; now all I had to do was get him down.

I thought of half a dozen ways of doing it. But by far the quickest and easiest seemed to be the net method I had used in getting a rare clouded leopard in Johore. So I sent some men back to camp for a rope net I had brought along. It seemed to me at the time that an orangutan up a tree could be captured in the same way as a leopard. I found out differently later.

When the men came back with the net I had a dozen of them hold it directly under the limb on which the orang was perched. The idea was simply to shoot the limb out from under the ape, and by the law of gravity he would naturally fall into the net where he could be neatly entangled and, for all his brute strength, rendered helpless in rope meshes.

The only trouble was that my orang ignored the law of gravity. He refused to be bothered by such natural conventions. I am not an expert shot, but I can hit a four- or five-inch limb 150 feet in the air nine times out of ten, and hit it just about where I want the bullets to land. I hit this one exactly eight times with a high-powered rifle bullet, and the limb cracked and fell. But the orang didn't fall with it. When he felt the limb snap under him he simply launched his bulk in the air, caught another limb with his strong hands and swung onto it. And he sat on that limb and stared down at me disdainfully.

There was nothing to do but try it again. I tried it three more times. And each time as the limb was shot from under him my orang flew through the air with the greatest of ease, and swung safely onto a new branch of that durian tree.

I gave it up finally. Obviously this king of all orangs was too smart to be captured in this way. He defied the law of gravity; but there was one law of nature he could not long defy—hunger. I had him up a tree, a tree from which there was no escape. Sooner or later he must come down to feed and drink.

If you've never lived in a jungle lean-to for five days you won't know what I went through. No chairs, no mosquito netting, no cot. A lean-to roof of palm leaves to keep off any rain that might come and that is all. Earth for a bed, leaves for a roof, and the open jungle for walls. But I was willing to put up with it all if only I could capture this *orangutan besar* that still clung to the top branches of that durian tree. Sooner or later I knew he must come to earth for food and water. And when he came, with the aid of the *pangkulu*'s men and the net, I knew I would get him.

Yet when he finally came I did nothing of the sort.

It was on the fifth day that he ventured down his tree. He was pretty well starved by this time, and mighty thirsty. I could tell by the way he lowered himself from limb to limb in that durian tree that he was coming down to fight his way out. Every gesture, every movement of his massive hairy arms said: "I'm going to get some food or know the reason why! And you're not going to stop me!"

I had the *pangkulu*'s men well prepared for this moment. For five days I had drilled into them what they were to do.

The net was ready; the moment the orang touched the ground they were to pile on top of him with that net, toss it over his head, roll him over, and get him so tangled in its meshes that he would be helpless.

The plan worked beautifully except for the orang. The men ran forward in the prescribed manner. They tossed the net over him as expertly as fishermen casting into a run of shad. But the *orangutan besar* ignored the net. He pushed it aside with one sweep of his powerful arms. With the same sweep he knocked one man ten feet away in a sprawling heap. And in the same motion he was back up his durian tree again, climbing limb after limb as an old-time sailor used to go up the rigging of the main mast.

So my orangutan was up a tree again. And so were we.

I decided then to use different methods. By this time I actually felt that this was a personal war between the huge orangutan and myself. It was a question of wits, of brain, and I knew that sooner or later the mind of man must conquer the natural instincts and strength of the animal.

So I ordered the *pangkulu*'s men to build a trap. It was to be a heavy trap of solid, hardwood logs; a trap and a cage both, strong enough to catch the orang, and strong enough to carry him back to Singapore. At least, this was the idea.

The trap was the usual kind of animal trap, a sliding door that would drop when bait and trigger were touched. The only problem was, I couldn't use it in the usual way. I knew that if I set that trap on the ground my orang, instead of going in it, would be off in the jungle as fast as his legs could carry him. At all costs I had to keep him in that segregated durian, and it looked as if we would succeed in keeping him there as long as we remained in force on the ground below. The only way to catch him was to set the trap in the tree.

I got four ropes over a high branch, tied them one to each corner of the trap, and the men hoisted it up. It was a tough pull and took the concentrated efforts of every native we had on the job. Ali, a monkey where trees are concerned, climbed along with it, guided it, and finally fastened it solidly on two parallel limbs. He then put in the bait, adjusted the trigger, and slid down the tree.

All the while the orang, high above, watched the proceedings with mingled anger and curiosity. Occasionally he would break off a limb and throw it at us furiously. Then he would merely sit and stare thoughtfully at this strange log box that had invaded his tree.

All monkeys and apes are curious by nature. Never having heard the story of what curiosity did to the cat, they investigate anything new that comes their way. However, I doubt if the orang would have ventured near that trap if he hadn't been so hungry. He was a wise old ape, and unlike most oversized animals he seemed to have a brain in proportion to his bulk. But he'd been without food for six days now, and the luscious fruit inside that log box was calling.

It was plain that he suspected the box. When he finally ventured down the tree to the limbs it was on, he sat for a long time and studied it. Then, very cautiously, he attempted to reach the bait with one of his long arms. I had foreseen this maneuver and placed the food in the rear of the trap. The only way he could possibly get those tempting morsels was to go all the way in.

Sitting there looking at that food he went through all the temptations of Satan. His starved animal stomach said, "Go get it!" His cautious animal instinct said, "Careful!"

Stomach won. Into the trap he went, reached for the bait, and down slid the door with a roaring of logs. He dropped the fruit he had snatched and flung his weight against the door. He tore at the bars with all his strength. I had a few bad moments as I watched that trap tremble and rock. But those hardwood jungle logs were solid and strong. And the rattan that bound them together was tough and tied by expert Batik hands. It wasn't until my giant orang stopped his struggles, and began to fill his stomach that had betrayed him with the bait that had caught him, that I breathed easily and ordered the men to lower the cage to the ground.

They say the way to a man's heart is through his stomach. Well, the way to the capture of the biggest orangutan in the world was also through his stomach.

CHAPTER III

JUNGLE LAUNDRESS

Of the thousands of monkeys and apes I've brought to America from Asia perhaps the most interesting was a female orangutan I picked up in Pontianak, Borneo. She was sold to me along with four other members of her species by a Malay trader who'd been up bartering among the Dyaks.

I did not know at the time that I'd bought anything as unusual as Gladys proved to be. (That's the name my favorite ape later achieved, though I couldn't possibly tell you how or why.)

Of the five orangutans I took off the trader's hands, two were little babies in baskets, two were about half grown, and the other, Gladys, was almost full grown. She was about two or three years removed from the age of eleven to twelve when members of her sex and species, dismissing the follies of youth, take upon themselves the cares of motherhood. A carefree young lady, with a genius for sociability, she devoted herself to the business of making friends and keeping them amused.

When I pick up a group of orangutans in this fashion I don't know whether they're fresh from the jungle and wild or whether they are animals that were raised as pets from infancy. The natives of British North Borneo and Dutch Borneo will never pass up an opportunity to raise a baby orangutan and hold it till some trader appears to acquire it for a few guilders or an ax, tobacco, salt, cotton cloth for *sarongs,* or any of the other staple articles used in bartering for local goods. Such animals come to the collector tame and are easy to handle.

It is useless to ask the trader who in turn sells to the collector whether he is offering tame or wild monkeys for sale. Half the time he doesn't know; and, when he does know, he won't tell for fear he'll give the wrong answer and spoil a sale. The collector who knows his business can generally answer for himself the more important question: are these sound and healthy specimens? Once he is reasonably sure of himself on this score (it is impossible, of course, to be absolutely sure) he takes his chances on all other points.

After a person has spent as many years in the trade as I have, he forgets to worry about whether an animal is wild or not. In the course of handling hundreds of the jungle's most ferocious inhabitants, animal savagery becomes a commonplace. There's a way of handling the worst of them.

But it's convenient, in handling animals you haven't trapped yourself or bought under circumstances that give you some idea of their characteristics, to know something about them. This is particularly true in the case of orangutans. One that has been raised as a pet, for instance, will have a much better chance of thriving in the collector's compound if it is given the liberties one can safely give a domesticated ape of this variety.

The only safe course until you've had a good chance to observe your orangs and classify them, if they are anywhere near full grown, is to treat them all as rascals, which is what most of them are. Put your hand too close to the bars of one of these tree-dwellers that resents his captivity, and there's a good chance that you'll get only part of it back; or, if you get it all back, it won't be in working order.

Along with many other animals, these five orangutans found their way before long to my compound in Katong. As I supervised the job of installing them in the shed, one of the five reached out through the wooden bars of its cage and gently touched my arm.

The approach of a tame orang is unmistakable. There is no grabbing, no frantic reaching, none of the quick stealthiness that one finds in members of this simian family that have evil intentions.

I stopped to observe the movements of the animal that had touched me in this friendly fashion. I was getting my first real impression of Gladys. Moving a little closer, but ready to withdraw in an instant in case I was mistaken, I encouraged the lady to show how sociable she could be. Again she reached out and stroked my arm.

Continuing the experiment further, I took an ax and smashed a few of the wooden rungs, much like heavy broomsticks, that bar up the boxes used in caging orangutans. She poked her head, or part of it, through the opening and nuzzled against me as I moved closer. Not once was there a display of teeth. The animal was as tame as they come.

In a few minutes I had Gladys out of her cage. Never have I seen such ecstasy in an ape, and I've seen some happy ones. She gently put her arms around me and held me for a minute, rubbing her face against my hand when that was over. Then she stroked me again with her hands, completing her display of joy by dancing up and down in front of me and eagerly looking up as if to say, "Where do we go from here?"

Soon I had Gladys installed under the house, which stood three feet off the ground. She was almost four feet high when she stood upright, but that did not matter, for I put a collar around her neck and gave her ten feet of chain, and she used the space under the house merely for sleeping quarters.

While Gladys had no desire to escape, she frequently pined for more liberty than her chain afforded and usually she knew what to do about it. In fact, she managed to free herself from every collar I put on her until I resorted to one that was fastened on with a padlock.

I would have cheerfully given Gladys her liberty, but she worried the servants and the two friends who shared the house with me. In fact, Andy Mack told me that if Gladys didn't stop entering his room and throwing his things around he'd have her arrested for disturbing the peace. He didn't mind what she did to the things a fellow couldn't trip over, like socks and ties, but when she started scattering his shoes all over the floor, complicating his 3 A.M. tipsy entrances, that was serious, and he wouldn't stand for it.

Gladys also had a playful habit of climbing all over the house, the roofs of the sheds in the compound and occasionally a neighbor's dwelling. In fact, once she almost scared the wits out of the young man next door who worked in a bank in Singapore. She peered in at him one morning while he was bathing, unladylike conduct, I was forced to admit, though I had to correct the lad when he insisted that it was a gorilla he saw at his window and that "he" (the gorilla) had "his" teeth bared and was about to break through the window when he scared the monster off by pounding. I will not here correct all the inaccuracies in this statement. I will say, however, that I emphatically pointed out that Gladys always let closed windows alone. She never hesitated to climb through an open window to say hello but forcing her way into a place was out of her line. Those who didn't think enough of her to provide access to their quarters simply had to do without her society. She had her pride, did Gladys.

Then there was the complaint from our *tukang kebun* (gardener). He once caught Gladys rubbing her face against the cheeks of his little baby. Gladys, her maternal instincts asserting themselves, had developed quite a fondness for the child and would mother it whenever she got a chance. She enjoyed swinging the child's hammock back and forth, and so did the child, for that matter, but the *tukang kebun* objected, and as I didn't want to lose our gardener I was forced to curb these attentions of my affectionate orangutan.

One of Gladys's favorite pastimes was looking for me around the compound. Once she decided she wanted to put her arms around me, she would hunt all over the place, and when she failed to find me around the compound she would try the house. This always annoyed the servants, who thought that the place for an orang, tame or otherwise, was in the jungle.

Gladys, however, was a determined girl, and once she made up her mind she wanted to see me she would continue her search until she found me. These searches were sometimes complicated by the fact that I was in Singapore while Gladys was trying to find me in Katong. Once I found her waiting for me at the road. She had got used to seeing me drive home in my car; and failing to find me on the premises, she waited (for how many hours I'll never know) till I drove up, joyously scrambling over the door and taking a seat beside me.

Although Gladys was as harmless as a kitten, I eventually found it necessary to secure the padlock mentioned above and restrict her to such territory as her original ten feet of chain permitted her to roam. She was probably puzzled by the curtailment of her liberty for only the day before she had performed an act of real usefulness. Ali had opened the door of one of the bird cages too wide, and one of the mynas flew out. Filling the air with triumphant chatter (it will be recalled that the myna is a chattering bird that can outtalk a parrot when in a garrulous mood), she flew all over the grounds with Ali in frantic pursuit. After a half-hour's chase, Ali and the bird were all fagged out, and when Ali made a final weary dash, driving the worn-out bird in Gladys's direction, it was a simple matter for the orangutan to grab the squawking myna, which she did very gently, holding it so carefully that not a feather was rumpled.

As Ali came running up, Gladys handed him the fugitive, stroking it tenderly by way of farewell, the noisy bird replying unfeelingly by pecking at the hand that was petting it.

Gladys was philosophical about her confinement. After all, it was better than life in a cage. She was able to exercise and get the sun, and probably that is why, after a few days, she seemed to forget that she had a padlocked collar, and she was again her exuberant self. I've never seen an animal with a similar capacity for enjoying life. Everything that went on around her interested her. Keen, alert, responsive, she was closer to the human species than any other ape I've ever handled.

Gladys, among other things, was an excellent chambermaid. She got the maximum results out of the bundle of straw and the blanket I gave her for her bed. In fact, she made a ceremony lasting about a half-hour out of the nightly business of making her bed. She would spread out the straw, step back a few feet and survey her work, rearrange the straw, step back again for another look, and repeat the performance over and over again till she decided that all was well. Then she would lay out the blanket on top of the straw and lie down, rolling over until she was completely wrapped up. Sometimes the end of the blanket would not wind up at a point that enabled her to tuck herself in securely, and when this happened she would unroll herself and go through the performance again and again until she was so rolled up that there was no chance of the blanket coming loose while she slept.

Whenever I would see Gladys go through a performance of this kind I would find myself growing curious about her past. These amusing little customs and habits were, of course, traceable to her early life in captivity. What was that life? I would never know exactly, but this did not prevent me from speculating on it and trying to piece Gladys's story together.

Needless to say, I am not an animal trainer. Many animals that I have sold to circuses have been converted into fine performers, but I have no interest myself in teaching animals tricks or stunts. It is out of my line entirely.

This is not by way of saying that I am not interested in trained animals. I am; but I must add that I find it much more absorbing to watch an animal like Gladys go through some routine she has picked up herself than to watch the antics of animals trained to do certain tricks after rigorous discipline.

One day I was passing Gladys's place under the edge of the house on my way to the compound. In my hand I carried a tin wash pan of water in which was soaking a square piece of ordinary cotton cloth that I was about to use in washing a minor wound on the leg of a small animal. As I went by, my favorite orangutan reached up and stopped me. Curious to see what she wanted, I stood by and did nothing. She was obviously interested in what I was carrying. (It was customary for her to examine anything I had in my hand. I never discouraged the practice as I was on the lookout for reactions that would throw some light on the past life of this animal that interested me so.)

With both hands Gladys reached up for the wash pan. I let her take it. She carried it two or three feet and then sat down on the ground with the pan in front of her, between her legs. She removed the rag from the water and began to scrub it with her fists like a laundress. Then she doused it in the water again, swished it around, removed it, put it between her fists again and rubbed away vigorously as before. There was about five minutes of this, winding up in a final dousing of the rag. After first soaking it thoroughly she picked it up with both hands and proceeded to wring it out like an experienced washerwoman.

She carefully unfolded it and shook it out. Then, putting one corner between her teeth she stretched it out flat with her hands. This done, she ran her eyes over it carefully to see if it was clean all over. Satisfied that it was, she walked over a few feet out of the shadow of the house to where there was some sun and spread the rag out neatly on the grass.

Gladys had gone through all the motions of an Asian woman washing clothes, winding up with the method of drying that they use. Partly, at least, I could now piece together Gladys's story. She had been raised in a native village, right in the bosom of the family. How she got there has to remain a matter for speculation; although a reasonable enough supposition is that when a baby she accompanied her mother in a raid on a durian tree on the outskirts of the village. (The durian is a jungle fruit about as large as a medium-sized cantaloupe, the favorite fruit of both apes and natives; it has a hard, prickly rind, containing a soft, cream-colored pulp, of a most delicious flavor, though somewhat offensive odor.) The natives, as frequently happens, might have speared the mother to get the suckling babe.

More than once in a Borneo village have I see a woman nursing a baby on one breast and an infant orang on the other. Always there is the hope that a trader will come along and buy the ape.

Gladys probably grew up with the children of the family, playing with them and accompanying their mother to the river bank on wash day. There it is customary for the children to help, and Gladys, not to be outdone, doubtless decided she would do her bit too. It was probably somewhat in this fashion that she learned the gentle art of laundering.

Gladys got to be so much fun that frequently I took her to Singapore with me where she became a familiar figure. She enjoyed nothing more than an automobile ride, and when I would unleash her and let her climb into my car for one of those trips to Singapore she would embrace me so completely that I would have to disengage myself before I could drive. Then she would sit back in the seat like a lady out for an airing, confining her displays of affection to an occasional pat with her hand or a rub of her cheek against my arm.

My business over, Gladys would sit down with me in the bar of the Raffles Hotel while I had a gin sling. Occasionally I would let her have a small glass of beer. Once, to see what she would do, I removed all chairs but one, in which I sat down, pretending to be unaware of Gladys's existence. Undaunted, she slid a chair over to the table and seated herself, reaching for my glass by way of announcing that she was ready for her beer.

On the way back to America, Gladys was the pet of the *President Cleveland*. I had her installed on the boat deck where her chain gave her plenty of room for exercise.

As soon as the women on board heard of Gladys's accomplishments as a laundress they made regular trips to the boat deck with water-soaked handkerchiefs, which Gladys would rub with her fists, wring out, and spread out on the deck in the sunshine.

The news also spread that my amusing orangutan was fond of tea, and at tea time many ladies would have their afternoon cup with Gladys. As much as Gladys liked beer, it was as nothing compared with her fondness for tea.

Once a lady on board accused Gladys of snubbing her offer of tea-time refreshments. The orang drained the proffered cup of tea but refused the sandwiches and cakes that accompanied the offer. It was necessary to explain that Gladys had gotten into the habit of eating out of a plate. I had taught her this at Katong, and, unless very hungry, she would ignore food that was placed on the bare deck. After all, that's no way to treat a lady. The food was placed on a plate, and Gladys ate it.

The wireless operator of the *President Cleveland* developed quite a fondness for Gladys. In fact, some of his frivolous associates referred to her as his "girl." He would pet the orang and feed her apples and bananas, and she in return would rub her head against him, and, in her more affectionate moments, embrace him.

One day Gladys, who still knew how, resorted to her old trick of unfastening her collar, which I had forgotten to padlock. A few minutes later she was in the wireless operator's quarters, looking for her friend. Failing to find him, she looked around to see what mischief she could do, and, evidently deciding that the bed was not properly made, pulled it apart. She was making a neat pile of the bedding in the middle of the bunk in an effort to arrange it like her own straw bed when the operator entered.

He let out a yelp of dismay, for overhead was a high-voltage wire that ran through his quarters into the wireless room, and if this animal, that was in the habit of climbing all over everything, decided to investigate the wire, she'd be a dead orangutan not long after she touched it.

The operator sent a boy to get me, and I came running in and claimed the exploring Gladys. The operator afterwards told me that he sweated blood in the few minutes that intervened between the time he sent for me and my arrival. He stood there, he told me, ready to stun his favorite monkey with a water pitcher if she made a move in the direction of the wire.

The officers of the ship kidded the operator for the rest of the trip and accused him of secret *tête-à-têtes* in his cabin with Gladys. "He tried to steal Buck's monkey," was the way one of them put it. "Buck had to break down the door to get her out."

Before the trip was over Gladys also made a reputation as a bookworm. A lady visitor brought a book with her and sat beside the orang and read. When the woman put the book down, Gladys picked it up and, opening it up, held it for a full minute in the manner of a person reading. The fact that she held it upside down did not seem to affect her interest in what she found on the pages.

My parting with Gladys was the saddest animal farewell I've ever known. I hated to part with her. As she required the kind of attention she could get only in a good zoo, I had to let her go. She went to the Municipal Zoo in Madison, Wisconsin. In Madison I knew that she would have a good home and that her affectionate nature and interesting character would make her many friends.

CHAPTER IV

CHIPS LENDS A HAND

I was in Dallas, Texas, laying out plans for a zoo with Director of Parks Jacoby. The Al G. Barnes Show was in town, and, once I had concluded my arrangements with the municipal authorities—an order involving the complete stocking of the type of zoo that I suggested—I found myself hanging around the lot where my friend Al G. was entertaining the local citizenry with his performing animals.

Having provided Barnes with the bulk of his collection, I had an interest in his show that went beyond my normal interest in animals. These were my animals—at least they were mine in the days when I brought them out of Asia—and I always got a kick out of hearing how they were getting along. Had this tiger or that elephant developed into a good performer? Was that black leopard any better natured than he was in the days when I brought him and dropped him, a snarling rascal who'd as soon claw you as look at you, on Al's doorstep? . . . And a hundred other questions that were on the tip of my tongue whenever I ran into this old friend who for years ran the best all-animal show America has ever seen.

Al G. and I had a long talk one day in which he mentioned his needs in the way of new specimens. He was particularly anxious to get a good-sized orangutan, not necessarily full grown but large enough to make a good showing. Joe Martin, his famous orang, had "gone bad" on reaching sexual maturity, as most anthropoid apes in captivity do. He had attacked several people, and Al did not want to take any more chances with him. This meant that the most famous of all performing orangs had to be kept in his cage, where he was now a member of the nonperforming group, a mere exhibit in a traveling menagerie. What a comedown for Joe, who had once been featured in the movies and starred in the Barnes Show, one year capturing the place of honor on the billboards. No longer was it safe to lead him out into the center ring, where for so long a time he had earned the plaudits of the mob. Knowing something about the problems of a sensitive animal of this kind when full sexual ripeness suddenly arrives to complicate his life, I appreciated what a tough time Joe Martin must have had, and I sympathized with him in his uneven struggle against the demons of maturity.

The king of circus orangs dethroned, another animal had to be found to take his place. But perhaps I should alter that. Al Barnes was not hopeful of securing another Joe Martin. He told me so. "If there's ever another one like him I'll be the most surprised man in the business." (The nearest approach to Joe Martin in my own experience was Gladys, the orangutan described in these pages in the chapter "Jungle Laundress," the most lovable, intelligent member of the species I ever handled.) Barnes said he would be satisfied if I could secure for him a specimen tame enough to lead out into the ring or one that had been partly tamed. The animal need not be one capable of developing into a performer. The main thing was to secure an orang that knew how to behave himself, or at least had a nucleus on which to found a career featuring good behavior.

On my next trip to Asia I looked around everywhere for an animal that would meet Barnes's requirements. When I would run into an animal that was tame enough he would be too small. When I would get on the trail of one that sounded as if it was of the right age and the prescribed docility, it would turn out to be crippled or in delicate health. Always a hitch somewhere.

Chop Joo Soon, a Chinese animal trader in Singapore, with whom I had done considerable business and who knew of the type of orang I needed to fill my Barnes order, notified me one day that he had just the thing. His specimen proved to be an excellent one, although he had apparently forgotten the tameness clause. His animal was of the right age and the right size, but he was about as tame and manageable as a fresh-caught panther. In fact, he had just been brought in from the Borneo jungle. He was so fine an orang, however, that I decided to take him regardless of whether or not he would do for Barnes. If I could not land a better-behaved specimen, I would try to tame him down sufficiently to make him a useful member of my friend's show. If this proved impossible I would bring him back anyhow and place him in a zoo.

The shipment of which this orang was a part was a very sizeable one. It was one of the many floating zoos with which I have returned to the United States. As I needed more help than Lal, my capable Hindu assistant, could give me, I asked the mate of the ship on which I was crossing the Pacific to select another helper for me from among the sailors. I often do this, never having any trouble getting the assistance needed. There is always some member of the crew whose duties are light and who welcomes the opportunity to pick up a little extra change.

Having mentioned the fact that I needed a man who was husky, the mate suggested the ship's carpenter, a hulking, powerful American. Chips—he was known by no other name—had more spare time than any other available member of the crew and would be just the man, the mate said.

Chips, I afterwards learned, was the bully of the forecastle, and I suppose one of the reasons the mate suggested him as my helper was a secret hope that the extra work would keep the burly braggart so busy that he wouldn't have time to make trouble for his brother sailors, which had long been his specialty. Proud of his strength, the carpenter would perform feats that none of his comrades could match and then proceed to call them a lot of weaklings. Many fights resulted, Chips invariably coming out on top. His specialty was beating up smaller men and boasting about it. He had lost favor with the officers and was due to be dropped as soon as a good man could be secured to take his place.

The mate was so anxious to keep the roughneck busy that he was even willing to let him pick up a little extra change. I imagine he would also have been glad to see him pick up a few little injuries in his work with my animals.

Chips's standing with his fellow sailors, however, was no concern of mine. I had asked for a husky helper, and the mate had supplied one.

The carpenter was a rare bird. Shortly after I was introduced to him he asked me to feel his muscle. This I did, withdrawing my fingers too quickly to suit him.

"You hardly felt it," he said, taking hold of my hand and placing it on the bulging biceps of his right arm. "Feel again."

I obliged. "Some muscle," I said.

"You bet it's some muscle," Chips agreed.

"How much do you suppose I can lift?" Chips asked.

"I haven't any idea," I replied.

"Well, what would you guess?"

"Oh, I guess you could do some pretty heavy lifting. Those are fine muscles you've got there."

"You said it. Like iron. Feel!"

"I just did."

"I know, boss. But feel again. It's bigger now."

Again I obliged. After all, I was crossing the Pacific with this man as one of my helpers, and we might as well get acquainted.

Chips was at me again, trying to make me guess the number of pounds he could lift. As I stood there trying to frame a suitable reply, one that would convey my confidence in his ability to walk off with the Pyramids on his back, I heard one of the elephants straining at his chain. This animal was tied up on the aft deck between the bulkhead and the No. 4 hatch.

As the restless pachyderm kept rattling his chain and stamping his feet, I said, "I wish that elephant would stop milling around."

"Do you want me to put a stop to it?" asked Chips, who knew as much about elephants as I know about Greek dancing.

"Never mind the elephant, Chips. I've got other things for you to do."

"We ought to teach him a lesson, boss."

I had a hard job convincing him that he'd better do as I said. He was all for grabbing an elephant hook and showing the animal "a thing or two."

"Never mind the hook, Chips. Throw him some hay. That may quiet him down."

"Don't you think I'd better jab him a couple too, boss?"

"No."

Chips looked crestfallen.

"Just the hay?" he asked.

"Yes, just the hay."

A half-hour later the elephant had quieted down. Triumphantly Chips came over to where I was working on some birds and announced the fact that he had made the elephant behave.

"That's fine, Chips."

"If he makes any more trouble, boss, let me handle him. I've got his number."

"Swell. I . . . By the way, what did you do besides throw him some hay?"

"Well, you see—oh, I just—well, the first thing I did—"

"That's wonderful," I interrupted, not wanting to embarrass him too much. "There's nothing like having a system." Then I quickly gave him another job to do to spare him—and me—the pain of further explanation.

A few days later I was forced to admit that Chips wasn't overestimating his strength. I wanted some tigers shifted around, and the carpenter, unaided, moved them about in their heavy cages as if they were so many kittens in baskets.

"That's outstanding work, Chips." (There really had been no need for Chips to do the job alone. Lal was there to help, but Chips spurned assistance. "This is man's work," was the way he put it.)

"There's no one else aboard that could 'a' done it," was how he received my compliment.

"I'm sure of that."

"Osgood thinks he's strong, boss. Have I told you about him? He's a roach, is Osgood. That's what—a roach. Thinks he's got muscle. I'll bet if he was asked he'd say he could 'a' done it. He's that lousy, is Osgood. Ask him, boss, willya? It'll be a real joke. If he says he could 'a' done it I'll clip him on the snoot. I'll point him out to you, boss, and you ask him. It'll be wonderful sport."

I declined the invitation. This left Chips gloomy, for he was obviously aching for an excuse to "clip" Osgood. But I cheered him up when I said, "You needn't tell me you're stronger than Osgood, or anybody else. You're the strongest man I've ever seen, bar none." And it wasn't far from true. The necessity of having to keep on telling it to Chips, however, grew a bit painful after a while.

One day I said to the carpenter, "Chips, I've got a real job for you."

"I'm your man, boss."

"It's a job that takes strength and nerve, Chips. I wouldn't think of asking anyone else to do it. There's no one else on board that's got the muscle to do it. Certainly Osgood couldn't do it." I knew this would make Chips feel good.

"That roach!" was all he said.

I explained to Chips what the nature of his task was. "I'm going to take the orang out of his cage, and you're going to help me do it."

I wanted to see if I couldn't tame down this little demon before reaching San Francisco. After all, Barnes wanted a manageable specimen, and, if possible, I didn't want to disappoint him. If I could get a collar around the animal's neck and take him out of his cage daily, in the process getting him used to the idea that I was a friend, not an enemy, some progress would be made toward taking the fight out of him. Once he got it through his head that he was safe in my company, and saw how much fun it would be outside of his cage for exercise in the warm sun, he'd be a different animal. One can't ever be sure about these things, but that was my guess about this particular orang.

"We're gonna take Shrimpo out of his cage?" asked Chips. This was the name he had given the ape.

"Yes."

The carpenter's disappointment was obvious. "Hell! I thought you had a real job." Chips had never taken the orang seriously on account of its shortness of stature. It was less than four and a half feet in height, which was no reason to assume, as Chips had done, that this was not a formidable creature. An orang can't be judged by its height. The short back legs give an impression of squatness that has more than once resulted in an underrating of the fighting powers of these dangerous apes.

Chips had evidently not taken the trouble to notice that Shrimpo's arms, for instance, were all out of proportion to his height. They were enormous, with huge bulging muscles.

I thought I had a pretty sizeable pair of biceps. I weighed about two hundred pounds at the time, most of it bone and muscle, thanks to years of strenuous work that was death on fat, but Shrimpo's biceps were much bigger around than mine. Chips had also failed to notice the animal's mouth and wicked teeth, or, if he had noticed them, he had lacked the perception to see that this orang was not to be taken lightly. As a matter of fact, Shrimpo was a good match for the average two or three men.

"This is a tough job, Chips," I said. "You'll find that out when we get started."

"Quit your kidding, boss," said Chips, as he disdainfully eyed Shrimpo, in front of whose cage we were standing. "If that little feller got fresh I'd put him on my knee and spank him."

"Don't be so sure, Chips. But we'll go into that later. I want to explain how you and I are going to get the ape out of his cage and hold him while Lal puts on the collar."

"What!" exclaimed Chips. "Three people to put a collar on that little runt! Gimme the collar. I'll do it myself."

Lal started grinning.

"What the hell's he laughin' at?" roared Chips. "I suppose he thinks I can't do it alone. He thought I couldn't move those tiger cages alone either."

"Calm down, Chips. This is different from moving tiger cages."

"You ain't tellin' me that monks is worse than tigers, boss, are you?"

"When they're loose, and the tigers are boxed, yes." Chips didn't seem capable of getting anything through that thick skull of his. "We're going to get started now, Chips," I said. "Here's the dope. First we'll knock the front of the cage out. I'll make a quick reach for him and grab a wrist. Then—"

"Let me do that part, boss. I'll show the little shrimp."

"I'll grab him first. I've done it before. Looks easy, but it isn't. It takes experience. I'll drag him out of his cage with a swift yank. Your job is to grab the other wrist quickly. We'll stretch his arms out straight, like this. [I stretched out my arms till they were parallel with the deck.] Then, while we're holding the little devil, Lal will snap a collar, with chain attached, around his neck from behind.

"Then we'll all let go together, jump back, and run the end of the chain around a stanchion."

"There's nothing to that," said Chips.

"It'll take every bit of strength we've got to keep that animal's arms stretched out. Don't fool yourself about that. He's a powerful little cuss. If I should let go he'd make a quick lunge for you, to break your hold. He could snap your wrist with one bite. But I'm not going to let go. How about you? If you let go, I'd be in the same danger."

"Say, boss, you don't think that little roach is going to bother me, do you? I've handled bigger roaches than him. Take Osgood. One day . . ."

"Never mind about Osgood. We've got to get busy. Do you understand what you're to do?"

"Hell! There's nothing to understand. It's as easy as . . ."

"Remember what I said before. If one of us lets go the other will probably get hurt. Maybe badly hurt."

"There's a swell chance of me letting go, boss! If I couldn't hold a flea like that I'd . . ."

"Let's go!" I said.

I proceeded to pry off the iron bars of the cage with a crowbar. The occupant didn't wait to be yanked out. The idea of getting out of his cage appealed to him. With an angry grunt, which was his way of saying, "Get out of my way!" he stepped forth. As he did I grabbed one wrist, Chips grabbing the other. We pulled his arms out straight, firmly holding him as we had planned. The carpenter had followed instructions and seemed to have a very good grip on the wrist he was holding.

The orang, boiling over with rage, was making frenzied efforts to reach us with his teeth, violently twisting and bobbing his head. His struggles to get at us were nothing to worry about, for we were holding him securely; but that head was moving in all directions in a perfect riot of twists and squirms, making it impossible for Lal to get the collar on. The only sounds that came from the animal were the alternate grunts and sucking-in of air that are characteristic of an orang on the warpath.

"Again, Lal!" I yelled after he had made five or six unsuccessful attempts to get the collar around the struggling ape's neck. Once more Lal tried but failed.

"Don't take all year, Blacky!" came from Chips, whose breathing was an indication that the animal was giving him more work than he had expected.

"Hold on, Chips!" I yelled. The carpenter, normally the most talkative fool I had ever encountered, made no reply except a muttered oath. The strain was beginning to tell on me, and I knew the carpenter must be feeling it too. I gave Lal a cussing he didn't deserve, imploring him to snap that infernal collar around the animal's neck.

Chips was heaving and panting as if he had been running a marathon. Suddenly I saw him go white. Instantly I knew he was going to let go. He did. I lost no time in following suit. It would have been silly to try to hang on alone.

I jumped back, the orang coming after me with those powerful arms outstretched. I'm keen for affection, but I didn't want one of those embraces. The orang's method of fighting, described elsewhere in these pages, is to draw his victim to him in a hug and then tear him to pieces with his teeth.

As I cautiously backed away I could hear Chips yelling, "This'll fix him, boss!" He was holding up the crowbar with which I had opened the cage. The idiot was trying to hand it to me, nervously edging up.

"Get out of here, you!" I yelled.

Chips was committing the added crime of trying to get my attention while the animal was closing in on me. As if he hadn't sinned enough in letting go of that arm.

The orang, as I kept scrambling for position, made a sudden rush at me. He had the advantage of a longer reach, but I knew more about boxing. As he spread out his arms to grab me he gave me a beautiful opening. I waded in and let him have it smack on the point of the jaw. It was one of those uppercuts that get results, a wallop that had all of my beef behind it. The collision with the enemy's chin came just as the arms were about to enfold me. Shrimpo smacked the deck with a bang while some sailors who had run over to see the scrap broke out into applause like fans at a prizefight.

It was a clean knockout. The orang, landing flat on his back, slept the sleep of the kayoed.

After Lal had snapped the collar around Shrimpo's neck, we fastened the ape to a stanchion by a short length of the chain. When we brought him back to consciousness by dashing a bucket of water over him, that was where he found himself.

Chips spent the rest of the voyage making excuses. One day his story was that his hands were perspiring so freely he had been unable to hold on. "No man," he bellowed, "could 'a' held on with his hands soppin' wet." His listeners, fellow sailors who taunted him for the rest of the trip, no longer fearful of his bullying, broke into a horse laugh.

The next day the carpenter's story was to the effect that he had shifted his fingers to get a better grip, the animal eluding his grasp as he did. This story was also greeted with derisive howls.

Chips ceased to be the bully of the forecastle. He had been unable to change the opinion of his mates that he had let go because he was scared. What really broke his heart, however, was the fact that Osgood ("that roach!") had witnessed his disgrace. Osgood was his hated rival, having once come close to licking the carpenter. Now Osgood acted as if he'd enjoy another chance at the champ. I often wondered whether the fight took place.

Shrimpo soon discovered that there was a lot of fun to be had basking in the sunshine on the deck. We had fine weather practically all the way back, and my orang got the benefit of most of it. There were one or two minor flare-ups, and when the animal discovered that these weren't getting him anywhere he decided to behave himself.

By the time we arrived in San Francisco the orang was conducting himself in such mannerly fashion that I was able to lead him over by his chain to where Al Barnes came up to meet me. The showman was pleased with the animal and took him then and there.

CHAPTER V

MAN-EATER

This is the story of a man-eating tiger, probably as vicious an animal as I'll encounter if I continue in my chosen field for another fifty years. I captured him alive; but that would hardly have been possible without the sultan of Johore.[†]

I have known the sultan of Johore since 1918. I met him in the course of my work as a collector, and we became good friends. We don't stand on ceremony in our relationship. The sultan doesn't want it.

The finest treat I can think of when I am in his part of the world is to be invited to the sultan's house for *tiffin* (a snack or light lunch). When one of the courses is Malay curry, as prepared in this Epicurean household, I become so enthusiastic that H. H., the nickname that His Highness likes to have me use, kids me unmercifully. One day he accused me of plunging into my curry like a man-eating tiger.

This gave me an opportunity to change the subject and to pick up one of my favorite themes: man-eating tigers. In my work as a collector I had brought back to the United States many unusual specimens, including animals and birds never before seen in America, but I had never knowingly brought in a tiger that had eaten human flesh. The subject of man-eaters fascinated me, the vaguest

---

†   Johore Bahru (or Johor Baharu) is the capital of Negeri Johor. It is the southernmost city of the Malay Peninsula, connected to the island of Singapore by a rail and road causeway. The road and rail systems of the peninsula begin here. Rubber, palm oil, pineapples, and bauxite are produced in the surrounding area, and the city has fruit-canning and oil-milling plants. Within Johore Bahru are a large mosque, the sultan's palace and gardens, and botanical and zoological gardens.

reference to it setting me off on an orgy of questions, recollections of what I had heard from others on the theme (little of it involving first-hand experience), and speculation on what I should find if I should ever realize a long-standing ambition to come face to face with one of these eaters of human flesh.

"You would run," opined H. H. one day when we were discussing the subject. "Very fast you would run. That is what you would do. Like a deer you would run. Swiftly as you do when I invite you to my house for curry."

"Some day, H. H.," I told his joshing majesty, "I'm going to land a man-eating tiger, and then the joke'll be on you."

"Have some more curry," replied the sultan with a chuckle.

"Wait and see! The first time I get a chance to go after a man-eater I'm going to bring him back alive. And if it happens anywhere near Johore, I'll bring the beast right to your house where you can look at him."

"You are eating hardly any curry." (I had had three helpings.) "Have some, or I will not believe you like it as much as you say. It will give you the strength to fight man-eating tigers." With this, the sultan blew himself to another laugh.

"How will you be able to prove your capture is a man-eater?" he added, with a twinkle in his eye. "You forget how difficult it is to make me believe anything."

"If necessary I'll stick an arm or a leg through the bars of the cage and let him chew it off."

"That will be fine," replied H. H. "Then I will know it is not a tame tiger. It is necessary to put you Americans to such tests. You are all such bluffers." Then he roared his enjoyment of his playful dig at me.

In less frivolous moments the sultan discussed the serious menace of man-eating tigers. The presence of one of these killers would demoralize a whole rubber district, putting the workers on edge and rendering them practically useless.

Perhaps more rot has been written about the tiger than about any other wild animal. Certainly no one will deny that the tiger has come in for its share. Much of this silly stuff has had to do with the subject of man-eaters.

In one year, tigers killed more than fifteen hundred people in British India, and the average annual mortality from this cause has not been much below this figure. In most cases the tigers responsible for these deaths are man-eaters, because it is unusual for an ordinary tiger, no matter how ferocious a specimen, to attack a man. In fact, he finds the smell of human flesh repulsive and will lose no time in vacating the spot where this offensive odor reaches his nostrils. Once in northern Perak I practically stumbled over a female tiger with a pair of sizeable cubs. We were not more than six or seven yards apart when we spied each other. She and her youngsters snarled and slunk away without any loss of time.

Man-eating in a tiger is a form of perversion. A normal tiger, cornered by a hunter and killing him in a fight, will seldom give a thought to eating the body. In isolated cases a tiger, in killing a man who had tracked it down and cornered it, has been known to develop a liking for human flesh in the process of mangling the enemy. Once this happens, the animal becomes a confirmed man-eater and may account for a dozen or more human lives before its wild career is checked.

The tiger is decidedly not a man-eating animal. Its normal role is to keep out of man's way. Man-eating is a depraved taste, developed under unusual circumstances. A tiger that sustains so severe an injury in combat with another animal that it is not strong enough or fast enough to knock down game will attack a native if opportunity arises, simply because it's easier. Most jungle beasts are too fast or too tough for a badly maimed tiger. A native that is unfortunate enough to stray into the path of a hungry tiger that is incapacitated is likely to be knocked down and devoured.

It would be appropriate to cite here the case of a hunt for a man-eater organized by the sultan of Perak and a British government official stationed there. The Briton headed the expedition that set out after one of the worst man-eating tigers that ever terrorized a native village. The vicious beast had accounted for several lives when the Englishman, heading a company of Malay soldiers assigned to him by the sultan, went out into the jungle to get the killer. After a long and strenuous chase, the man-eater was tracked down. The hunting party surrounded him in a little section of jungle and beat him out into an open space. Four soldiers fired, and the striped scourge toppled over dead. The Englishman examined the body carefully. The animal was a magnificent specimen, everything indicating perfect condition. There were no signs of incapacitation or impaired strength. "Pretty odd," said the Englishman. "Expected to find some sign of a wound that made the devil take to man-eating."

Suddenly one of the Malays cried, "See, *tuan,* see!" Holding up one of the paws he pointed to a prominent scar across the pad where the foot had been cleaved wide open. Once there had been a terrible wound there, and for at least a month or six weeks the tiger must have hobbled around on three paws. During that period he probably had to subsist on frogs and small rodents, and, more than likely, he failed to get enough of these to stave off hunger. In his half-starved condition some native might have crossed his path, or appeared in the jungle close to him. Under circumstances of this kind, the animal, desperate for food, would probably attack. It would be an easy matter for a tiger, no matter how badly he was limping, to catch up with a native and knock him down. In all probability this is what happened. The best local students of wild game with whom I discussed the occurrence interpreted it that way, their further belief being that the incident created in the animal a lust for more human flesh.

Old age, strangely enough, is also responsible for the development of the man-eating instinct. A tiger that is getting on in years is faced by a serious problem. His teeth are bad; a thousand fights have left him battered and bruised; he is worn out. He no longer has the strength nor the agility to keep his stomach filled through the normal process of killing game in the jungle. He has to keep alive. Anything will do, even a man. It's meat of a kind, certainly, and after a few meals of man-meat, the new diet takes on a peculiar fascination. Nothing else will satisfy. A craving for human flesh is developed, and the animal goes on the prowl for this new delicacy. A tiger, crazed by this desire, will enter a village at night, drag a native out of bed, and carry him off into the jungle. There the poor victim is consumed, the killer becoming a more dangerous beast with each mouthful. The more human flesh it eats, the more it wants; and when the pangs of hunger again are felt, there will be another manhunt.

The presence of a man-eater in a district is the signal for much excitement. The natives are in a state of terror, and the local industry, whatever it is, is at a standstill. Soldiers are immediately sent to the spot by the person in authority, either a British colonial official or the reigning prince.

One night the sultan of Johore was telling me of the trouble the ruler of a nearby state was having with a couple of man-eating tigers that had become active in his territory. We were standing at the bar of the Raffles Hotel in Singapore, an old haunt of the sultan's, where he had invited me to have a few drinks with him.

"I have no problem of this kind," the sultan told me. "That is very good, no? Yes, it is very good. Sometimes we have a bad tiger. He eats a man, and we have trouble. But it is no steady thing. We have not had any for two, three years now. That is good fortune. Yes."

"The next time a man-eater is spotted in Johore," I said, "give me a crack at him if I'm in this part of the world, will you? I'd like to have a try at catching one alive."

"It is agreed. The next time I have tiger that eats a man I send for you. You go up to tiger, say, 'Boo!' Tiger say, 'All is lost, it is Buck,' and lie down on back and cry like baby, and you go up and throw him over shoulder and swim back to America with him. In America everybody clap hands, and you become instant hero."

Again the sultan had seized an opportunity to kid me about man-eating tigers. Let me point out that what amused him was my wanting to catch one alive. He would have understood my wanting to hunt one down and kill it. But to catch one alive! It seemed such a needless risk. And besides, why prolong the life of one of these killers?

Some time after this session with the sultan, I was to sail for San Francisco. The owner of the house in Katong where I usually lived when in Singapore had sold it, making it necessary for me to move out, although I still maintained my compound there. After the sale of the house I invariably stayed at the Raffles Hotel when in Singapore. I had just returned to my room there when I was informed that the sultan of Johore was on the telephone and wished to speak to me at once. As the morning was still young I was puzzled, for it was most unusual for H. H. to telephone so early.

It was a very serious H. H. who spoke to me. He got to his business without any loss of time. Did I still want a man-eating tiger? Well, here was my chance. Breathlessly he told me that a coolie on a rubber plantation twenty-five miles north of Johore Bahru had been seized by a tiger while at work and killed. The animal, a man-eater, had devoured part of the body. Work, of course, was at a standstill on the plantation. The natives were in a state of terror. The sultan was sending an officer and eight soldiers to war on the killer. It was necessary to show some action at once to ease the minds of his frightened subjects. If I thought I could catch the man-eater alive he would be glad to place the officer and soldiers under my command, with instructions to do my bidding. If, after we looked over the situation, it became apparent that in trying to capture the killer alive we were taking a chance of losing him, he expected me to order the beast immediately shot. He wanted no effort spared in locating the animal. There would be no peace in the minds and hearts of his subjects in the district where the outrage was committed until the cause was removed. In a series of crisp sentences the sultan got the story off his chest. This was an interesting transition from his lighter manner, the vein in which I most frequently saw him.

Needless to say I leaped at the opportunity to try for a maneater. H. H. asked me to join him at the fort in Johore Bahru, which I agreed to do without delay.

At the fort, which is the military headquarters for the state of Johore, the sultan introduced me to the officer he had selected to assist me, a major with a good record as a soldier and a hunter. He was a quiet little chap, so well mannered that his courtesy almost seemed exaggerated. His soldiers were a likely looking contingent. It was obvious that H. H. had picked good men to help me with the job.

The major was not in uniform. He was dressed in ordinary rough clothes of European cut. I was interested in the rifle he carried. It was a Savage .303, which most hunters consider too small a gun for tiger-shooting. This capable Malay, however, had killed several tigers with the weapon, the sultan told me. It took a good man to do that.

The major's command were dressed in the khaki shirts and shorts affected by Malay soldiers. They wore heavy stockings that resembled golf hose. If not for the little black Mohammedan caps on their heads and their weapons—each was armed with a swordlike knife and a Malayan military rifle—they might have been taken for a group of boy scouts. A cartridge belt around each man's waist topped off the warlike note.

The major bowed two or three times and announced in his fairly good English that he was ready to start. We departed, the officer and his men piling into a small motor lorry, Ali and I following in my car.

The asphalt roads of Johore are excellent. Many of them are the work of American road-builders who did a wonderful job of converting stretches of wilderness into fine highways. Thus we were able to motor to within three miles of the killing. The rest of the journey we made on foot over a jungle trail.

I had requested the sultan to order the body of the slain coolie left where it was when the killer had finished his work. When we arrived we found a group of excited natives standing around the mangled remains. One leg had been eaten off to the thigh. The animal had also consumed the better part of one shoulder, and to give the job an added touch of thoroughness had gouged deeply into the back of the neck.

Other groups of natives were standing around not far from the body, some of them hysterically jabbering away, some making weird moaning noises, others staring down at the ground in silence. One has to have a good comprehension of the wild, world-old superstitions of these natives to appreciate fully what happens inside them when a man-eating tiger appears. All the fanaticism that goes with their belief in strange devils and ogres finds release when a tiger, their enemy of enemies, kills a member of their ranks. They act like a people who consider themselves doomed. Going into a delirium of fear that leaves them weak and spiritless, they become as helpless as little children. Under a strong leadership that suggests a grand unconcern about man-eating tigers, they can be rallied to work against the striped foe; but, until there are definite signs of a possible victory, this work is purely mechanical. The most casual glance reveals that each member of the terrified crew is staring hard at the jungle as he perfunctorily goes through the motions of doing whatever it is you assign him.

An investigation revealed that the victim of the tiger had been working on a rubber tree when attacked. His tapping knife and latex cup (in which he caught the latex, or sap) were just where they had dropped from his hands when the poor devil was surprised, mute evidence of the suddenness of the assault. Then he had been dragged fifteen or twenty yards into some nearby brush.

Bordering along the jungle wall—as dense and black a stretch of jungle, incidentally, as I have ever seen—was a small pineapple plantation. This was not a commercial grove but a modest affair cultivated by the estate coolies for their own use. An examination of the ground here revealed marks in the dirt that unmistakably were tiger tracks. The tiger's spoor led to a fence made by the natives to keep out wild pigs whose fondness for pineapples had spelled the ruin of more than one plantation. There was a hole in this fence, which could have easily been made by the tiger or might have been there when he arrived, the work of some other animal. Through the hole, the killer's movements could, without the exercise of much ingenuity, be traced in the soft earth across the pineapple grove into the coal-black jungle some fifty yards away.

It is no news that a tiger, after gorging himself on his kill, will return to devour the unfinished remains of his feast. If there is no heavy brush within convenient reach he will camouflage those remains with leaves and anything else that is handy for his purpose and go off to his lair. Confident that he has covered his leftovers skillfully enough to fool even the smartest of the vultures, jackals, hyenas, and wild dogs, he curls up and enjoys one of those wonderful long sleeps that always follow a good bellyful and that I have always believed to be as much a part of the joy of making a good kill as the actual devouring of it.

I felt, as I studied the situation, that when the tiger returned for the rest of his kill—assuming that this creature would follow regulation lines and revisit the scene of the slaughter—he would again make use of that hole in the fence. It was a perfectly simple conclusion. Either the animal would not return at all, or if he returned he would retravel his former route.

"*Changkuls! Changkuls!*" I yelled as soon as I decided on a course of action. A *changkul* is a native implement that is widely used on the rubber plantations. It is a combination of shovel and hoe. With the assistance of the major I managed to make it clear to the natives what I wanted them to do.

My plan was to dig a hole barely within the borders of the pineapple plantation, so close to the hole in the fence through which the tiger had traveled on his first visit that if he returned and used the same route he would go tumbling down a pit from which there was no return, except in a cage.

I specified a hole four feet by four feet at the surface. This was to be dug fourteen or fifteen feet deep, the opening widening abruptly at about the halfway mark until at the very bottom it was to be a subterranean room ten feet across.

Soon we had a sizeable gang of natives working away with the *changkuls*. The helpful major, to whom I had given instructions for the pit that was now being dug, bowed a sporting acquiescence to my plan when I knew full well that this accomplished *shikari* (hunter), who had brought down many tigers with the rifle, was aching to go forth into the jungle in quest of the man-eater.

The pit finished, we covered the top with nipa palms. Then we made away with the pile of dirt we had excavated, scattering it at a distance so that the tiger, if he returned, would see no signs of fresh soil. The body was left where it was.

Ali returned with me to Johore Bahru, where I planned to stay overnight at the rest house adjoining the United Service Club. Before leaving I placed the soldiers on guard at the coolie lines with instructions to keep the natives within those lines.

The coolie lines on a rubber plantation correspond to the headquarters of a ranch in this country. There is a row of shacks in which the natives live, a store where they buy their provisions, etc. My idea was to give the tiger every possible chance to return. Too much activity near the stretch of ground where the body lay might have made him overcautious.

Early the next morning the soldiers were to examine the pit. If luck was with us and the tiger was a prisoner, a Chinese boy on the estate, who owned a bicycle that he had learned to ride at a merry clip, was to head for the nearest military post—there is a whole series of posts, very few jungle crossroads in Johore being without one—and notify the authorities, who in turn would immediately communicate with the fort at Johore Bahru.

The next morning no word had been received at the fort. At noon I drove back to the rubber plantation to see if there was anything I could do. The situation was unchanged. There were no signs of the tiger. No one had seen him, not even the most imaginative native with a capacity for seeing much that wasn't visible to the normal eye.

The body of the mangled victim was decomposing. Though I did not like to alter my original plan, I acquiesced when the natives appealed to me to let them give their fallen comrade a Mohammedan burial (the Malay version thereof). They put the body in a box and carried it off for interment.

The major did not conceal his desire to go off into the jungle with his men to seek the killer there. He was characteristically courteous, bowing politely as he spoke and assuring me that he had nothing but respect for my plan. Yes, the *tuan*'s idea was a good one, doubtless it might prove successful under different circumstances, but it was not meeting with any luck, and would I consider him too bold if he suggested beating about the nearby jungle with his men in an effort to trace the eater of the coolie?

What could I say? My plan had not accomplished anything, and we were no closer to catching our man-eater than when we first got to work. I readily assented, stipulating only that the pit remain as it was, covered with nipa palms and ready for a victim, though if the animal returned after the number of hours that had elapsed, it would be performing freakishly.

There was no point in my staying there. So, when the major went off into the jungle with his men, I left the scene, returning to Singapore with Ali.

I felt badly all the way back to Singapore. Here was the first chance I had ever had to take a man-eating tiger, and I had failed. Perhaps I was not at fault—after all, the business of capturing animals is not an exact science—but just the same I was returning without my man-eater, and I was bitterly disappointed. Ali did his best to cheer me up, but all he succeeded in doing was to remind me over and over again that I had failed. Using words sparingly and gestures freely, he tried to communicate the idea that after all a person could worry through life without a man-eating tiger.

When we returned to Singapore I kept in touch with the situation by telephone, the fort reporting that though the major and his men had combed every inch of the jungle for some distance around, they found no trace of the killer. The major gave it as his opinion that the beast had undoubtedly left the district and that further search would accomplish nothing.

"Well, that's that," I said to myself as I prepared to contend with the many tasks that were waiting for me in my compound.

The third day, very early in the morning, just as I was beginning to dismiss from my mind the events that had taken place on that rubber plantation, I received a telegram from the sultan of Johore that, with dramatic suddenness, announced that the tiger had dropped into the pit. No one knew exactly when. "Some time last night." Would I hurry to the plantation with all possible haste? He had tried to reach me by phone and failing this had sent a telegram.

Would I? What a question! Perhaps it is unnecessary for me to say how delighted I was over the prospect of returning to the plantation to get my man-eating tiger. Ali ran me a close second, his joy (much of it traceable to my own, no doubt, for Ali was usually happy when I was) being wonderful to behold.

We climbed into the car and set out for the plantation at a terrific clip. At least half the way we traveled at the rate of seventy miles an hour, very good work for the battered bus I was driving.

When we arrived the natives were packed deep around the sides of the pit. Never have I witnessed such a change in morale. There was no suggestion of rejoicing, for natives endow tigers with supernatural powers. They do not consider themselves safe in the presence of one unless he's dead or inside a cage, but they were again quick in their movements. A determined-looking crew, they could now be depended upon for real assistance.

In addition to the crowd of coolies, the group near the pit included the major and his soldiers and a white man and his wife from a nearby plantation. The woman, camera in hand, was trying to take a picture. Even in the wilds of Johore one is not safe from invasion by those terrible amateurs to whom nothing means anything but the occasion for taking another picture. I distinctly recall that one of my first impulses on arriving at the scene was to heave the lady to the tiger and then toss in her chatterbox of a husband for good measure. This no doubt establishes a barbarous strain in me.

I plowed my way through the crowd to the mouth of the pit. The natives had rolled heavy logs over the opening, driven heavy stakes, and lashed the cover down with rattan.

"*Apa ini?*" I inquired. "*Apa ini?*" ["What is this?"]

"Oh, *tuan! Harimau besar!*" came the chorused reply, the gist of it being that our catch was an "enormous tiger." I loosened a couple of the logs, making an opening through which I could peer down into the pit. Stretching out on my stomach, I took a look at the prisoner below, withdrawing without the loss of much time when the animal, an enormous creature, made a terrific lunge upward, missing my face with his paw by not more than a foot.

This was all I needed to convince me that the natives had shown intelligence in covering the mouth of the pit with those heavy logs. I did not believe that the beast could have escaped if the covering was not there; yet he was of such a tremendous size that it was barely possible he could pull himself out by sinking his claws into the side of the pit after taking one of those well-nigh incredible leaps.

The business of getting that tiger out of the pit presented a real problem, due to his size. I had not expected a monster like this, a huge cat that could leap upward to within a foot of the mouth of the pit.

Ordinarily it is not much of a job to get a tiger out of a pit. After baiting it with a couple of fresh-killed chickens, a cage with a perpendicular slide door is lowered. An assistant holds a rope that when released drops the door and makes the tiger a captive as soon as he decides to enter the cage for the tempting morsels within, which he will do when he becomes sufficiently hungry. A variation on this procedure, though not as frequently used, is to lower a box without a bottom over the tiger. This is arduous labor, requiring plenty of patience, but it is a method that can be employed successfully when the circumstances are right. When you have the box over the tiger and it is safely weighted down, you drop into the pit, slip a sliding bottom under the box and yell to the men overhead to haul away at the ropes.

It was obvious that neither of these methods would do. I simply could not get around the fact that I had underestimated the size of the man-eater and had not ordered a deep enough pit. Our catch was so enormous that if we lowered a box he could scramble to the top of it in one well-aimed leap and jump out of the hole in another. Ordinary methods would not do. They were too dangerous.

I finally hit upon a plan. As a good part of the morning was still ahead of us, I decided to tear off to Singapore for the supplies I needed, race back post haste, and get that striped nuisance out of the pit that day. I could not afford to spend much more time on the plantation. I had so much work waiting for me in connection with a shipment I was taking to the United States.

My first move on arriving in Singapore was to get hold of Hin Mong, my Chinese carpenter, and put him and his assistants to work at once on a special long, narrow box with a slide door at one end. When I left for my next stop, Mong and his helpers had cast aside all other tasks and were excitedly yanking out lumber for my emergency order. Knowing Hin Mong's fondness for needless little fancy touches, I assailed his ears before departing with a few emphatic words to the effect that this was to be a plain job and that he was not to waste any time on the frills so dear to his heart.

Leaving Mong's, I headed for the bazaars, where I bought three or four hundred feet of strong native rope made of jungle fibers. Next

I went to the Harbor Works and borrowed a heavy block and tackle. Then I hired a motor truck.

When I added to this collection an ordinary western lasso, which I learned to use as a boy in Texas, I was ready to return to the rubber plantation for my tiger. While on the subject of that lasso, it might be appropriate to point out that the public gave Buffalo Jones one long horse laugh when he announced his intention of going to Africa and roping big game, and that not long afterwards the laugh was on the public, for Buffalo serenely proceeded to do exactly what he said he would.[†] I have never gone in for that sort of thing, but my rope, which is always kept handy, has been useful many times. I even lassoed a crane, a rare animal, on the wing as it sailed out over the ship's side after a careless helper had left its shipping box open.

When the box was made—and though Hin Mong and his assistants threw it together hastily it was a good strong piece of work—I loaded it and the coil of rope and the block and tackle onto the truck and sent this freight on its way to the rubber plantation, putting it in charge of Ali's nephew, who was then acting as his uncle's assistant at the compound. I gave him a driver and two other men and sent them on their journey after Ali had given his nephew instructions on how to reach the rubber plantation. Four men were needed to carry the supplies the three miles from the end of the road through the jungle trail to the plantation.

My own car, which had carried Ali and me on so many other important trips, carried us again. Our only baggage was my lasso, which I had dropped on the floor of this speedy but badly mutilated conveyance of mine that for want of a better name I called an automobile.

As I had not seen the sultan since the day he turned his major and those eight soldiers over to me, I decided to drop in on him on the way to the rubber plantation. Having learned he was at the fort, I headed for these glorified barracks, where H. H. greeted me effusively. He came out of the fort as we pulled up, leaning over the side of the car. Two or three times he congratulated me on my success in getting the

---

† Charles Jesse "Buffalo" Jones (1844–1919) went to Africa in 1909, where he captured and photographed wild animals. *Roping Lions in Africa* by Guy H. Scull documents Jones's safari. Jones also caught buffalo calves in Oklahoma and Texas. He raised the animals on his Kansas ranch and used them to restock depleted wild herds. In 1959 he was elected to the Cowboy Hall of Fame. Zane Gray wrote about him in *The Last of the Plainsmen*.

tiger into the pit. Then, very solemnly—and for half a second I didn't realize that he had reverted to his bantering manner—he said, "Glad you stop here before you go take tiger from pit. I would never forgive you if you did not say good-bye before tiger eat you."

Laughing, I told H. H., whose eyes were resting on the lasso at the bottom of the car, "You don't seem very confident, do you?"

"Confident?" came the reply. "Sure! You going to catch tiger with rope like cowboy, no? Very simple, this method, no? Very simple. Why you don't try catch elephant this way too? Very simple." Then the sultan broke into one of those hearty roars of his, slapping his thighs as he doubled up with laughter.

"Don't you think I can do it, H. H.?" I asked.

Tactfully, he declined to answer with a "yes" or a "no." All he said was, "This is tiger, not American cow." His response was more eloquent than a dozen "no's."

"I'll tell you what, H. H.," I said. "I'll make a little bet with you, just for the fun of it. I'll bet you a bottle of champagne that I'll have that tiger alive in Johore Bahru before the sun goes down." H. H. never could be induced to make a wager for money with a friend; that's why I stipulated wine.

"I bet you," he grinned. "But how I can collect if tiger eat you?" (Turning to Ali with mock sternness.) "Ali, you do not forget that your *tuan* owe me bottle champagne if he do not come back!" Then he blew himself to another one of those body-shaking laughs of his.

We were off in a few minutes. Clouds were gathering overhead, and it looked like rain. I wanted to get my job over with before the storm broke. Stepping on the gas, I waved a good-bye to H. H., and we were on our way.

I was worried by the overcast skies, but I did not regard the impending storm as a serious obstacle. It looked like a *Sumatra*, a heavy rain and wind storm of short duration, followed by bright sunshine that always seems freakish to those who do not know the East. The chief difficulty imposed by the storm, in the event that it broke, would be the slippery footing that would result. A secondary problem would be the stiffening of the ropes. Rope, when it has been well exposed to rain, hardens somewhat, although it can be handled. If it rained, my job would be so much tougher.

We tore along at maximum speed, my engine heralding our approach all along the line with a mighty roar. Considering the terrific racket, I had a right to expect the speedometer to indicate a new speed record instead of a mere seventy miles an hour. My bus always got noisy when I opened her up, reminding me of a terrier trying to bark like a Saint Bernard.

The skies grew darker as we raced along, and when we were a short distance from the point where it was necessary to complete the journey on foot, a light rain started to fall. By the time we were half-way to the plantation it was raining hard, and Ali and I were nicely drenched when we arrived.

The rain had driven many of the coolies to cover, but at least a score of them were still standing around when we pulled up. The major and his soldiers, soaked to the skin, stood by faithfully, the major even taking advantage of this inopportune moment to congratulate me again (he had done it before) on my trapping of the man-eater. I appreciated this sporting attitude after the failure of his search in the jungle. However, I didn't feel very triumphant. The tough part of the job was ahead of me. Getting a tiger out of a pit into a cage in a driving rainstorm is dangerous, strenuous work.

I got busy at once. Taking out my knife, I began cutting my coil of native rope into extra nooses. This done, I knocked aside some of the stakes that secured the pit's cover, rolled away some of the logs, and, stretching out flat with my head and shoulders extending out over the hole, began to make passes at the roaring enemy below with my lasso rope. One advantage of the rain was that it weakened the tiger's footing, making it impossible for him to repeat the tremendous leap upward he had made earlier in the day when I took my first look down the pit. As I heard him sloshing around in the mud and water at the bottom of his prison, I felt reassured. If the rain put me at a disadvantage, it did the same thing to the enemy.

With the major standing by, rifle ready for action, I continued to fish for the tiger with my rope, the black skies giving me bad light by which to work. Once I got the lay of the land I managed to drop the rope over the animal's head, but before I could pull up the slack (the rain had made the rope "slow") he flicked it off with a quick movement of the paw. A second time I got it over his head, but this time his problem was even easier for the fore part of the stiffening slack landed close enough to his mouth to enable him to bite the rope in two with one snap. Making a new loop in the lasso, I tried over and over, but he either eluded my throw or fought free of the noose with lightning-fast movements in which teeth and claws worked together in perfect coordination as he snarled his contempt for my efforts.

The rain continued to come down in torrents. When it rains in Johore, it rains, an ordinary occidental rainstorm being a mere sprinkle compared to an honest-to-goodness *Sumatra*. By now I was so thoroughly drenched I no longer minded the rain on my body. Only when the water dripped down into my eyes I found myself growing irritated.

After working in this fashion for an hour till my shoulder ached from the awkward position I was in, I succeeded in looping a noose over the animal's head and through his mouth, using a fairly dry fresh rope that responded when I gave it a quick jerk. The noose accomplished my purpose, which was to draw the corners of his mouth inward so that his lips were stretched taut over his teeth, making it impossible for him to bite through the rope without biting through his lips. I yelled to the coolies, who were standing by ready for action, to tug away at the rope, which they did, pulling the crouching animal's head and forequarters clear of the bottom of the pit. This was the first good look at the foe I had had. The eyes hit me the hardest. Small for the enormous head, they glared an implacable hatred.

Quickly bringing another rope into play, I ran a second hitch around the struggling demon's neck. Another group of coolies, also working under Ali's direction, pulled away at this rope from the side of the pit opposite the first rope-hold. It was no trouble, with two groups of men holding the animal's head and shoulders up, to loop a third noose under the forelegs and a fourth under the body. Working with feverish haste, I soon had eight different holds on the man-eater of Johore. With coolies tugging away at each line, we pulled the monster up nearly even with the top of the pit and held him there. His mouth, distorted with rage plus what the first rope was doing to it, was a hideous sight. With his hind legs he was thrashing away furiously, also doing his frantic best to get his roped forelegs into action.

I was about to order the lowering of the box when one of the coolies let out a piercing scream. He was No. 1 on the first rope. Looking around I saw that he had lost his footing in the slippery mud, and, in his frenzied efforts to save himself, was sliding head first for the mouth of the pit. I was in a position where I could grab him, but I went at it so hard that I lost my own footing, and the both of us would have rolled over into the pit if Ali, who was following me around with an armful of extra nooses, hadn't quickly grabbed me and slipped one of these ropes between my fingers. With a quick tug, he and one of the soldiers pulled us out of danger.

The real menace, if the coolie and I had rolled over into the pit, was that the other coolies would probably have lost their heads and let go of the ropes. With them holding on there was no serious danger, for the tiger was firmly lashed.

I've wondered more than once what would have occurred if the native and I had gone splashing to the bottom of that hole. Every time I think of it, it gives me the creeps; for though the coolies at the ropes were dependable enough when their *tuan* was around to give them orders, they might easily have gone to pieces, as I've frequently seen happen, had they suddenly decided that they were leaderless. It wouldn't have been much fun at the bottom of the pit with this brute of a tiger.

The coolies shrieked, but they held. The rain continued to come down in sheets, and the ooze around the pit grew worse and worse. Self-conscious now about the slipperiness, the men were finding it harder than ever to keep their footing.

The box would have to be lowered at once. With the tiger's head still almost even with the surface of the pit, we let the box down lengthwise, slide door end up. Unable to get too close, we had to manipulate the box with long poles. The hind legs had sufficient play to enable the animal to strike out with them, and time after time, after we painstakingly maneuvered the cage into position with the open slide door directly under him, our enraged captive would kick it away. In the process the ropes gave a few inches, indicating that the strain was beginning to be too much for the men. If we were forced to let the animal drop back after getting him to this point, it was a question if we'd ever be able to get him out alive.

Quickly I went over the situation with Ali. I was growing desperate. With the aid of the major and three of his soldiers we got the box firmly in place. The tired men at the ropes responded to a command to tug away that lifted the animal a few inches above the point where his thrashing hind legs interfered with keeping the box erect. I assigned the three soldiers to holding the box steady with poles that they braced against it. If we shifted the box again in the ooze we might lose our grip on it, so I cautioned them to hold it as it was.

"Major, I'm now leaving matters in your hands," I said. "See that the men hold on and keep your rifle ready." Before he had a chance to reply I let myself down into the pit, dodging the flying back feet. Covered with mud from head to foot as a result of my dropping into the slime, I grabbed the tiger by his tail, swung him directly over the opening of the box and fairly roared: "Let go!" Let go they did, with me leaning on the box to help steady it.

The man-eater of Johore dropped with a bang to the bottom of Hin Mong's plainest box. I slid the door to with a slam, leaned against it, and bellowed for hammer and nails. I could feel the imprisoned beast pounding against the sides of his cell as he strove to free himself from the tangle of ropes around him. His drop, of necessity, had folded up his hind legs, and I didn't see how he could right himself sufficiently in that narrow box for a lunge against the door at the top; but the brute weighed at least three hundred pounds, and if his weight shifted over against me he might, in my tired condition, knock me over and . . .

"Get the hammer and nails!" I screamed. "Damn it, hurry up!" I leaned against the box with all my strength, pressing it against one side of the pit to hold the sliding door firmly closed.

No hammer! No nails! Plastered with mud, my strength rapidly ebbing, I was in a fury over the delay.

"*Kasi paku!*" ["Bring nails!"] I shrieked in Malay, in case my English was not understood. "Nails! *Paku!* Nails!" I cried. "And a hammer!" I felt the tiger's weight shifting against me, and I was mad with desperation.

The major yelled down that no one could find the nails. The can had been kicked over, and the nails were buried in the mud. They had the hammer. . . . Here she goes! I caught it. . . . But what good is a hammer without nails?

"Give me nails!" I screamed.

Ali finally located the nails, buried in the mud, after what seemed like a week and was probably a couple of minutes. Over the side of the pit he scrambled to join me in a splash of mud. With a crazy feverishness I wielded the hammer while Ali held the nails in place, and at last Johore's coolie-killer was nailed down fast. Muffled snarls and growls of rage came through the crevices left for breathing space.

Then I recall complaining to Ali that the storm must be getting worse. It was getting blacker. The *tuan* was wrong. The storm was letting up. Perhaps I mistook the mud that splashed over me as I fell to the floor of the pit, too weak to stand up, for extra heavy raindrops.

Ali lifted me to my feet, and my brain cleared. I suddenly realized that the job was all done, that the man-eater of Johore was in that nailed-down box. I was overjoyed. Only a person in my field can fully realize the thrill I experienced over the capture of this man-eating tiger, the first, to my knowledge, ever brought to the United States.

Ropes were fastened around the box. No one feared entering the pit now, and with the aid of the block and tackle, our freight was hauled out of the hole.

Eight coolies were needed to get our capture back through the slime that was once a dry jungle trail to the highway leading to Johore Bahru. More than once they almost dropped their load, which they bore on carrying poles, as they skidded around in the three miles of sticky muck between the rubber plantation and the asphalt road, which now reflected the sunlight, wistfully reappearing in regulation fashion after the rain and wind of the *Sumatra*. Finally, we loaded the box onto the waiting lorry, which followed Ali and me in my car.

About forty minutes later, as the sun bathed the channel in the reddish glow of its vanishing rays, I planted the man-eater under the nose of the sultan in front of the United Service Club in Johore Bahru.

With more mud on me than anyone who ever stood at the U.S.C.'s bar, I collected my bet, the hardest-earned champagne I ever tasted. The sultan was so respectful after I won this wager that once or twice I almost wished I hadn't caught his man-eater. H. H. is much more fun when he's not respectful. I enjoyed his pop-eyed felicitations but not nearly so much as some of the playful digs he's taken at me.

The man-eater of Johore, by the way, eventually wound up in the Longfellow Zoological Park, in Minneapolis, Minnesota.

CHAPTER VI

BABY BOO

It all started when an animal dealer in Los Angeles cabled me in Singapore asking me to secure for him a female baby elephant under three feet in height. The animal was wanted for work in the movies.

This may not sound like a very difficult assignment. It was every bit of that, however. In fact, I was being asked to produce an elephant shorter in stature than any in the whole United States. If the cable had read, "We want elephant smaller than any now in captivity," it would have meant exactly the same thing as asking me to secure one less than three feet tall.

Some years before, I had brought back from Asia as small an elephant as I had ever known to find its way to these shores, a little lady named Mitzi who became quite a famous vaudevillian. Mitzi stood three and a half feet high. For years she played with the well-known vaudeville act, Singer's Midgets.† She traveled with the troupe till she outgrew the midgets.

---

† Singer's Midgets were the Munchkins in *The Wizard of Oz* (1939). Leo Singer was a German immigrant who found and trained his midgets as acrobats, singers, dancers, and wrestlers in Germany and Austria. "Singer didn't fool with American midgets," according to Henry Kramer, a five-foot-nine man married to four-foot-one Dolly Kramer, "Queen of the Midgets." Between 1936 and 1952, the Kramers headed their own troupe of ten midgets. "American midgets were too independent for Singer," Kramer told Aljean Harmetz, "and they wanted too much money." "Singer had a reputation for cheating his midgets," said another former Munchkin. "Some of those little guys didn't have the intelligence to know the value of money. And they were foreigners, too. Half of them couldn't speak English. Singer fed them and clothed them. And when they didn't work, Singer was still giving them a couple of bucks to spend. They thought that was great." Aljean Harmetz, *The Making of the Wizard of Oz*, Alfred A. Knopf, New York, 1977.

I couldn't for the life of me figure out how I was going to produce a baby elephant smaller than Mitzi, the most diminutive member of the species I had ever secured.

However, an order is an order, and I was more than willing to make a determined effort to secure what the Los Angeles dealer wanted. I had other specimens to collect, and, in the process of gathering them, I planned to make inquiries wherever I went—my program promising to carry me practically all over the map of Asia—in an effort to locate a trunked shrimp short enough to meet the specifications.

Ali, who accompanied me on this trip, was instructed to be on the lookout for small elephants and to give me any and all information he picked up. I've been at this business of collecting animals and birds so long that I am known to scores of Asian traders, *shikaris,* headmen, and others. Wherever I go people come to me, and the assistant who's traveling with me, with information about specimens of all kinds that are available.

In Siam we heard that the *keddah walla* [chief] north of the town of Alostar, with whom I had traded in the past, had some very small elephants in his sheds. However, when I arrived to inspect his stock, I found that he had nothing under four feet eight inches. Wherever I went it was the same. Small elephants were available but nothing under four or four and a half feet.

Collecting activities brought me back to Calcutta, and while there I heard that a work elephant at Siliguri had given birth to a calf. As soon as I could get away, I made the trip to Siliguri, only to find the youngster had not survived.

All in all, I investigated at least a dozen tips, none of them yielding what was wanted.

It was now necessary for me to go to Singapore with the various animals and birds I had collected on these trips. While there I wired the Los Angeles dealer that I had had no success but that I would keep on trying. I wasn't very hopeful of securing the Lilliputian he sought, and, while I was perfectly willing to continue the search, I didn't want this dealer to be too optimistic about the prospects.

A few weeks later Ali and I were in Sumatra scouting around for pythons, gibbons, binturongs, and other specimens for which I had orders. We were at Domji, a port on the west coast of Sumatra, north of Palembang. The news of my arrival had spread, and several native trappers sought me out with their wares, most of them specimens that were undesirable.

After I had turned down a number of animals, reptiles, and birds that I did not want, I was approached by a Batik native who had a few specimens that were worth picking up, although they were not important contributions. In front of the nipa house where I was staying, he set down the two baskets that he bore on his shoulder on a carrying pole.

He proceeded to show me his wares. One basket contained a pair of fine hornbills, the other housed a monitor lizard, a five-foot creature that was rolled up in the container with its feet trussed up over its back.

These specimens were in excellent condition, and, as I knew I could dispose of them, I was glad to pick them up.

"*Berapa?*" I asked, pointing to the hornbills. ("How much?")

The reply was a question. Did the *tuan* have any tobacco?

I nodded my head. I always carry plenty of tobacco because it is frequently very useful in trading with the natives.

With the aid of Ali (my own knowledge of the Malay dialect this fellow spoke proving inadequate) I learned I could have the birds for eight ounces of tobacco. The tobacco available in that part of the world comes in twisted sticks, three ounces to the stick. I would have gladly given him three sticks, or nine ounces, but I was afraid he might decide there was something wrong with the tobacco, something of the sort having happened to me before, so I decided to give him exactly what he wanted. I sent Ali into the house for three sticks of tobacco. Then I took out an old pocket knife and proceeded to cut one of the pieces at the two-thirds mark, two and two-thirds sticks totaling the eight ounces he named as his price.

I handed him his tobacco, and he handed me the birds. He was pleased with his bargain, promptly spitting out his betel nut and biting off a mouthful of tobacco to take its place. (Many Asians are more interested in tobacco as something to chew than they are in its smoking possibilities.)

Next I asked this native what he wanted for his lizard. He suddenly became very coy, looking down at the ground and putting his hand to his face as if to conceal a blush.

"*Berapa?*" I repeated.

No answer.

I suggested five guilders.

He shook his head.

I was puzzled. Five guilders was a good price for that lizard. I asked him what he wanted.

Looking up, he beckoned to Ali, who walked over to where he stood. Leaning over, he whispered something in Ali's ear.

Ali looked up, grinning.

"What does he want?" I asked.

Ali, still grinning, told me that the native wanted my knife. He had taken a fancy to it when I took it out to cut the tobacco. He didn't feel right about asking for it, Ali told me, but would deeply appreciate it if I could bring myself to part with it for the lizard. He didn't want my five guilders. He knew that he was asking a lot in suggesting that I part with my precious knife, but if I would consent to the deal, he would be so happy. Perhaps some time in the future when I returned to this part of the world there would be some way in which he could reciprocate.

Ten years before I had bought that knife in America for seventy-five cents. Yet this fellow preferred it to the five guilders ($1.80) that I offered him for his lizard. Of such strange turns is the business of trading with natives comprised.

I readily agreed to trade the knife for the lizard. The simple fellow was delighted with his bargain. He eagerly grabbed the knife, an ordinary bone-handle affair, with a sizeable main blade and two smaller ones, fondling it as if it were something of infinite worth. Finally he put his treasure in his pocket and jauntily started away.

About ten yards off, he turned around and shouted, *"Berapa ada kecil gajah?"* ["How much would you give for a little elephant?"]

I had ceased to think about my need for a midget pachyderm. Although I had not given up, the subject had slipped out of my consciousness. The press of other business, involving specimens that were more available, was responsible.

Both Ali and I were excited when the subject was so unexpectedly reopened. We called the native back.

We asked him how tall the elephant was. With his hand he indicated a height of about four feet. I shook my head, and Ali, resorting to his favorite method of registering disgust, wrinkled up his nose.

That was too tall, we told him. Whereupon the obliging soul started protesting that the animal he had in mind wasn't that tall at all. It was only so tall, indicating a height of about two and a half feet, which he gradually decreased until finally his hand was not more than ten inches from the ground.

I was so amused by this exaggeration that I started laughing. Ali was not ready to be as amused as I was, having his private opinion of natives who lied so outrageously. He did decide that the occasion did not call for too much seriousness, for he actually stopped wrinkling up his nose when my laughter reached his ears. He confined himself to spitting at the ground, his method of registering fair-to-middling displeasure. When I continued to chuckle, as I eyed the Batik liar who was still stooped over indicating with his hand a height of ten inches, Ali even smiled faintly.

I started questioning the native about his ten-inch elephant. Pressed for a description of the animal, he mentioned the fact that there was hair all over it. This had the effect of making us take the fellow seriously. Regardless of the beast's exact measurements, if it was covered with hair it was bound to be a fairly recent calf and might easily be under three feet. Another thing that encouraged me was the fact that in answer to my question he told me, without hesitation, that the animal was a female. He had no way of telling that what I wanted was a female.

I decided to take a chance and investigate. The Batik's village, it developed, was about fifteen miles off. He had walked all that distance to dispose of his hornbills and his lizard.

Within half an hour Ali, the Batik, and I were seated in a bullock cart on our way to investigate the little elephant with the fuzz on it. A baby elephant, when born, is covered with hair, which gradually falls off as the animal grows up.

Ali was suspicious of our new acquaintance. He even hinted that this native was holding out the promise of a rarity merely to get us so excited we would want to make the trip at once, thus enabling him to get a ride home and rest his weary bones after his long walk to Domji. A rascal capable of promising you a ten-inch elephant was capable of anything, he insisted.

I'm all for taking chances. I've secured some of my finest specimens that way. Needless to say, I've been hoodwinked too, but I always set forth on a mission of this kind willing to trust to luck. If I get the breaks, fine; if I don't, what of it? I know one man, a German collector, who might have made a reputation if he had been less suspicious, who very often failed to investigate tips from natives for fear that someone might be trying to put something over on him. He was so careful not to let anyone send him off on a wild goose chase—he'd show those natives whether they could fool him—that on several occasions he just missed picking up some very rare specimens. I know because I beat him to it on more than one of those occasions.

My Batik tipster was wreathed in smiles all the way back to his village. The pleasure he got out of acquiring my knife was almost incredible. He would turn it over in his hand, hold it out and regard it ecstatically, turn it over again, and finally put it away. Then he would suddenly think of it again, and out it would come, this time perhaps for a few minutes of whittling, or for use in cutting off a piece of tobacco. In fact, he got so much fun out of keeping the implement in use that he cut and chewed more pieces of tobacco on that trip than he probably used in the course of two or three normal days.

After a journey of four hours we arrived at our destination. The native took us to a tapioca garden in back of the village headman's shack. There, with a rope around its neck, and looking terribly thin and emaciated, stood the smallest baby elephant I had ever seen. With the carpenter's rule I had taken with me I measured it and found it to be just two inches under three feet, at the shoulder, which is how elephants are measured. As my informant had told me, it was a hairy little tot and couldn't have been over ten or twelve days old.

Weak and wobbly, the little babe, a female, as the native had said, seemed to be supporting herself with difficulty. Her trembling and starved appearance suggested that the headman and his four partners, who owned the elephant jointly, had not had much success in feeding their captive. The task of getting food inside a baby elephant that has been suddenly taken away from its mother usually presents real difficulties.

I said to the headman, "What good is your elephant? She's going to die of starvation." I'd have given the creature two more days to live under the conditions that prevailed when I found her.

I was mistaken, the headman insisted. The animal was in excellent condition, the finest, strongest, best-nourished baby elephant he had ever seen. The fellow evidently thought I was a greenhorn. Never had I seen a baby animal in worse shape.

Yes, the baby was in splendid condition. (The gist of what the headman was feelingly shouting.) Hadn't she been eating bananas? (His four partners nodded their heads.) And was there anything more nourishing than bananas? (Again the four yesmen did their stuff.) Wasn't it a heart-warming joy to see the sweet little thing take a banana in its trunk and eat it? (This time the ever-ready quartet chorused their affirmation, struggling for a note of wistfulness as they okayed the tender picture projected by the spokesman.)

The more the headman spoke, the worse his story got. An elephant as young as the one that stood tottering before us doesn't know what its trunk is for. It is so much loose flesh limply dangling from its head, and it has a tough time getting it out of the way when it sucks its mother.

"All right," I said, "let's see you feed her a banana." I got tired of hearing the old man tell me that the elephant could take *pisang makan* (banana to eat), and I decided to call his bluff. A banana was secured, and the headman proceeded to demonstrate. This consisted of an effort to wrap the end of the animal's trunk around the fruit. The bewildered little pachyderm was unable to give the faker any cooperation, having no control over her floppy little trunk. Time after time the banana would fall to the ground.

After five or six failures, in the course of which Ali and I swapped winks, one of the partnership quartet came to the rescue. The animal had eaten six bananas just before my arrival. He'd forgotten all about it. Then his comrades came to life, and they remembered the incident too. Why, of course! That explained everything. One couldn't very well expect a little elephant like that to eat a banana so soon after it had consumed the other six.

"You see?" smiled the headman after the convenient four had explained all.

I nodded, restraining a smile, for I didn't want these rogues to know how much fun I was getting out of their crude efforts to fool me. Yes, I saw. (The headman beamed happily, thinking he had convinced me.) I was dealing, I quickly added, with a cheat who was trying to sell me an animal that he knew to be doomed on account of his inability to get food into its stomach. (The headman's expression changed. Again he took on his protesting manner, vowing by all that was sacred that he was an honest man who was being grossly misunderstood.) He turned and asked his partners if it wasn't a fact that he was an honest man. (They almost nodded their heads off.) Was there a more honest man in the whole district? (Four emphatic shakes of the head.)

"See?"

I still didn't see.

I wanted the elephant. It was in very bad condition, but I felt I might be able to save it. Naturally I did not feel like paying a good deal. The risk was unacceptable. It wouldn't have surprised me if the shaky little creature had curled up and died that very day. It was as frail as a Christmas tree ornament unless I could devise some means of making it eat.

The headman's object, of course, was to establish that he was selling me an elephant in perfect health and to be paid accordingly. I didn't know what the market price that day was for food-refusing, half-dead baby elephants, so I was forced to consult my own index of values. I quickly decided what was a fair price to pay for this wobbly little pachyderm and resolved that once I made my offer I would stick to my story.

The headman, switching tactics, decided to feign independence. If I was unwilling to buy the animal as a perfect specimen, he knew someone that was. He and his associates were rattan gatherers, and they were anxious to return to the jungle to resume their work. If he did not get his price from me, he would have to start negotiations with another prospect who was in the district.

I decided to call his bluff. "All right," I said, "go ahead . . . Come, Ali." We started to go. As we left, a violent argument broke out among the headman and his four partners. Evidently they were accusing him of gumming up the deal. There was much name-calling, and for a while it looked as if they would come to blows. Ali, looking over his shoulder, told me that the native who had brought us there was trying to pacify them, evidently in an effort to earn the commission that would be his if a deal took place.

Suddenly the headman started running after us, inspired no doubt by the words of our Domji friend. With the four partners following him, the spokesman pulled up alongside me and pantingly pleaded with me to take the elephant off his hands. I knew he realized full well that anything he got would be so much velvet, for the animal could not survive much longer in the state it was in. None of them knew enough about the species to figure out a way of making a food-declining baby elephant eat; and there was apparently no one in the district who could or would help them solve this problem of providing nourishment.

I decided to close the deal without wasting any more time. Taking out ten ten-guilder notes (I had fixed on one hundred guilders as the maximum that a half-dead baby elephant was worth) I handed them to the headman, saying: *"Bagi lima."* ["Divide this among the five of you."]

The headman counted the money and smiled, apparently pleased with the deal. His partners, pleased too, added their smiles to their spokesman's, and soon everybody was happy, including the native who had given us the tip, this chap proceeding to collect his commission.

Their problem was over, but mine had just began. I had to get some food into that elephant's belly, and without much loss of time. I sent Ali out to scout around for a milkgoat. He brought one back and hurriedly milked it. I tried to pour some milk down the stubborn pachyderm's throat, but I couldn't get her jaws open. Once or twice I managed to get them partly open, but before I could pour the milk down she closed them again.

I considered five or six different plans for feeding that animal, dismissing them as impractical as fast as they popped into my head. Then I got an idea that I thought was worth trying. The first step was to send Ali to a nearby clump to cut me a length of bamboo. As is commonly known, a stick of bamboo is made up of a series of joints, the wood being hollow between joints. Ali brought back exactly what I had sent him for, a piece of bamboo about two inches in diameter. I cut off a piece about nine inches long, leaving the joint to form the bottom. This gave me a device that I planned to use as a feeding tube. I sharpened the opening till it came to a point, and, satisfied that I was on the right track, I proceeded with the next step.

Before this could be carried out we had to get our elephant—we practically carried her—to the shack where we had arranged to spend the night. I instructed Ali to boil some rice in water. When the rice was cooked I mixed some goat's milk with it, the result being a thin but nutritious gruel. Then I proceeded to fill my bamboo tube with this substance.

This done, Ali got his shoulder right under the elephant's forequarters till she was almost standing on her back legs. Then I forced the point of the bamboo tube between her tightly closed jaws, gradually working it in until I could tip it up and dump the contents down her throat. Stubborn to the last, she tried to keep from swallowing, giving in after a few seconds of gurgling. A second tubeful was prepared, and the operation was repeated, this time the task proving less difficult. In all, I fed her three tubes of gruel that session.

An hour later I put the obstinate little girl to bed, covering her up with some old gunny sacks. The following morning there was a definite improvement in her condition, some of the wobbliness having disappeared. We gave her her breakfast, repeating the performance with the tube. This time it was unnecessary to prop her up.

A little later in the morning we put her on a bullock cart and took her back to Domji, from where she was transported, along with my other specimens, to Singapore. We had no trouble feeding her en route, the bamboo feeding tube working perfectly.

As soon as I reached Singapore I cabled the Los Angeles dealer that I had a female baby elephant under three feet. I installed the midget pachyderm in my compound, and within a week after her arrival there, she had developed so complete an interest in food that if I took out the bamboo tube she would follow me all over the lot. By the time I was ready to return to America she was in splendid condition, full of life, alert, and a wee bit mischievous. A lovable animal, she became a favorite on board ship, the crew taking a particular fancy to her.

I exercised her regularly on deck, one of my principal difficulties being to get her past the full-grown elephants I was bringing back. She would try to get chummy with them, nuzzling against their legs and making other friendly advances.

She was an amusing sight when she began to learn to use her trunk. She developed a sudden consciousness of the uses to which this part of her, till now a dangling impediment, could be put. Gaining control of it, she would swing it in all directions, delighted with the discovery that this was something she could make do her bidding, like her legs. All the way across the Pacific she kept it in action, like a child captivated with a new and interesting toy. For the benefit of "company" she would promptly show off, swinging that little trunk till I thought it would come off.

When I arrived in San Francisco the dealer who had ordered this baby elephant was waiting for me on the dock. He was delighted with his acquisition, the little lady from Sumatra being exactly what he wanted. I turned her over to him together with three of my bamboo feeding tubes, instructing him how to use them.

Not long afterwards she became a movie queen, under the name of Baby Boo. Someone gave her this sobriquet in Los Angeles, and it stuck.

One day Baby Boo was being filmed in a picture [*Pink Elephants*, 1926] in which Al St. John[†] was the featured player. To create a desired effect, it was necessary for the camera to catch the little elephant on the run. Baby Boo was not in the mood for running. Coaxing availed nothing. Either she didn't get the idea, or she had decided that she didn't want to run, as she had once decided that she didn't want to eat.

The cameraman was frantic. The director was in a frenzy of despair. Both appealed to the animal's keeper. Wasn't there something that could be done?

The keeper said he would see what he could do. When Baby Boo had been turned over to him, with her came a magic wand that had proven helpful more than once in handling her: one of my bamboo tubes, which the keeper always carried with him. Getting out of range of the camera, he took out the tube and called to the balking elephant. Baby Boo caught sight of the bamboo, and as she did, she started to run, making a hurried beeline after him. Once more the tiniest elephant I have ever brought back to America was under the spell of the bit of bamboo that had saved her life.

The cameraman got what he wanted.

[†] Al ("Fuzzy") St. John (1893–1963) starred in his own comedy shorts at Paramount and Fox, many of which he directed and wrote himself in the early 1920s. He later played character parts in feature films. In the 1930s, St. John began a new phase of his career as a grizzled sidekick of various cowboy stars in countless low-budget Westerns. One of the characters he played frequently was called "Fuzzy Q. Jones," hence his nickname. In all he appeared in hundreds of films. He was a nephew of disgraced film comedian Roscoe "Fatty" Arbuckle and was married to Hearst writer Adela Rogers St. John.

CHAPTER VII

MONKEY MOTHERS

I had some orders for crocodiles. Not being fond of these reptiles —a vicious lot at best, with none of the color and imaginative appeal one frequently finds in savage creatures—I had put off securing the specimens until I had gathered most of the other items of a collection that I had rounded up at Singapore and Calcutta for shipment to the United States.

I was in Calcutta when I decided to land my crocodiles and get this dull chore out of the way, little knowing that these reptiles were going to provide an opportunity to witness as touching an example of the maternal instinct at its heroic best as I have ever seen, in a species that had nothing to do with my mission.

I left with Lal for the Sunderbunds [Sundarbans], that vast lowland studded with innumerable islands and marshes, where the Ganges splits into many rivers and enters the Bay of Bengal. This district is easily accessible from Calcutta and was the ideal place to go for my crocodiles.

Until recently the Sunderbunds were one of the game paradises of Asia. Most of the big game has been killed off, although there are still some tigers and leopards. Thousands of monkeys inhabit this territory, however, and it is also alive with crocodiles, cobras and wild pigs.

The Sunderbunds cover an area of over eleven thousand square miles. Some is heavy jungle, but in the main it is not the thick black jungle of other parts of India and the Malay country.

There are several lighthouses in this district. An old *shikari* who used to get crocodiles and other specimens for me lived with one of the lighthouse keepers, and I was on my way to see him, having notified him of my needs and arranged for a meeting place.

Zoos are the only market for crocodiles. Hardy creatures, they live a long time, and practically every sizeable zoo has at least one specimen to round out its reptile exhibit.

The natives have many ways of catching crocodiles, but the one most commonly used is to take a live monkey and tie a stout hardwood stick about the same length as the monkey along its back. The stick is sharpened at both ends. Attached to the center of this stick and set crosswise upon it is another of about half its length. The monkey is then tied out on a leash in the mangrove bushes that grow in the shallow water along the edge of the streams where the crocodiles are found. When the crocodile grabs the monkey, whichever way it takes its prey, either sidewise or perpendicularly, its jaws clamp down on the two sharp ends of the stick, which hold its mouth open. Being unable to close its mouth, the crocodile cannot swim, so it immediately makes for the banks, where its tracks can easily be followed by the trappers, who have no difficulty in catching the monster on land.

As little enthusiasm as I have for crocodiles, I am always glad to pick one up for a zoo that wants it. It is all in the day's work; and usually it is part of an order that includes more interesting assignments.

I'll say this for crocodiles: once you get 'em boxed for shipment they cause very little trouble. I recall one that I brought back for the St. Louis Zoo that declined food and drink for forty-five days and yet had the good grace to be in perfect condition when I delivered him. I mention this by way of giving an idea of how hardy these strange reptiles are.

Another specimen that I brought back had no interest in food for almost as long a period, but in this case the long fast was more understandable as the creature had consumed a native woman before he had been caught. The woman victim had gone to the river bank to do the family washing when the reptile felled her with a terrific blow of its tail. Then the killer dragged her off into the mud and finished the job. Crocodiles are among the worst of the man-eaters. In some sections the local governments pay a reward for the killing of these vicious reptiles. For instance, in Sarawak, North Borneo, which is ruled by Rajah Brooke, the only white rajah, a bounty of twenty-five cents (Straits money) per foot is paid for all crocodiles killed and captured, and for man-eaters a larger bounty is paid. The depredations of these murderous creatures have reached sizeable proportions in that district, and for some time past everything possible to stamp them out has been done.

Most of the specimens brought in by those claiming bounty money range from ten to fourteen feet. (The longest crocodile I ever saw was a sixteen-footer that got into a drain ditch on a rubber estate in Johore and was killed by coolies.)

A native claiming bounty money usually goes through this outline: First, of course, he catches his crocodile. (Experts tell me that is the most important step, and I guess they're right.) Next the question of transporting the captive arises. The reptile's front legs are trussed up over its back and tied, then the hind legs are treated in a similar manner. The prisoner is lashed to a pole, and two men carry it on their shoulders to the nearest village, where it is taken before the headman, the local police magistrate, or anyone else in authority.

In the presence of the Authorized One the reptile is cut open, and then his insides are explored for signs of a human feast. Practically all the natives wear trinkets of some kind, usually pewter, brass, or silver bangles. The first object of the search is to look for the bangles, which a greedy crocodile does not hesitate to cram down his throat along with the flesh. These ornaments become embedded in the reptile's insides and apparently do him no harm. I know of one case where a crocodile that was caught and killed was found to have bangles so deeply embedded in his flesh (which had completely grown over the trinkets) that it was the opinion of the headman that the ornaments represented a killing made twenty or twenty-five years before.

If signs are found indicating that the captured reptile has been feasting on human flesh, the special "man-eating bounty" is paid. If not, the smaller reward applies.

Lal and I traveled by bullock cart the last seven or eight miles of our journey to meet the *shikari,* there being no other means of conveyance. If I could have expected something besides crocodiles on my arrival I would have found the trip more enjoyable. As it was, I was bored by the necessity of retraveling this familiar ground, which did not promise to yield anything in the way of a new experience. My one thought was to meet my man, get my crocodiles, and return to Calcutta with all possible haste. I couldn't have been less interested in my mission if I were on my way to collect a herd of cows, although that's an unfair comparison. I find cows more interesting than crocodiles.

As we rumbled along I found myself mentally cussing out the driver for not making better time, although I knew full well that he was doing all that could be expected of him. Suddenly as we passed a spot where there was a small clearing on one side of the jungle, the driver let out an excited yell in his best exclamatory Hindustani. As he did I heard crashing sounds near the side of the road. Then I saw a monkey jump frantically from a gnarled twisted tree trunk that leaned out over the roadway and scramble across the trail some ten or twelve yards ahead of us. Obviously the frightened creature was making for the trees on the other side of the clearing. When the monkey was halfway across the road I could see what was happening. There was a yellow streak in pursuit . . . a leopard! The pursuer had no doubt dashed up the sloping tree after the little rhesus, and having failed to make its capture there, was now after the elusive simian on open ground. The unlucky monkey had barely reached the other side of the road when the cat, coming on in a rush, pounced upon it. There was an agonized screech, and in a fraction of a second the monkey population was reduced by one.

Just before the leopard seized the shrieking monkey and disappeared with it into the jungle on the other side, I thought I saw a small dark object drop to the ground a few feet away. I had no idea what I had seen—in fact, I wasn't sure I had seen anything—but my curiosity was aroused. I halted the driver and with Lal went over to investigate. Lal wasn't sure what I was looking for, which wasn't surprising since I wasn't either. He had kept his eyes on the leopard.

For several minutes I looked around on the ground, my search yielding nothing. I was about to give up the hunt and decide that I had been imagining things when I suddenly spied something in the grass, a baby monkey not more than four inches long. I picked it up and examined it. It couldn't have been more than a few days old. Its head was about as small as a good-sized marble, its face and hands were pink, and its very thin hair was a further indication that it had only recently arrived on Earth.

I wrapped the little baby in a handkerchief and placed it in one of the pockets of my jacket. Then we were off again.

What had happened was obvious. With the breath of the leopard on its back, the last thought of the doomed mother was to throw her babe to safety. This she had done.

A monkey mother carries its babe in a peculiar way. The infant, facing the parental stomach, puts its little arms, as far as they'll go, around the body from which it sprang and hangs on for dear life in this fashion. The mother moves from place to place, on the watch for food and looking after its other concerns, knowing that its babe will instinctively cling to her. When the heroine of the episode I have just described realized that she was faced by certain death, she tore the young one loose and threw it to a place on the grass where she hoped it would be safe. I hadn't any doubt that this is what had happened.

At the nearest point along the line, I stopped and got some goat's milk, which I fed with difficulty to the little child of my favorite jungle heroine.

I met my *shikari* and picked up my crocodiles, but they received scant attention from me. I assigned to Lal the job of looking after them. My little monkey was my primary concern.

When I returned to Calcutta I found it easier to feed the little infant, for there I was able to secure an eye-dropper, a device to which I have frequently resorted as a means of getting milk into the stomachs of tiny animals. The little fellow thrived, and I made a pet of him all the way back to America, and for some time afterwards. I didn't like to part with him as I had grown very fond of the tiny cuss, as amusing a handful of rhesus monkey as I'd encountered in some time, but eventually it became inconvenient for me to keep him.

His best chance of surviving was to put him in a place where there were attendants to look after his needs, so I gave him to the San Diego Zoo, where I knew he would have excellent care. On only a few occasions have I parted with an animal more regretfully.

Ali and I were in Pontianak, Dutch Borneo, where I found myself bargaining with a Malay trader for some specimens he had on display in front of the nipa shack where he made his headquarters.

I had heard from a member of the crew of one of the boats that ply between Singapore and the Borneo coast that this trader had recently come down from the jungle with a pair of orangs and a number of other interesting catches. Tips of this kind having resulted profitably in the past, I decided to investigate. It is a short trip from

Singapore, where I was at the time, to Pontianak. The boat remains only one day, long enough to pick up a cargo of rattan, which eventually finds its way to Grand Rapids, Michigan, then goes directly back to Singapore.

So here I was in Pontianak, looking around for bargains, and more particularly for something unusual. Your dyed-in-the-wool collector is ever on the lookout for something that has never before been seen in the country where he disposes of his specimens. There is no more exquisite thrill in the game than bringing back rare "firsts," and on every trip I've ever made since I got started in my chosen field I've always kept my eye peeled for novelties. Nothing delights me more than to place under the nose of an eminent zoologist a bird or a beast or a snake he has never seen before, something that up to then had been only a name, perhaps a ponderous Latin one, in the natural history books or the zoological dictionary. A phlegmatic scientist suddenly come alive is always a treat to me. There is one, a chap who normally seems as devoid of emotion as a flounder, who, when I show him a rare zoological specimen, becomes so animated I begin to fear that the quick transition from his usual state of bloodless calm may prove too much for him. He jumps up and down, waves his arms, shouts, and acts for all the world like an astronomer who has discovered a new planet. These bursts of scientific joy are one of the real compensations of my work.

The Malay trader had a fairly interesting collection but nothing that I had not brought back many, many times. Still, I had orders for most of the species he showed me, and as his specimens were in good condition I started bargaining with him for the lot. The exhibits on display constituted his entire collection, he told me, and he preferred to sell the whole business for a flat price. As I was about to close the deal, Ali, who had been snooping around, came over and whispered something in my ear.

The information Ali gave me was decidedly important. Instantly I turned and went up into the house, the trader chasing after me protesting. There, in the place where Ali told me to look, I found as unusual a sight as I'd witnessed in years of collecting—a pair of proboscis monkeys! These are the rarest of simians and had never been seen in the United States. It was the first time I had ever beheld the species.

The male was about three feet high, its nose sticking out from its face about two and a half inches. The female was somewhat smaller in size, but she too had a very prominent proboscis. The animals were tan brown in color.

Ali had done an excellent piece of detective work, a very necessary part of the business of dealing with native traders. Very often they hold out their best specimens. When I buy out a person's stock I feel entitled to a look at everything he's got. As these traders can seldom be depended upon to tell the truth, it was part of Ali's job to snoop around and see what else he could find while I bargained for whatever I selected.

With more indignation than I really felt—for the trickiness of traders was something that I had grown accustomed to—I demanded to know why he had been holding out on me. What was the idea of telling me he was showing me everything when he knew full well that the pair of monkeys in the house would interest me more than anything he had shown me?

He was sorry. But the proboscis monkeys were not for sale.

Not for sale? Then he could keep his other stuff. . . . Come, Ali. . . . Together we started walking away. (Of course, we were bluffing. It is all part of the business of dealing with a trader.)

The trader ran after us, needless to say. Would I please return? He would explain.

Yes, I would return for a moment, but he was wasting his time. How could I believe anything that came from the lips of a person who said he was selling me everything and then held back his best goods? Bah! (I did my best to restrain a chuckle as I made this show of disgust with having encountered the appalling trait of deception. No, not until I had come to Pontianak did I realize there were people who were capable of such dastardly conduct.)

Would the *tuan* please listen. I nodded, shrugging indifferently as I did. . . . The *tuan* would soon see that he, the trader, had not been trying to practice deception. He had merely been following the advice of the Dutch resident who had told him that the proboscis monkeys were very valuable. If they could be got to Batavia, there they could be sold to the Amsterdam Zoo for a handsome price. Surely the *tuan* understood. The trader might never again acquire another monkey like that pair. He would have to have at least fifty guilders ($21) apiece for them.

To close the deal in a hurry I offered the Malay trader a thousand guilders for his whole collection, including the proboscis monkeys. He was overjoyed. This was a fortune to him. He had probably secured that pair of rare simians from the Dyaks for five cents' worth of salt or a few ounces of tobacco. I know of one instance where a trader left a group of Dyak natives in a delirium of joy by giving them a dozen yards of cotton cloth and a hatchet for a fine collection of animals and reptiles. When he threw in a little salt and tobacco for good measure, they decided they had been dealing with the most generous man in the world.

Ali and I departed, with the blessings of the Malay ringing in our ears. A few hours later my purchases were at the dock; and when the little interisland packet heaved anchor at Pontianak, I was having a much-needed sleep on a pile of loose rattan under the shade of a matting awning that had been rigged up for me. Ali sat upon the poop deck peacefully chewing his ever-present betel nut. He was surrounded by two orangutan cages, four baskets containing argus pheasants, a crated leopard cub, two gibbon apes looking out of crude native containers, a box containing a twenty-four-foot python, and the cage housing my rare firsts.

The trip back to Singapore was a happy one, for I couldn't help reveling in the fact that I had picked up the only proboscis monkeys, with one exception, brought out of Borneo in several years. The single exception I knew of was the proboscis monkey captured for the prince of Wales on the occasion of his visit to India and the Straits during 1921–1922, when a good-sized zoological collection was presented to him by both the Indian and Straits governments for the zoo at Regents Park in London. This proboscis monkey, however, died a few days after arriving in Singapore. I kept in close touch with such matters, having been on the hunt for this species for some time and having failed to find one after consulting practically every trader and trapper along the Borneo coast.

When I got back to Singapore, the rare pair of monkeys was not installed in the compound with the balance of the collection. Ali, who was almost as pleased over securing them as I was, decided he could take better care of them and keep a closer watch on them by taking them out to his own house. So the two quaint little long-nosed simians became members of his household. A roomy cage was built for them on his nipa-thatched veranda, and they were made as comfortable as if they were in their jungle home. Ali fixed up the cage with log perches and swings and watched the pair's diet and general welfare as carefully as a mother might look after a delicate child. A couple of weeks after they were installed at the Malay house, a little baby proboscis was born to the female, so when I went up to Calcutta some days later I left quite a family on Ali's front porch.

Ali's main problem, and it was this that I stressed more than anything else before leaving, was to find a steady palatable substitute for the food these strange creatures were accustomed to. In their wild state they live mainly on three or four varieties of thick, waxy jungle leaves obtainable only in Borneo. A sudden change of diet is dangerous in handling animals, especially in the case of monkeys, with the exception of the hardy little rhesus chaps that eat practically anything.

Ali finally fixed on a thick-leafed water plant, used by the natives in salads. My long-nosed simians soon grew very fond of it. The faithful Malay daily had his army of grandchildren out gathering these plants. Raw carrots also proved popular, and occasionally a meal of bread and boiled rice.

All went well until we transferred my lucky finds to my compound, just before I returned to the United States with my entire collection. At the compound Ali continued his careful supervision of these odd little creatures from Borneo. Our first mishap took place when, without warning, the male decided he had seen enough of this world and died. Only a few hours before he had been as gay and chipper as could be. It was one of those sudden casualties about which it is possible to theorize at length but that are never fully explained.

The female, of course, was affected by the loss of her mate, but her little baby kept her so busy and filled her life so completely that she had no difficulty in retaining a very healthy interest in life. Spry and energetic, she kept fussing over her little child, obviously as proud of it as any human mother could be of her offspring. It was a charming little infant, about the size of a marmoset and very much like a human baby. Its long nose had not yet formed, which made it impossible for me to tell the mother, regardless of how much I wanted to flatter her, "Your child takes after you." Without the long nose of its species, it looked like anything but the child of the female that was nursing it so tenderly.

Along with the rest of my collection, this proud mother and her babe, hale and hearty in a brand-new roomy cage, were placed aboard a small freighter bound for Hong Kong, where I was trans-shipping. There the twain from Borneo were placed in a protected place on the aft main deck of the *President Wilson,* the boat on which I was returning to the United States, alongside other monkey boxes that housed, among others, some rare Wanderoo monkeys, those queer black fellows with manes and tufted tails like lions. Rare, yes, but not "firsts" like the long-nosed lady from Borneo.

I've seen many monkey mothers, good ones too, but never have I seen one nurse her little one with such tender solicitude as my Pontianak purchase displayed. When strangers came to have a look at her she would draw to the back of her box, pulling the babe over with her and encircling it with her arms as if to prevent someone from stealing it. A contented look on her face, she would sit by the hour hugging her little treasure, feeding it, gently stroking it, and showing it every conceivable attention. More than one passenger, come to visit Lady Cyrano, the name by which this monkey came to be known, was moved by the demonstrations of affection.

One morning, a few days after we sailed, I noticed that most of the cages in the monkey sector, including the one that housed the proboscis, were water-soaked. In washing down the decks, an early morning ritual on board ship, the crew had been careless, and some of my best specimens had received a dousing, which didn't do them any good.

I complained to the boatswain in charge of this gang, an officious man who strutted about like an admiral. Give a person a little authority, and there's more than an even chance that he'll swell up till there's no dealing with him.

In all my years of sea travel I have had very little trouble with ship people. Usually they're easy to get along with, a reasonable, good-natured, understanding lot.

I did my best to convince the boatswain that he'd have to tell his men to be more careful with the hose that was used in washing down the deck. I didn't want my collection to get any more saltwater baths. All I succeeded in getting out of him was a shrug of the shoulders and a stupid statement to the effect that his men were doing the best they could and that if any damage was being done, he couldn't help it. This didn't sound very reassuring, so I decided to keep an eye on the fool.

When I got a good look at my long-nosed monkey and her babe I was fighting mad. Both were shivering after their soaking with the hose. The mother, who had grown to know me and would get chummy when I looked in on her, deciding at last that I had no designs on her young one, made no response when I approached her now. She sat slumped back in a corner of the box, eyeing me sluggishly as she wrapped her trembling arms around the cuddling infant in an effort to keep it warm. I promptly replaced the wet straw in the cage and threw over the barred opening the canvas covering that normally was put into use only at night. My prizes from Borneo were soon warm again, but I was worried about them. Animals that are used to tropical warmth don't thrive on treatment of this kind.

Every morning I was on deck at five o'clock, the hour the washing-down was started. The boatswain, realizing that I was watching him, would eye me sourly, striding past me stiffly without a sign of recognition as he ordered his men about.

One morning the man at the hose let it go wild, the water shooting straight at my monkey cages and giving a number of my specimens, including the proboscis and babe, another thorough soaking. After the first experience, this certainly did not look like an accident. If ever an act had the earmarks of deliberateness, this was it.

Angry enough to throw him overboard, I tore over to where the boatswain stood. I called him fifteen kinds of a lowdown skunk, consigned him to hell, and promised to knock his front teeth out, upper and lower, if that hose squirted another drop of water on any of my animals. If I didn't know what serious business it is, rightly or wrongly, to strike a member of a ship's personnel while at sea I'd have knocked that idiot as cold as last week's soup.

"Speak to him," said the boatswain, pointing to the man with the hose, "he's the one that did it." Then he grinned crazily and strode away. I afterwards learned that this numskull was making his last voyage with the ship. Other complaints had resulted in a decision to dispense with his services, undoubtedly accounting for his defiant manner. He was quitting the vessel, so to hell with me and my animals.

I called the mate as soon as I had seen to it that my dripping monkeys were again dry and comfortable. I told him what had happened, making the air blue with various opinions I expressed of the conduct of that damnable boatswain. The mate was a decent chap. He volunteered an opinion of the boatswain besides which even my most violent outburst seemed tame. He called him a—but perhaps I'd better not set it down here. The mate reported the matter to the captain, and shortly afterwards that boatswain was up in the "old man's" quarters hearing some plain language, which of course fell on deaf ears.

Even if the boatswain had decided to behave himself, it would have been too late. That night the baby proboscis died.

This was the start of one of the saddest animal tragedies I have ever witnessed. The mother of the dead infant started pining away. I'll never forget her grief. As I approached her cage, after the death, she was shaking the lifeless body, not yet ready to believe what had happened and striving to stir it into being. I stepped back a few paces, too touched to violate the privacy of Lady Cyrano's suffering. After shaking the body for a few minutes, she picked it up and embraced it as I had seen her do a hundred times when it was alive. The idea, I suppose, was to hug it back to life.

Convinced, finally, that her efforts were useless, she slumped back in a corner of her cage, spiritless and heart-broken. As I removed the body she looked up at me pathetically in a manner that seemed to say, "I'm dead too. Better dispose of me also."

From then on Lady Cyrano was a real problem. Her chin down in her chest, she would sit motionless by the hour. She lost interest in everything, including food. Even such dainties as raisins and fresh bananas, which normally would have been joyously received, were ignored.

When I visited her she did not even look up. We had become such good friends that usually when she heard my voice she would run to the bars of her cage to meet me. Now there was no response when I greeted her. Chin buried in her chest, she sat silently mourning. It was a pathetic sight, this picture of an animal tortured by the sudden death of the babe that comprised her whole life. With her mate gone too, she was now all alone, and hour after hour, without budging an inch, she sat brooding over the cruel fate that had befallen her.

After she had skipped several meals I began to grow worried. Starvation was hardly the right program for this rare animal with which I hoped to delight the zoological world. Coaxing availed nothing, and I was finally reduced to forcing a little food down her. Mechanically she swallowed a few mouthfuls, again sinking her head in her chest and forlornly staring down at nothing as soon as the brief unwanted meal was over.

Lady Cyrano got over her dousing. I carefully watched her temperature for signs of fever, which did not develop, but she never recovered from the loss of her youngster.

I figured that if I could keep her alive until I arrived in America and put her in a busy zoo where new and interesting surroundings would help her take her mind off her troubles, she had a good chance of developing a new interest in life and of taking her place among the rarest exhibits in the world.

All the way back to San Francisco I worked on her. I arranged her cage so that when the weather was good she was sure to get the benefit of all the sunshine there was. When the weather was bad I took the necessary precautions to keep her cage warm and comfortable. I continued to ransack the galley for choice morsels in the hope of finding something so exquisitely tasty that she would eat voluntarily. But her interest in food was gone. Practically everything she ate for the rest of the voyage had to be forced down her.

Her brooding continued. Day after day she sat in that one position till her chin and her chest seemed to have merged and her bowed head suggested an attitude she had been ordered to strike and must not change for fear of punishment.

Poor Lady Cyrano was having a tougher time than any animal I had ever handled. I was having a pretty tough time myself. It is no fun to have to witness the slow pining-away of a fine, sensitive animal.

We finally arrived in San Francisco, and when I view the trip in retrospect it is no exaggeration to say that of my many Pacific crossings none provided more worry. There were far more exciting crossings but none that occasioned quite so much mental anguish. The sufferings of Lady Cyrano got under my skin to such an extent that the whole trip took on an air of tragedy.

A careful physical examination of my mourning proboscis monkey revealed, curiously enough, that she was in good physical condition. I had managed to do enough forced feeding to provide ample sustenance. Sometimes on a trip of this kind, an animal fares better if it does not eat too much. Physically Lady Cyrano was in better shape than some of my monkeys that had had far more to eat. It was the old girl's mind that was sick. She was as listless as ever when we docked, showing no interest in anything.

I wired the Bronx Zoo in New York that I had a rare proboscis monkey. Did they want her?

Did they! I received an immediate reply asking me to ship the animal at once. But Lady Cyrano was dead within an hour of the time I received my acceptance.

This is the only instance I have ever encountered, in all my years as a collector, of an animal dying of a broken heart. The monkey mother never got over the loss of her child.

CHAPTER VIII

ELEPHANT TEMPER

In my business a tame-sounding order often makes the most trouble. When Herbert Fleischhacker, well-known banker and president of the Park Board in San Francisco, told me that he wanted an elephant for presentation to the wonderful children's playground he founded on the city's ocean front, I naturally classified the assignment as routine business. It eventually proved to be far from routine.

Mr. Fleischhacker had made Golden Gate Park a present of two smaller elephants that were in constant use. Each of these pachyderms carried six children at a time (in *howdahs* that I designed). The animals developed such popularity that it was growing difficult to accommodate all the children who wanted a ride.

Mr. Fleischhacker, pleased with the success of his elephants, asked me one day if I couldn't bring back an animal capable of accommodating more children than the medium-sized elephants he had. He wanted one on whose back a much roomier howdah could be placed so that the little boys and girls of San Francisco would not have to wait in line too long for a ride. He discussed the matter as gravely as if it were an important banking problem, and I couldn't help feeling that the children of the city had a marvelous friend in this wealthy citizen who had not forgotten his boyhood days, who, in fact, revealed so much knowledge of what children consider good sport that you'd have thought it was only the day before yesterday that he was twelve himself.

I suggested that a good way of accommodating several children at a time would be to build an ornamental wagon, as colorful as a merry-go-round, and capable of carrying twenty little passengers, or more. I would supply the right elephant to pull them around. Mr.

Fleischhacker was delighted with the suggestion, and I was commissioned to deliver a good-sized elephant.

Up in northern Burma an influential Burmese went to the British Colonial Forest officials in the district in which he lived and made a contract with them to *keddah* (or corral) the elephants in that district. This meant, among other things, that he had to visit native villages throughout this territory and make a thorough canvass of the various stretches of jungle with a view to determining where the different herds of wild elephants were and approximating the number of animals in each herd.

The Burmese *keddah walla* had many things to bear in mind. Only elephants of a certain size could be taken, and only a fixed percentage of those from each district in the territory covered by his contract. There were other taboos that stipulated that the male leader of a herd could not be taken, nor a full-grown breeding female. ("Male herd leaders" are mentioned here with reservation. An adult male is the real boss of every herd of elephants, though an old female actually leads the herd as it moves from one feeding ground to another.)

Males that were not herd leaders and young females comprised the main group of allowable captures, the size range taking in animals between four and eight feet in height, although sometimes the *keddah*ing of bigger specimens was permitted.

When he had the lay of the land—when, in other words, he had taken a reliable census of the elephants in the area of jungle covered by his contract and had a good idea of how these animals were distributed over the stipulated territory—the *keddah walla* fixed upon the best location for centralizing the beasts, and here he built an enormous corral known as a *keddah*.

Elephants being a government concession, the Burmese had an arrangement with the government whereby he was to pay a fixed price for each animal he selected that came under the head of allowable catches.

Had he been in Siam or the Malay country, the Burmese gentleman would have gone through practically the same operations to get his pachyderms. The points of variance would have been few. Siam being an independent country, he would have dealt, of course, with the king instead of a British colonial official, but the rest of the procedure would have been practically the same.

Siam, by the way, has as well organized an elephant industry as there is in all of Asia (the operations are on so grand a scale they may fairly be described as an industry). Its Forestry Department is one of the best-regulated government bureaus I know. They can tell you almost the exact number of wild elephants that are to be found in any section of Siam you are minded to name.

All his arrangements made, the Burmese proceeded to build his *keddah.* Huge posts were driven into the ground a few inches apart and firmly lashed with rattan and wire cable. These posts covered an area of several acres that comprised the *keddah.* Connecting with this, by means of a gate, was a smaller corral.

At one end of the corral was a huge sliding door or gate that, for want of a better name, might be designated as the main entrance. It was into this opening that the elephants were to be driven, some of them never to return to the jungle.

When the *keddah* was finished, an army of native trackers, expert in the business of keeping elephants on the move, was sent out to drive the pachyderms in. By the time the drive began, the checkers had provided a reliable map indicating the approximate location of the different herds and an accurate census of each of them.

Hundreds of natives, in the charge of lieutenants appointed by the *keddah walla,* or chief, take part in an elephant drive. Too much is at stake to permit of any but wholehearted methods.

My Burmese, an important man in his district, had secured financial backing for his elephant enterprise in Rangoon. A tremendous investment (certainly in terms of Burma) was involved. It was up to him so to conduct his drive that he would be able to round up the elephants he wanted with as little loss of time as possible.

He had a payroll that must not get out of hand. While each man received a very small sum for his services there were so many trackers and checkers that it would not be difficult to get "in the red" if the enterprise was sloppily conducted.

Disposing of his elephants was the least of the Burmese's problems. His main job was to round them up at a minimum of expense.

Export sales (orders like mine, for instance, regardless of how extensive my operations as a collector) are a drop in the bucket. The local market for elephants—a considerable one—was what the Burmese was figuring on to make his investment pay. Every tea estate has one or two elephants to do hauling and other rough work. Many elephants are also used in India for road building and other tasks. Then there is the "ceremonial trade," scores of elephants being regularly sold to princes, rajahs, and sultans for use in court functions. The teak business is another important outlet for elephants. Hundreds of them are used in this important industry that supplies the fine hardwood that goes into the decks of practically all ships that sail the seas.

His army of trackers and checkers in motion, my Burmese was receiving bulletins at his headquarters on the progress of the roundup as a general receives communications on the progress of a battle. One messenger would come tearing in to report that this herd, consisting of so many elephants, was working in this direction; another courier would come on the run to report that such and such a herd had veered off the path that had been set for it but that the trackers, beating on their tin pans and making the other noises that were expected of them, were again in back of the off-course group and could be depended upon to work them back to the path that would lead straight to the *keddah*.

I have been asked many times whether other animals do not interfere when a herd of elephants is being rounded up. The answer is no. To all other animals in the jungle, a herd of elephants in motion is regarded as an elemental force that is not to be disputed. The thing to do is to get out of the way, as when a storm comes.

There are few sights stranger than that of an army of trackers working behind a herd of elephants. No weirder combination of noises ever reached human ears, no more fantastic sight ever greeted human eyes. Gesticulating wildly and moving along like figures in an unearthly dance, the tin-pan pounders pummel their discordant instruments into masses of dents. Some of the panless men pound anything else that will give off a noise. A few of the elect, natives with old muzzle-loading guns, superiorly brush past their unarmed comrades and shoot holes in the air by way of making their presence felt. Other natives, bearing firebrands and depending exclusively on lung power for their contribution to this jungle movie with sound, shriek and scream and screech and howl like so many demons out of hell.

Forward, forward move the elephants. Closer and closer to the *keddah* they come, their movements in most instances as accurately controlled as if someone were working a steering wheel that sent them now to the right and now to the left. The helmsman—the lieutenant selected by the *keddah walla* to direct the din barrage—directs his forces by signals, swinging the tumult this way or that to suit the needs of the moment.

Usually the elephants are rounded up one herd at a time. This may mean anywhere from ten to twenty animals. Sometimes two herds are brought in together, the deafening armies behind them converging and driving the double catch in together.

In their joy over participating in a holiday-like swing through the jungle that means money in return for noise, the natives sometimes forget that rounding up elephants is not without its dangers. My Burmese has had many proofs of this.

In the course of the drive that netted him the wild herd from which my Fleischhacker specimen was selected an overaggressive native was wiped out so quickly his comrades hardly had a chance to realize what had happened. In fact, it was over so soon many of them didn't know about it until afterwards.

The herd had been driven to a position directly in front of the huge open door of the *keddah*. In a final assault on the ears of the all-but-trapped pachyderms, tin pans, guns, lungs, and what not were called upon for a last epic outburst designed to stampede the frantic beasts through the opening of the prison.

The demoniac hullabaloo had its effect, most of the elephants tearing forward madly according to the lieutenant's plan. They stirred a real breeze into being on a hot and windless day with their headlong rush into captivity, knocking against one another as they came on in a mass formation. It would have been a clean job of *keddah*ing the whole lot if not for a female elephant that lagged behind with her calf, keeping three others from going in, including a fine young specimen that was particularly wanted.

An overzealous native—the poor devil I just mentioned—conceived the foolish notion of using a long bamboo pole to prod the lagging lady, who was half-crazy with the din and in a panic lest something happen to her little one.

Normally that native would have known better than to do anything as foolish as that. Emboldened no doubt by the fact that the other elephants were in the pen, signifying one more victory for man over beast, and with the absence of fear that is common among natives at such a moment, the reckless one advanced with his pole and let the elephant have it. With a tremendous shrill trumpeting that gave voice to all the rage in her being she whirled around and charged her tormentor, grabbing him and raising him up and stamping on him with her forefeet as she swung him back to earth. Before anyone could interfere she had pounded him into an unrecognizable mass, her trumpeting achieving a piercing high falsetto as she broke every bone in that luckless body. In record time the population of Burma had been decreased by one.

After some clever maneuvering by the lieutenant and a picked squad, the stragglers, including the killer and her calf, were driven into the *keddah* and the door was locked.

The elephants were then worked from the corral into the small pen, where the *keddah walla* gave the whole herd a careful inspection (there were seventeen in all) to see how many of the animals complied with the clause of his contract with the British officials governing purchasable specimens and how many of these eligibles he wanted. He selected seven out of the lot, healthy young specimens that would fetch good prices at Rangoon, where he marketed most of his elephants.

Four *mahouts* (keepers), on tame elephants accustomed to participation in such work, were sent in to perform the ticklish task of tying up the ones that were wanted. Cautiously they worked their mounts in among the herd, selecting the first animal to be tied, and carefully avoiding the tusks of the old bull herd leader that acted as if he had a burst of indignation coming on. They sifted their way through the captives, cleverly surrounding the elephant that was to be one of the seven nominees to be put through the process of taming. Jockeying for position with the skill that only a trained *mahout* possesses, the expert four continued their maneuvers until they had their prisoner's side against the pen, two of them getting alongside, lining up parallel to him, a third lining up in front at right angles to the side pair, and a fourth lining up in the rear and completing the square. Thus the captive was unable to move forward or backward or to either side. One of the *mahouts* —the most skillful and fearless of the quartet—then quietly slipped off his elephant, and, with a chain that he carried so deftly that it didn't rattle once as he alighted, got a quick hold on the back leg nearest the fence. A long stout rope was quickly tied to the chain and thrown out between the posts of the corral to a group of natives in charge of a pair of heavy work elephants. Speedily the rope was manipulated so that the elephants outside were tugging away until they had brought the wild specimen inside flush against the wall of the pen. The captive's other hind leg was then quickly tied and his front legs hobbled.

The six other prisoners were put through the same process until there were seven fine elephants tied up in the corral.

The gates were then thrown open, and the rest of the herd were driven back into the jungle to breed more elephants to be *keddah*ed in future years.

A man schooled in the art of handling wild elephants was assigned to each of the seven. The captives were nicely treated, food and water being regularly brought to them.

As soon as one of the captives showed signs of becoming manageable he was lashed to two tame elephants with ropes and chains and taken out of the pen to a nearby shed that was divided into stalls. Here his keeper put him through a further process of taming. With his front legs hobbled (and a rope tied to the back legs as a safeguard in case he tried to make a getaway) he was taken for an occasional walk, at the start for a very short distance, this being increased as the animal grew tamer.

It was not long before the animal was resigned to his lot and doing whatever his *mahout* was asking of him. The same was true of the other six. There were a few rebellions, but these were minor and quelled without any serious consequences. Once subdued, the rebels decided that they had more to gain by behaving themselves, which they did. By this I do not mean to say that these seven elephants, comparatively fresh from the jungle, could be classified as tame specimens. They were moderately manageable, responding to the as-yet-simple commands of their *mahouts*. While this taming process was going on other wild herds were being driven up to the *keddah* to be handled in the same manner.

Two of the seven were purchased by buyers representing teak yards located at Moulmein, two others were bought by representatives of interests at Bangkok, and three were picked up by the Rangoon Zoo.

I came down to Rangoon from the interior about the time the three elephants were brought in and installed in the zoo. They still showed signs of wildness, but they were not hard to handle for animals that were practically fresh from the *keddah,* permitting themselves to be led about without much coaxing.

Not long before, I had delivered to the Rangoon Zoo an American buffalo, or bison, which they had ordered of me. This was the second animal of its kind ever seen in Asia. The first was one that I had presented to the sultan of Johore, who for years had been anxious to secure a specimen to keep in his deer park adjoining the palace in Johore Bahru. The sultan had read extensively about the American buffalo, and when I finally secured one for him he was delighted with it, this species having captured his fancy the very first time he had heard about it.

The officials of the Rangoon Zoo had offered me a worthwhile trade for the buffalo, and now that they had something I wanted, I decided to collect. One of those three new elephants, after the process of taming had been carried further, would be ideal for the Fleischhacker playground. The zoo officials agreed to let me have one of them in an even swap for the buffalo. I selected a fine healthy young lady that stood about eight feet in height. The animal I picked, with a little more training, would be just right for the job of hauling the kids around in the ornamental wagon that I had suggested to Mr. Fleischhacker.

The deal closed, I arranged with the British India Steamship Company at Rangoon to take the elephant (she afterwards became known as Babe) to Singapore, where I would install her in my compound. Little Ali, nephew of Old Ali, my number one Malay helper, accompanied me on the trip.

In loading an elephant onto a ship a heavy canvas sling is fastened around the belly, the hold on the animal being further secured by ropes passed around the neck and under the tail. We had a hard job getting the sling around Babe on the dock at Rangoon. There was nothing in her conduct to indicate rebelliousness or a mean disposition, but it was hard to get her used to the idea of something new. We finally got the sling around her and hoisted her on board, but she trumpeted plenty of displeasure over the business of being swung through space. She didn't like it a bit.

However, once we got her installed in her place on deck, she was again herself and gave all the signs of being the manageable animal I knew her to be. We reached Singapore without mishap, and Babe was walked out to the compound. She conducted herself en route in lady-like fashion and behaved very well for so new a captive. We placed her in the temporary home, which she shared with four smaller elephants that I had secured from a *keddah walla* in Siam. The Siamese pachyderms were more used to captivity, having been caught several months before Babe was driven in from the jungle. They required less attention than the lady from Burma, who was naturally friskier, her jungle freedom being still a recent memory.

But Babe made no trouble for us beyond the normal difficulties involved in completing the adjustment of a wild elephant to the idea of captivity. By way of preparing her for her career on the Pacific Coast I had a breast-band and traces made and hitched her to a heavy log that she pulled around daily. After a while she was going through this performance with a good deal of zest, starting to pull without waiting for the command to show what a smart girl she was. So good-natured was her response that I was surer than ever that she would be perfect for the role of pulling little children around the Fleischhacker playground in the gaily colored wagon that was to be made for her.

Big Ali came out to assist me, and, to round out Babe's education, he taught her to lie down and get up; and with Little Ali on her back he walked her around the compound daily till she had done about a mile. She seemed to enjoy these workouts, responding with a good will as soon as she understood what was wanted of her.

When all the specimens I had collected at Singapore were ready for shipment to the United States I arranged for passage on a cargo boat that was lying out in the bay about three miles from shore. This meant loading my collection (many varieties of animals, birds, and reptiles) onto lighters from which we would transfer them to the ship.

We loaded all my crates and boxes into motor lorries and bullock carts and started for the dock. The elephants, some led and some ridden by men, brought up the rear.

At the dock we quickly transferred the crates and boxes to the lighters, saving the elephants for last.

Then I made a mistake. I should have loaded Babe first. Instead I started with the other four elephants.

When the first of the four was lifted into the air by the dock's gear she started squealing and trumpeting. By the time she was lowered onto the lighter she had made quite a commotion. The other three were just as noisy, kicking up a fuss the second they were lifted off the ground. There are few elephants that do not yell blue murder when you suddenly lift them into the air.

It was Babe's turn next. Not only had she demonstrated at Rangoon that she didn't enjoy being swung through space but also she had been listening to the protests of her predecessors. The others were too small to cause much trouble, but Babe was a husky lady, with a capacity for making trouble if sufficiently frightened. Having seen her balk at Rangoon, I should have loaded her first instead of giving her a chance to remember that this was a business she did not like.

The girl from Rangoon had made up her mind that she was not going to be swung aboard the lighter. She balked the second we tried to get the sling around her belly. She would not have any of it. That was her story, and she stuck to it.

We struggled, and we struggled, but we could not get the sling around her. She'd either raise up a foot and push the device away or get down on one side to keep us from slipping it under her. Over and over, she repeated the performance, first fighting the sling with her feet, then getting down on her side. She had a chain tied to one front leg and a rope fastened to a back leg, but there was enough play to enable her to go through this performance, which she did until I found myself perspiring and cussing freely.

The captain of the freighter (the only sea captain I've ever wanted to choke) kept yanking out an enormous watch and shouting that if I didn't hurry he'd have to leave without me. At the height of his peevish outburst Babe decided to get down on her belly and stay there, thrashing around with her trunk and trumpeting angrily as a warning that she wasn't enjoying this business at all.

To aid me the captain kept bellowing that he was getting tired of waiting. So far I had held him up about twenty minutes, and I was sorry; but I was doing everything I could to speed the loading of that stubborn elephant, and the foolish skipper wasn't helping any with his repeated wail that we were losing time. I wouldn't have minded that, however, for I knew that he had to leave while the tide was high, but I felt like aiming for his jaw when he said, "I thought you knew your business. I wouldn't have let you ship with me if I thought it was going to be like this."

Having loaded scores of elephants onto lighters and ships without mishap, I had a right to resent his attitude, as well as his superiority about carrying my freight—several thousand dollars' worth of
business that his company was glad to get.

We finally managed to get Babe off her belly and back on her
feet. Ali and I took counsel. We agreed that the chances of getting
the elephant harnessed in the regular manner were slim. We would
have to try something else. The captain continued to storm and
swear that he wouldn't wait another minute. No, sir! Not for a
damned elephant.

With that infernal skipper, a lanky sour-faced Yankee, behaving
like a lunatic there was no chance to work out a careful plan. I would
have to take a long chance and be quick about it.

I figured that if I could get between the animal's front legs, Ali
could throw me the end of the sling quickly and we could get it on
her. Ali got close to her on one side, two Siamese men, experienced
elephant hands who had helped me get my group of five to the dock,
getting on the other side so they could grab the sling as I passed it
through to them.

When everyone was in his appointed place—it was a tense moment, only the captain's curses breaking the silence—I got ready to
dive between Babe's front legs. Having successfully played crazier
and riskier roles in my dealings with animals, I thought there was a
pretty good chance of accomplishing my purpose now.

I rushed in, and as I did Babe reached down with her trunk and
raised me straight up in the air over her head as if to say, "Well, how
do *you* like being lifted off the ground?" I was about ten feet up in the
air but not for more than a second. She let go, throwing me straight
forward with every bit of strength she had, which was plenty, sending me a distance of ten to twelve feet. I landed smack on my bottom,
sitting down with enough vehemence to dislocate a less-battle-tried
posterior, and sliding forward four or five feet on the loose gravel
with which the dock was covered. Good upholstery is all that saved
me. If there were ribs in that part of the human form all of mine
would have been broken.

Above the shouts and screams of the men who came running
over to pick me up, I heard a laugh. For the first time the captain
was enjoying himself. Anyone who can laugh when a person is
heaved violently into space by an enraged elephant has a queer

sense of humor. I got a few laughs out of the whole business later myself (as, for instance, when the gravel that had embedded itself was painstakingly picked out of my stern), but I could not understand the show of captainly mirth that reached my ears as the ground and I collided. With less luck I might have suffered a broken neck or a snapped spine.

While the men bent over me to see how much damage Babe had done, the bad girl from Burma was struggling to free herself. Ordering the men to look to the elephant, I got up with difficulty and hobbled over to join them. As I came up, Babe, having managed to shake herself loose from the rope that had held her hind leg fast, came running forward. When she reached the end of the twenty-four-foot play she had, now that she was no longer held from behind, the impact of her forward rush snapped the chain on her foreleg, nine or ten feet of it remaining fastened to the foot.

The chain dragged along after Babe as she ran, annoying her and slowing her up. When she was about ten yards ahead of us she stopped to pick it up with her trunk; and as we came up she started whipping it around like a bull whip.

It was not my lucky day. As I stood there telling the men what to do with their elephant hooks (I was too wobbly to wield one myself) the whirling chain struck me on the leg, wrapping itself around me in a rattle of metal. With the chain around my leg, Babe started to run, dragging me on one knee across the gravel that seemed all at once to become a series of saw-like points.

Luckily the two Siamese men, as good a pair of elephant hands as I've ever known, didn't forget what to do with their hooks. Staying in front of the would-be runaway they kept jabbing her in the trunk and forehead until they stopped her, after she had dragged me some fifty or sixty feet. The flesh was off my knee, and I was a wreck, unable to stand up, when I was released from the chain that had crazily bound me to the elephant. I don't mind adding that I had had a bad scare and that this, added to my physical troubles, left me shakier than I had been in some time.

The captain, waving his watch in the air in a frenzy of despair, called upon heaven to witness that this was my last chance to leave with him for his boat three miles away. He would give me five minutes more and would go without me if I was not ready then.

I was licked. It was the first time in several years that I was faced by the prospect of leaving behind an animal that I had set out to bring back to America. There was nothing else to do. All my crates and cages had been loaded on the freighter, and my four elephants were in the last lighter below, the only part of my collection that had not been taken down the bay and hoisted on board.

I would have to leave; but I had no intention of abandoning that elephant. She was a fine animal. Her erratic conduct proved nothing except that fear of dangling by a sling in midair, a sensation that probably gave her a sickish feeling the first time she experienced it, was capable of making her seem like a vicious pachyderm.

As soon as she saw that no further efforts would be made to put a sling around her and lift her off her feet, Babe quieted down. The Siamese men, keeping their hooks handy, had her well in hand by the time I had used up only half of the captain's five minutes. I ordered Babe back to my compound, adding that I would send instructions later telling what I wanted done with her.

We reached the boat with time to spare, the condition of the tide being such that we could have left a half-hour later without doing any damage to the jumpy captain's schedule. I might have been able to overlook his time-craziness if he had taken the trouble, even once, to drop in at my quarters to see how I was getting along. After all, I had boarded his vessel too weak to negotiate the ladder—so helpless, in fact, that it had proven necessary to swing me over the side like one of my animals—and it wouldn't have done the old fool any harm to look in and say hello. I didn't exactly miss him. But I'd have thought more of him if he'd showed himself to be that human. As it was, I was unable to decide whether he was a fish or a reptile.

"What's the matter with that damned captain of yours anyway?" I asked the mate the day after we sailed. I got to know him quickly for on a boat of this kind there is no doctor, and the mate (who is required to know something about first aid and some of the other fundamentals of healing, such as ministering to a gravel-inlaid posterior, etc.) acts as medical officer.

"You asked a question?" said the mate, a likable chap with an amusing habit of repetition, as he dislodged from my right lower cheek the tenth bit of gravel in five minutes.

"Yes, I did," I replied.

"I believe you asked, 'What's the matter with the captain?'"

"That's right," I said.

"Yes, that's right," he echoed. "That's what you asked." He dug out another bit of gravel as he solemnly made this statement. "Well, sir, if you ask me I'd say—"

"Yes, I'm asking you."

"Well, sir, it's a question. What's the matter with anything? Take, for instance, a mud turtle. What's the matter with a mud turtle? Take a bedbug. What's the matter with a bedbug? Or take something simple. Take a dead fish. An old dead fish. One that's good and ripe. What's the matter with it? It stinks, sir. That's what's the matter with the captain."

His work on my bottom concluded, the mate turned his attention to my knee, replacing the neat bandage he had made the day before with a fresh one.

"That's what I thought," I said.

When the mate left I found myself thinking of Babe. I was determined not to lose her. She was a valuable property, and I had no intention of letting her remain in Singapore. If I had considered her capable of running amuck under ordinary circumstances I'd have felt differently. I had had enough experience with the species to know that the gentlest of elephants will act badly if sufficiently scared. For an animal fresh from the *keddah,* Babe had made wonderful progress. She was not to be judged by an erratic performance involving her pet prejudice: belly slings.

To this day my right knee bears Babe's trademark. Perhaps it seems strange that, with the wound still fresh, I should have been so tolerant of her misconduct. The answer is that I had seen so much freakish conduct in animals mistaken for viciousness. I had a hunch about Babe, and I was going to play it. I was soon busy putting into effect a plan that I considered worth trying.

I sent a wireless to a close friend in Singapore asking him to give Ali these instructions: He was to see Hin Mong at once and order the Chinese carpenter to build a platform strong enough for Babe to stand on. He was then to lead the elephant on to the platform, keeping her standing there while Hin built a crate around her out of heavy timbers with iron reinforcing bars, using the platform as the floor of the crate. If the elephant could be quickly crated, she was to be shipped to Manila on the first boat sailing, with ample food for a six-day trip. The *President Cleveland* was due at Manila a few days after my boat was scheduled to arrive; so, in sending the animal to Manila, the thing to do was to have her consigned to the Dollar Line, which I did.

When I arrived at Manila I found a telegram from Singapore advising me that the elephant was on its way aboard a Spanish boat. This vessel was due in Manila a few days after our departure and about the time the *President Cleveland* was scheduled to arrive. I arranged with the Dollar Line to ship the elephant from Manila to San Francisco, leaving a long letter of instruction for Bill Morris, mate of the *Cleveland,* a likable and intelligent seaman. I arranged for Bill to get at Hong Kong the food that Babe would need for the trip, this to be charged to me at a local ship's chandler where I carried an open account.

At Manila I had another job to do. I had been unable to pick up sufficient hay at Singapore, a commodity difficult to secure there in large quantities. I needed more than I was carrying to keep my elephants fed on the long trip across the Pacific in a cargo boat. I had arranged by wireless to secure some hay at Manila that was to be brought in from an army post fifteen miles in the interior. When we arrived the hay was not at the dock. There was a message for me saying that there had been some delay but that the hay would be delivered.

A half-hour before the time set by our Yankee skipper for our departure from Manila the hay had not arrived. I telephoned the army post and learned that the trucks were on their way and would arrive in an hour.

I asked the captain if he could not wait a little longer, telling him that if I did not pick up this hay I wouldn't have enough food for my elephants.

"You should have thought of that before," he told me.

I told the captain that I had, adding a few details about the difficulty of buying hay in Singapore. All I had been able to secure there was a small quantity of Australian hay that I was able to divert, after much effort, from the racing stables that had ordered it.

Although I learned in confidence from the mate that another hour's wait was perfectly feasible, the captain was unrelenting. He raved about the unreasonableness of landlubbers. (At the time of this occurrence I had crossed the Pacific over thirty times and was rated a pretty fair sailor by some hard-boiled sea captains.) No, he would not wait. Not for any danged hay! I had held him up long enough at Singapore. He'd be blowed if he'd let me delay him again.

We left without my hay, which gave me a real problem. I would be without anything to feed my elephants toward the end of the trip.

My problem was complicated when we got up into the North Pacific. The captain received a wireless from the owners instructing him to cut down to the most economical cruising speed, which in the case of this freighter was eight knots.

This meant several more days on the ocean and, of course, aggravated my food problem. The situation was now serious. I had to find some way of getting more food for my elephants or face the prospect of losing them.

I discussed the matter with the engineer, with whom I had struck up quite a friendship. In the course of our conversations it developed that we had many mutual friends on the sea, and we spent a good deal of time reminiscing about them. After we'd been out four or five days we were calling each other by our first names.

The engineer was sympathetic. The captain was a dirty thus and so for not waiting a little longer at Manila. But what are you going to do with a skipper like that? Nobody liked him. In all his experience the engineer had never known so unpopular a ship's captain. Mean, that's what he was, mean. Why, do you know, Frank—and then he launched a series of stories that more than proved his point. "What are you going to do?" he asked me when he had concluded.

"Damned if I know. But I've got to figure out something. I don't intend to let those elephants die."

Suddenly the engineer brightened. "I've got an idea," he said. "It may work and it may not. But it's worth trying."

"Swell! Let's hear it."

Then the engineer, a true scout, if I ever knew one, told me his scheme. He would let some fresh water out of the tanks and report to the captain that with the ship's speed reduced to eight knots the fresh water on board would not be sufficient for the rest of the trip. We were about two hundred miles off the Japan coast, and the following morning we would be just opposite Kobe. He would suggest that we put in there for water. This would give me a chance to get my hay. I could wireless ahead for it. We would be at Kobe three or four hours if the captain fell for the scheme, giving me plenty of time to load my hay.

"I know what the louse will tell me. 'Ration each man's water and use your condenser.' But I've got an answer. The condenser is in bum condition. I have my doubts as to how much fresh water could be made with it. I've been trying to get the owners to buy a new one, but they're a stingy lot. That's why we're crawling along this way. They're trying to save a dollar's worth of fuel oil."

There was much feeling in this outburst, despite which I found myself smiling through it. The idea of putting one over on the captain appealed to me.

The engineer didn't lose any time putting the scheme into effect. The tanks tapped, he left for the bridge to report the water shortage to the captain.

I saw the engineer an hour later. "What's the verdict?" I asked.

"Not sure yet," he replied, grinning. Forgetting to be indignant, as before when his peevishness over the line's stinginess got the better of him, he was now enjoying himself. "But it looks pretty good."

"That's fine."

"When I showed him what the gauge registered he blew up. 'I don't understand it!' he roared. 'There ought to be more water than that.'"

"'It is kind of funny,' I said. 'I could have sworn there was more water in that portside tank only a little while ago.' He nearly had convulsions. Told me I was a hell of an engineer. If I was any good I could fix the danged condenser so she'd work right. 'Don't stand around doing nothing,' he wound up. 'Go and have another look at it.' So I went and had a look. That's what he told me to do, wasn't it? Having looked the condenser square in the eye for twenty minutes, I'm now on my way back to report that after trying everything, I've decided it's hopeless. If he doesn't like it, he can get a new engineer. I'm sick of this old tub anyhow."

Before I could reply he was off.

Twenty minutes later the engineer announced his victory. The captain was boiling mad—ready to kill someone, in fact, but that didn't mean anything. All I was interested in was that we were going to stop at Kobe. I lost no time in getting off a wireless to the Japanese port ordering plenty of hay. This commodity is easy to secure there, and I knew that my supply would be on the dock when we arrived.

A few hours after I got my message off I bumped into the skipper. "I see you're taking on some hay at Kobe," he said. On a freight boat all wireless messages have to pass the captain, which is why he knew that I had ordered the hay.

"That's right," was all I could bring myself to say.

"Why don't you figure out before you start on a trip what you'll need in the way of supplies and carry that much?" (This after all I had told him about the difficulty of securing hay in Singapore.)

"I understand you're going to take on some water at Kobe," I replied. "One of the sailors told me."

"Yes," came the irritable retort, "we're stopping for some danged water."

"Well," I responded, "why don't you figure out before you start on a trip what you'll need in the way of water and carry that much?" The effort to say this with a straight face was almost too much for me.

The captain stomped off in a rage, saying unprintable things about the ignorance of landlubbers. I caught a few phrases to the effect that if I knew anything about the sea I'd understand such emergencies. These phrases were mixed with a jumble of oaths in as weird a cocktail of angry words as my much-assailed ears have ever been called upon to drink in.

We stopped at Kobe. The captain got his water, and I got my hay. Also a good laugh. So did the engineer.

A week after I reached San Francisco, rested and almost entirely mended, the *President Cleveland* arrived, with Babe on board riding on top of the poop deck. The only elephant I had ever shipped by crate (and the only one, to my knowledge, ever transported in this fashion) made her American debut in splendid condition, furnishing one more proof of the hardiness of her species. Not long afterwards, harnessed to the glittering wagon that I designed, reminiscent of the circus, Babe, the most mannerly of elephants, was pulling the children of San Francisco up and down the Fleischhacker playground and enjoying the work. She's doing it to this very day, and if there is a better-behaved elephant anywhere in the country I'd like to know its name.

Every day of the year Babe goes through her paces, delighting hundreds of children. The last time I saw her at work I couldn't help enjoying the comment of an ecstatic mother who said, "Isn't she the gentle dear!" as she watched the Lady from Burma pull her little boy around along with several other children. It was a warming confirmation of my own belief in the fundamental good nature of this animal even after she had almost blotted me out.

Not the least amusing phase of this experience was the way the story of my encounter with Babe on the dock at Singapore spread. I'll never know who started it, but it certainly got under way. All along the coast of Asia the newspapers carried stories to the effect that I had been fatally injured in a tussle with the largest and most ferocious elephant ever seen on the island of Singapore, probably the most terrible animal of any kind ever seen anywhere, capable of wiping out a dozen tigers with a butt of the head or a stamp of the foot.

Proving once more the truth of the Hindu proverb that says, "If a person sneezes in Bombay it's a typhoon by the time it reaches Calcutta."

Frank Buck, 1937. Norman Rockwell originally produced this image for a Schenley Cream of Kentucky Whiskey advertisement. The ad appeared in *Life* (November 22, 1937) and *Collier's* (November 6, 1937). It was titled "Have You Eyes Like Frank Buck's—Seeking Happy Adventure?" Photo courtesy of United Vintners and Distillers North America and the Norman Rockwell Family Trust.

(Above and facing page) Frank Buck and the actor Sabu (Sabu Dastagir, 1924–1963) at Buck's jungle exhibit in Cleveland. A former stable boy at the court of an Indian maharajah, Sabu was discovered by the documentary film maker Robert Flaherty, who cast him in the title role of the film *Elephant Boy* (1937), a docudrama about a native boy who claims he knows the location of a mythic elephant herd. Sabu played exotic boys in several other British films, then went to Hollywood, where he had similar parts in a succession of popular Eastern adventure films at Universal. One of Sabu's best known films is *The Thief of Bagdad* (1940), in which he portrays a native boy outdoing an evil magician; Conrad Veidt played the magician, but is better remembered as Major Strasser in *Casablanca* (1942). When the public tired of Arabian Nights stories in the late 1940s, Sabu sought unsuccessfully to revive his career in Continental films. He died of a heart attack at 39.

Frank Buck and Muriel Reilly Buck in front of Tiger Temple in Johore, which was erected by early Chinese immigrants. These pioneer workmen, in one of the world's richest rubber districts, wanted an altar where they could go to implore their gods to protect them from the ever-present striped terror. The temple was built in the center of the heavy jungle then being cleared and consisted of one room, in the middle of which stood a Chinese hand-carved table with a receptacle for burning joss sticks. Against the wall was a wooden Chinese altar, studded with porcelain figures representing various gods. An aged Chinese priest (left) officiated for many years, maintaining the temple with the money he collected at the altar for the joss sticks and the paper prayers that the worshipers burned. The prevailing belief was that anyone who regularly burned joss at the altar—and who in so doing displayed the proper fervor toward the gods—was immune from attack by tigers.

Frank Buck ca 1940.

(Previous page) Premiere of
Bring 'Em Back Alive, Mayfair
Theater, New York, 1932.
(Top) Muriel Reilly Buck at the
microphone on Frank Buck's
radio program. (Below) Frank
Buck and Muriel Reilly Buck,
Los Angeles, ca 1940. Photo
courtesy of the Academy of
Motion Picture Arts and
Sciences.

(Top) Frank Buck and John Ringling North, head of the Ringling Brothers Barnum & Bailey Circus, 1938. Buck toured with the circus as their featured attraction, astride an elephant. (Bottom) Frank Buck in a scene from the motion picture *Bring 'Em Back Alive* (1932).

(Top) Frank Buck is poised to leap at a deadly king cobra, which has escaped from its box. Cornered, Buck has taken off his coat in order to make a flying tackle. The scene is from the motion picture *Wild Cargo* (1934). (Below) Frank Buck ensconced in his jungle camp.

Frank Buck ca 1925.

(Top) Frank Buck in his mid-twenties. (Bottom) Frank Buck (right) preparing to depart for the Asian jungles to film *Bring 'Em Back Alive*. Van Beuren was the name of his company. Photo courtesy of the Academy of Motion Picture Arts and Sciences.

Frank Buck and a tiger cub, ca 1935.

Frank Buck holding tiny mouse-deer only 8-in. high, at his Johore headquarters camp, while his pet white-handed gibbon looks jealously on

Frank Buck's Jungleland at N.Y. Worlds Fair

Page from a souvenir program, 1939.

Frank Buck ca 1940.

(Top) Frank Buck (standing far right) in a scene from the motion picture *Jacare* (1942). Photo courtesy of the Academy of Motion Picture Arts and Sciences. (Bottom) In loading an elephant onto a ship, a heavy canvas sling is used that is fastened around the belly, the hold on the animal being further secured by ropes passed around the neck and under the tail.

Classics Illustrated issue #104, *Bring 'Em Back Alive,* appeared in February 1953, cover illustration by Henry C. Kiefer. The series began in 1941 as Classic Comics, with a 64 page comic book version of *The Three Musketeers* by Alexandre Dumas. The series title changed to *Classics Illustrated* with issue number 35. Publication ceased with issue #167, *Faust.* Many factors caused the demise of *Classics Illustrated,* among them television, cheap paperback books, and *Cliff's Notes.* Classics Illustrated is a trademark of Frawley Corporation. First Classics, Inc., Chicago, IL USA, is the sole Licensee of said Trademark. All Rights Reserved.

CHAPTER IX

MONKEY MISCHIEF

I've brought back to America over five thousand monkeys. That's a lot of monkeys.

More than once I've marveled at the fact that they didn't cause me more trouble. If my luck had not been good, that army of simians could have got me into more trouble than any one lifetime ought to know. That's because monkeys are full of cunning and mischief. If two particular experiences I had with these impish creatures that enjoy man's discomfiture more than any other animals had been typical, I should have cheerfully retired from the monkey industry and let someone else take my place.

The rhesus monkeys of India are the hardiest of the small simians. They are less subject than any other species to the two scourges most common among the creatures: lung trouble and dysentery. These little animals weigh only six to ten pounds full grown.

The pigtailed rhesus is a much larger variety, the males weighing as much as thirty-five to forty pounds. This type of monkey has to be handled very carefully, what with the formidable canine teeth that they bring into play in settling arguments. The males are particularly savage and require considerable taming.

One of these Borneo pigtailed chaps, an ill-natured male, once raised the devil on board ship in a manner I'll never forget. I was on the Pacific, several days out on my way from Asia to America. The boat was the *West Caddao*.

The pigtailed rhesus to which I refer managed to get out of his cage by working away cleverly at a loose slat. Regardless of all the precautions one takes, an occasional specimen will escape. Alongside the total of tens of thousands of birds and animals I have brought back to America, the number of escapes I have had to combat is small indeed. But most of them caused me so much trouble I'm not likely ever to forget them.

A person who collects many live specimens can't inspect and test all his crates and cages himself. Some of the work has to be done by others, and sometimes this assistance isn't as thorough as it might be. Invariably I order a new box when I know it is needed—Hin Mong has made hundreds of them for me at Singapore—and I have old boxes repaired when they show signs of needing it. Even so, faulty cages get aboard. Careless inspection is not the only cause, either. Sometimes, in the process of loading, a sound cage is handled roughly and weakened. This does not always come to light in the inspection I make on shipboard before putting out to sea.

Other things happen—freakish occurrences that can defeat the best job of packing and loading—and all one can do is to be philosophical about them and accept them as part of the business of collecting live specimens, just as black eyes and swollen lips are part of the boxing profession.

When my pigtailed rhesus got loose aboard the *West Caddao* he did a thorough job of messing things up. At the outset, by staging some quick killings among my birds, he established that he was no mere playful monkey out for a lark. Reaching into one of the cages, he strangled a Shama thrush, one of the rarest birds I had on board, and to show that he wasn't fooling he killed off a few other feathered specimens that I had secured after much difficulty.

By the time I arrived on the scene—I was in the dining room when the cyclone from Borneo started his career of crime—several birds were loose, and three were dead. Overhead a quintet of Shama thrushes, released from their bamboo cages, flew round and round in nervous circles, and a brush-tongued parrot squawked weird sounds of protest or triumph, it was hard to tell which.

With escaped birds circling above me and a loose monkey raising hell on deck, I was not in an enviable position. My first impulse was to concentrate on capturing the birds, which were rarer than the pigtailed rhesus, but I downed that quickly. A monkey like this rascal from Borneo was too dangerous to leave to his own devices, even for a short time. Assigning to little Ali (nephew of Old Ali, whom I had left in Singapore) the job of working on the loose birds, I gave myself the task of recapturing the monkey. Sailors volunteered to handle the monkey chase for me, but I didn't think it fair to let them handle the job alone, as anxious as I was to recapture my birds. An inexperienced person trying to grab one of these treacherous Borneo tree-dwellers has a fair chance of coming off with a badly torn wrist. The vicious canine teeth of the pigtailed rhesus have done plenty of damage of this kind—and worse—in their time.

Recruiting some sailors as assistants, I set out after the most troublesome forty pounds of monkey I've ever encountered. Our ambitious idea was to corner the wretch. He didn't think much of our efforts, scampering all over the deck and easily eluding us. He'd get about ten yards ahead of us and turn around and eye us contemptuously over one shoulder; and as we'd come up on him he'd be off with a burst of speed. The sailors were more willing than helpful, confining themselves in the main to tossing pieces of dunnage, not especially well aimed, at the simian foe.

We weren't getting anywhere this way, so I instructed my lumbering aides to reverse themselves and meet the monkey head on, the idea being to make the creature turn and run straight at me. I waited at the appointed place on the deck. The scheme was a success up to a certain point. The men managed to drive the little villain toward me, where I was prepared to stun him with a stout stick and drag him back to captivity; but the wily cuss had a plan of his own. He took a flying leap against my chest, hitting me with such force he knocked the wind out of me and almost spilled me. Then he disappeared for five or ten minutes, and when he returned it wasn't hard to guess that he'd paid a visit to the galley coal hole. The *West Caddao* is an oil-burner, but she carries a bunker of coal for the galley stoves where the cooking is done. Covered with coal dust, the monkey, with a perfect instinct for making the maximum amount of trouble in any given situation, had a sudden inspiration to mess up the mate's nice new paint job. During the last two weeks of a trip like this on a cargo boat, all hands are assigned to cleaning the ship and painting her spick-and-span for arrival at her home port. From forecastle to poop the *West Caddao* was being painted till she started looking like a brand-new vessel. My sailor assistants had been recruited with the mate's permission from among the renovating crew.

What an opportunity for a monkey black with coal dust! The scamp from Borneo, even if he had had the capacity for figuring such things out, couldn't have done more damage. In a flash he was all over the poop deck, seeming to run in four directions at one time. It wasn't long before the freshly painted funnels and rails were smeared here and there with coal dust, and it wasn't long before the mate's curses—and I didn't blame him—were ringing in my ears.

At this point, spurred on no doubt by the mate's cussing and a fervent desire to earn his blessings, the sailors resumed the target practice they had started on the main deck. With tin cans, lumps of coal, and other odds and ends they fired away at their elusive target, one of them, the star marksman of the group, actually coming within a foot of the monkey's head. Then, to show that if he couldn't hit the roughneck from Borneo, he could hit something else, this fusilier sent a lump of coal crashing through a port window. As if I wasn't already sufficiently in bad with the mate!

If groaning was in my line I would have groaned then, although I suppose I did give off a couple, mentally.

The interesting thing about that monkey was the fact that he was entirely unafraid. Curiously enough, a much more savage animal in a similar situation might have been full of fear on account of the strangeness of his surroundings. This was true of my leopard that got loose aboard the *Granite State*. He was frightened because he was at a disadvantage, and though this didn't mean that he wasn't dangerous, I had the upper hand because it was a tip-off on how to handle him.

No monkey is at a disadvantage where there is scampering space and there are things to climb up, over, and around. Instead of being scared, this little pest actually seemed to be laughing at us. As he'd duck a grenade tossed by one of my marines, he'd suddenly right his head and stand still, as if to say, "Well, here I am. Let's see you hit me!" Then there'd be another barrage, and the monkey, with what almost seemed like a grin of triumph, would scramble off to another point.

After he'd done a pretty thorough job of transferring the coal dust on him to the ship's fresh paint, we managed to get the tantalizing imp off the poop deck onto the main deck again. I suspect he came willingly, just to show how little he feared us. And then, as we chased him, he added the final insult by dashing right back among the cages and, before we could stop him, pulling the head right off a rare Impeyan pheasant.

A quick reach through the slats and this worst of all the pigtailed Borneos I've ever handled had killed a bird that was worth over twice as much as he was. It was pretty rough on the bird too, a rare fellow that was on his way to a zoo where he'd have had a good home and many admirers.

I had had quite a job landing that pheasant, and it was tough to lose him after I'd carried him all over Asia and more than halfway across the Pacific. As I pulled up to the scene of the slaughter I heard a series of crashes. The vandal had knocked over a stack of bird cages, but fortunately these were so stoutly built and so securely shut that no more of my feathered freight escaped. The jolting, however, didn't do the birds any good.

I came up in time to corner this destructive little demon against the side of the tarpaulin thrown tent-fashion over the hatch that served as a shelter for my cargo of birds. One of the sailors, in a sudden burst of usefulness after his failure as a marksman, got in and around and drove the monkey toward me. Before he could leap at me as he had done earlier in the chase, I brought down on his head the capable stick I was carrying. I put enough force behind the blow to knock the little terror cold but not enough to injure him. Back to his box he went, and this time he stayed there. The slats were reinforced, and in vain he worked all the way back home for another taste of life on the open deck where there were men to mock and birds to kill and where every day there was more nice fresh paint that any monkey would enjoy smearing up.

Meanwhile, little Ali, working with one of my landing nets, succeeded in capturing three of the Shama thrushes (little birds the size of a robin). Two of them, however, refused to listen to reason, and shortly after I got my monkey back into his box, the silly little things put out to sea, with as much chance of surviving as a deer has in a fight with a tiger. It was a heartbreaking spectacle, as is always the sight of helpless little creatures battling against forces that are too much for them and against which they have no chance of surviving. I will never forget the picture of these two beautiful little songbirds setting out to conquer the mighty Pacific. It was only a question of how many hours would elapse before, exhausted from the aimless flight deeper and deeper into the wilderness of water, with no place to stop for a rest and nothing to eat, they would drop to a salty grave. I stood watching the foolish little adventurers till they became tiny specks and disappeared. Once I thought I saw them falling, and I found myself, lost in reverie, starting forward against the rail and reaching out as if to grab them. Birds were my first love—it was as an amateur collector of them that I got started in the business in which I now find myself—and I have never ceased to be daffy about them. I have brought back over a hundred thousand of them, of nearly every known variety, some of them species never before seen in America, like the great black cockatoo, Pasquel's vulture-headed parrot, and the fairy bluebird of Borneo—and the experience has been full of genuine pleasure, replete with a kind of thrill that only the plumb crazy bird fancier understands.

The only other fugitive, the brush-tongued parrot, or lory, had perched himself high in the rigging, and there he remained for three days and nights. With a grand unconcern about food and drink (we left offerings at places that would be convenient for him to reach if he felt minded to leave his perch) he stayed there in his new-found home over our heads. It would have availed nothing to go up after him: he would only have flown out to sea and perished like the little Shama thrushes.

One day, when we were within a mile of an island (by a curious coincidence, it was Bird Island, the westernmost of the Hawaiian group), an idea involving the future of that parrot occurred to me. I put it into effect with a handful of nuts and bolts. These I hurled at the stubborn bird in the rigging until I drove him from his perch. He circled around a few times till he got his bearings, and then he put out to sea, heading for the island. I hope he had a good time when he arrived and that he found plenty of the kind of food he liked. For all I know he may be alive and squawking to this very day. If he is, I hope he doesn't feel unkindly toward the fellow that threw all those nuts and bolts at him. In my crude way I was trying to save his life.

The smaller rhesus monkeys—the little chaps from India—have also given me samples of the mischief of which they are capable, but never has there been anything vicious about it. Natural comedians, they confine themselves to antics that give rise to mirth rather than to wrath, although I must admit that once, when enough of them got mischievous at the same time, I felt like giving the little devils a spanking.

I was returning from Asia on the *Santa Cruz* with a shipment of birds and animals. Among my cargo were several boxes of small rhesus monkeys, twenty-five to a box. These boxes were stacked up in tiers, five to a tier.

We had hit a stretch of fine weather, enabling me to remove the canvas coverings that were used to protect the inhabitants of these containers from the wind. In this way I could give them the benefit of the sun and the balmy air. Without warning we ran into a quick blow that caused the lightly lashed boxes to shift. Before I could get every-thing firmly fastened, two of the top boxes, which had shifted with the sudden lurching of the ship, slid off and landed with a crash on the iron deck, a fall of about nine feet. They broke open, and in a few seconds there were fifty monkeys loose on that ship. They scam-pered off in all directions, up the masts, into the rigging, onto the cross beams, into the crow's nest, everywhere. Wherever your eye lit you saw a monkey.

Three of the little mischief-makers got up on the poop deck, where there were some potato boxes. The galley boy, who was carry-ing potatoes to the cook, had left the top of one of these boxes open, a natural thing to do as he was returning for more. When he returned he found the monkeys throwing potatoes all over the deck. They scurried off, looking back at him in the typical manner of prankish simians, tossing a last few potatoes around to make it clear that they didn't take the man very seriously.

One of the fugitives decided to visit the galley, where the baker had laid out some rolls, fresh from the oven, to cool. Before the baker could do anything about it, his unexpected visitor started scattering the rolls around, leaping on a stack of bread loaves in beating a re-treat and sending several loaves toppling to the floor. Dodging sun-dry missiles in the process the happy monkey, reveling in his new-found freedom, proceeded to investigate the work of some galley boys who were preparing vegetables for the cook. He dove right into a pail of cut-up carrots, upsetting it and disappearing with a mouth-ful before the awkward boys, too surprised to do anything but stare at each other, could do anything to stop him.

Other members of the escaped fifty decided to show their socia-bility by calling on passengers. There were about forty-five passen-gers on board, several of them women. Through a porthole one of the monkeys visited a lady who was dressing, scampering off with one of her stockings. As I chased after another one of my runaways I al-most ran into this lady, who, shoeless and wearing one stocking, was pursuing the little chap from India who had stolen the other stocking. "I want my stocking!" she frantically yelled as we almost collided. I'd have been glad to give her her stocking, having as little need for it as the monkey that had swiped it, but unfortunately there wasn't anything I could do about it. Stocking and monkey were off before anything could be done, and the lady never regained her property. What happened to that stocking I'll never know. I hope the monkey didn't eat it. It didn't look particularly digestible. I tried to pay the lady for a pair of stockings, but she refused. She said she would have her own stocking or nothing.

Another of the fugitives, preferring male society, called on an engineer who was returning to America and did his best to make this professional gentleman's trip memorable by knocking over a can of tobacco.

Still another of the sociable monkeys, with a fondness for face powder equivalent to its brother simian's leaning toward stockings, stuck its face into a box of the said powder (after another lady's privacy had been violated) and emerged with a nicely powdered face. Overzealous scientists have claimed the discovery of new species on the strength of less evidence than the powder on that monkey's face, and perhaps I lost an opportunity in not immediately taking a photograph and announcing the finding of the white-faced monkey of the forest of Singacutta.

All in all, the passengers had a thoroughly enjoyable time. There aren't many things that have more laugh-provoking possibilities than a half-hundred harmless monkeys loose on a ship and defying recapture. A few passengers made complaints. In fact, the lady whose face powder was messed up called on the captain and demanded that "those nasty monkeys" be put off the ship. To which the captain (an old friend with whom I had made several crossings) unfeelingly replied: "I'm afraid we'll have to catch them first."

Despite the fact that the captain was a friend and stood by nobly, I didn't feel any too comfortable on account of the glares of those members of the ship's crew whose work was being messed up by my frivolous fifty. To this aggrieved group, I soon had to add the Chinese stewards in the dining salon, particularly their chief. This chap claimed, and I had the misfortune to laugh as he hysterically voiced his complaint, that some of the monkeys had got into the dining salon and yanked the tablecloths and silver off four of the tables. I agreed that this was a most deplorable state of affairs, but the chief steward was unimpressed by my chuckling expression of sympathy, for he dashed off in a huff, announcing that the captain would hear of the matter in short order.

For me the choicest aspect of the whole episode was represented by the activities of an agent of the Standard Oil Company, an American in his early thirties, who started a contest among the passengers to see who could catch the most monkeys. This chap, who came to be known as the Monkey Tamer, got hold of a wooden box, which he converted into a trap. Turning the box over so that the opening faced the deck, he placed a wooden peg under one end to provide an entrance for his victims. Then he baited the trap with a banana. The idea was to lure a fruit-loving fugitive under the uptilted box and, just as he snatched the banana, to yank out the peg, which was controlled by a string. Down the box would come over the monkey, and he would be a prisoner.

Within a few hours of the time he got his trap going, the Monkey Tamer had made his first capture. The fun began when he raised the box and stuck his hand underneath to grab his monkey. The little fellow had no desire to be taken into custody, and he scampered around in his prison, which was about the size of an ordinary soapbox, eluding the grasp of his jailer. In working his hand around in an effort to grab his victim, the Monkey Tamer scraped one of his fingers against a nail and suddenly decided that he had been bitten. In his anxiety to get a quick look at the injured member, he raised the box too high, and the little animal dashed out, triumphantly carrying off the banana with him.

You'd have thought that young man had been nipped by a cobra. All I could see on his finger was a scratch. There were no marks of teeth. But the Monkey Tamer insisted he had been bitten, and within the next twenty minutes he doused his "wound" with three different kinds of antiseptic.

I'm always amused by the myths surrounding what is known as "monkey bite." There are all sorts of stories to the effect that if a monkey nips you, you're in danger. Having been bitten by monkeys hundreds of times, I naturally cannot take these stories very seriously. In fact, I don't know of a single case where monkey bite caused any real damage unless the victim happened to be in bad health. Even then the bite would have to be a real one.

In view of these facts I was unable to summon up much sympathy for the father of the monkey-catching contest who hadn't been bitten at all. I soon reassured him by telling him that every shipment of monkeys I had ever made had involved at least a dozen bites and that even granting that he had been savagely nipped, there was no immediate danger of death. His fears soon disappeared, and he was again busy with his trap. His "injured" finger bound up in gauze, I saw him a little later baiting his box with another banana.

His method was again successful, for less than an hour elapsed when I heard him excitedly shouting, "I've got another one!" The contest continued merrily. A scoreboard was rigged up, and a record was kept of each monkey that was captured. I caught four of the little rascals with a hook dip net that I always carried with me, but I decided to retire from the contest, letting a zealous passenger borrow my net. After all, my fellow travelers seemed perfectly willing to capture my monkeys, and I saw no reason why I shouldn't let them do my work for me.

At the end of the second day the Monkey Tamer had six monkeys, which left him in the lead, the nearest player to him having a score of two less. The high scorer was becoming cockier by the minute, telling highly colored stories of his captures to any listeners he could summon in the bar. In fact, this chap was becoming so puffed up with his success that he began to annoy the other passengers, a group of them putting their heads together and agreeing to pool their captures the following day and contrive to credit them to the score of an exuberant girl from California who ranked third on the list of contestants.

The contest wound up the following day, the Monkey Tamer winning with a score of eight, the girl from California finishing second with seven.

Only two monkeys were lost. One, in trying to elude a pursuer, went overboard. A second died freakishly of poisoning. A sailor was out on one of the hatches cleaning a pair of pants. Attracted by the picture of two ladies chasing a monkey, he broke into a laugh, and too amused to keep his mind on his work, he watched the spectacle on the deck. As he did, another of the loose fifty quietly paid him a visit. This foolish little fugitive decided to sample the cleaning fluid (an acid of some kind) that the sailor had placed on the hatch in a saucer. Before the seafaring gent could do anything to prevent the act, the monkey took a good swallow of the fluid, dying shortly afterwards.

When we pulled into San Francisco the local reporters interviewed me as they usually do when I arrive with a sizeable menagerie. One of the reporters, an old friend, called me over to one side and, pointing to the Monkey Tamer, asked, "Who the hell is *that* guy?"

"One of the passengers," I replied. "He represents the Standard Oil Company somewhere in China."

"What's this story he tells about capturing fifty wild monkeys?" he asked.

"I'd quite forgotten," I replied. "He's the hero of the trip. Saved several lives. Better get the story from him. Hot stuff."

At this point the Monkey Tamer looked over at me, and I broke into a laugh. Discouraged, the ace of monkey catchers walked off.

"Who're you trying to kid, Frank?" asked my reporter friend. As if I'd ever try to kid a newspaperman!

CHAPTER X

LOOSE ON BOARD

I had just left Calcutta aboard the *Granite State* with a shipment of animals and birds. On the way down the Hooghly [Hugly] River we stopped at Budge Budge [Baj Baj], an oil station just below Calcutta, to discharge a cargo of oil.

We remained at Budge Budge all day. Shortly before we left I negotiated an unexpected deal for a leopard. In fact, the gang ladder was about to be pulled up when a native came tearing up in a small motor lorry with a crated leopard on it. The box bounced around uncertainly as the driver suddenly applied his brakes and came to a halt.

The native arrived with such dramatic suddenness and gave vent to so much excited chatter that he seemed like the bearer of important tidings or a man on an epoch-making mission. Before anyone could stop him he was on deck making more wild noises and gestures there. It seems that he had to see Buck *Sahib*.

This was quickly arranged. In fact, he bumped into me as I hurried over to see who was paging me so frantically. Breathlessly the native told me (partly in broken English and partly in Hindustani, which my assistant Lal translated for me) that he had heard from Atool Achooli, the Calcutta bird and animal trader, with whom I did considerable business, that I was in the market for another leopard. He had one in the lorry below, an excellent addition to my collection, he assured me. In fact, it was the finest leopard in India, and if I didn't buy it I was making the mistake of my life.

I got hold of the mate. He was really too busy with his preparations for departure to be bothered, but he was good enough to give me a few minutes' grace before pulling up the gang ladder. Thus I was able to inspect the animal that the excited native had in the cage on the dock.

I went ashore, made a hasty examination, saw that the animal was a first-rate specimen, though not quite the finest leopard in India, and negotiated a quick deal. Lines were thrown over the side and made fast around the cage, and the latest addition to my floating menagerie was hoisted on board by hand.

My new cat was a full-grown male spotted leopard in perfect condition. He was a savage devil, raising a rumpus with his snarling and growling whenever I went near him. When Lal attempted to pass a few hunks of perfectly good beef into the cage, the leopard, in his attempt to get at him, lunged against the bars with a roar that resounded from the poop deck to the forecastle head.

I saw at once that it would never do to keep this screaming cyclone near my better-behaved cats. The others, leopards and tigers, were a fairly manageable lot, pretty much convinced that misconduct wouldn't get them anywhere, and I didn't want this rambunctious cuss to destroy the morale I had built up. With this villain to lead the rebellion there was much likelihood that the work I had done on all those other jungle tabbies would be undone. I therefore stowed his cage on the iron deck right down against the rail at the ship's side, a fair distance from the rest of my collection, which had been loaded on the tops of number one and number two hatches. There they were protected against the weather by a heavy tarpaulin flung tent-fashion over the cargo booms.

I spent a fair amount of my time on the bridge as the guest of Captain Harry Wallis, a friend of many voyages. Each of us thought the other had the most interesting pursuit in the world, and, when the sea was calm and we had easy sailing, we'd swap stories.

During one of these chats a blow came on. Whenever anything like this occurred I would beat a hasty retreat, for no sea captain, no matter how good a friend, wants to be bothered when he has to think about the weather. The best way to be reinvited to the bridge is to know when to vacate it.

As I started to go, I mentioned that it would be a good idea to play safe and move my new leopard to a more protected spot.

With a laugh, the skipper accused me of babying my latest arrival. "How do you expect to make a sailor of him if you coddle him that way?" he asked. "A little spray won't hurt him. That's all he's in for. We won't take any green seas over the forward deck out here at this season." We had left the typhoon area in and about the China Sea far behind us by this time and were somewhere out in mid-Pacific.

About five-thirty the next morning there was a furious pounding on my door.

"What's the matter?" I yelled, half asleep.

"There's hell to pay!" I heard through the door. "Open up!"

Groggily I stumbled to the door in the semidarkness. I didn't know whether I was being serenaded by a drunk, or whether we had another one of those practical jokers on board.

Opening the door and blinking, I discovered the third officer there. Pale and trembling, he looked like a man who had been having a bad dream.

"Come in and sit down," I sleepily greeted him. "You look all in."

"No time for sitting, sir," he replied. "There's hell to pay!" Not having anything specific to worry about yet, and being more asleep than awake, I could think of nothing to do but yawn and drop into a chair. At least, this is what the officer afterwards told me I did. Also, he didn't mind telling me that this was no way to act when a ship's officer paid you an emergency call. Now that I think it over, he was right. But I *was* sleepy.

"Put your clothes on, sir!" he barked. "Captain directs it. There's—"

My principal recollection of that sleepy session was that I had no desire to be told again that there was hell to pay. Fairly awake by now, I reveled in my triumph. I had frustrated the third attempt.

Mechanically I reached for my clothes and started to dress. "Faster, sir!" I was obviously not dressing very rapidly. "If you expect any speed out of me," I replied, "you'll have to tell me what's wrong."

The third officer was saving his news for a grand climax. He was a pleasant little chap on the whole, but he was so constructed that when entrusted with an important message he liked to nurse it along, loath to part with it until he had squeezed the last drop of excitement out of it.

"What's wrong, you ask?" he echoed. "What's wrong indeed! Plenty's wrong! Your leopard's loose! The one on the iron deck! That's what's wrong. And, if you ask me, it's a bad situation, sir. Bad!"

I fairly leaped from my chair. "My leopard's loose? I'll be damned!" Feverishly I finished dressing, firing questions at the third officer in the process.

Vicious seas breaking over the forward deck with a sudden rush had sent the cage on a ten-foot spin and turned it upside down. The officer on watch evidently thought that a leopard in a cage bottom side up was as safe as a leopard rightside up, as long as he was still inside his cage.

All went well until later when another tremendous sea came smashing over the upturned cage, pounding it amidships and completing the damage by dropping tons of water on the topside bottom, which was never meant to be as strong as the real top. The roof of the cage was gone. A bewildered leopard scampered out, mixed a few growls with the roaring of the sea, and pattered down the iron deck to think things over among some oil barrels lashed around the mast and against the bulkhead.

I had heard enough—more than enough. My visitor was right. There *was* hell to pay, although I'd have shot him if he had said so again. He turned to go. "Anything I can do, sir?" He really was a decent sort despite my murderous thoughts.

"Yes, send a quartermaster at once to rout out my assistant Lal. Have him chased here as fast as his legs can travel."

My early morning caller left, looking graver than ever. I could even hear him run down the hall, a remarkable performance in so dignified a chap.

The passengers were still abed. There was one thing that had to be done immediately. The midsection of the ship, the part occupied by the passengers, would have to be cut off from the foredeck and promenade deck.

In a few minutes Lal arrived, struggling to throw some clothes over himself as he entered on the run. I gave him some hasty commands. His principal task was to take a few dozen revolver bullets I tossed at him and pull out the lead noses with a pair of pliers. Then he was to stuff wadding into the empty ends to hold the powder in. He had done the job for me before.

I left on a hurried visit to the captain's quarters. He sportingly agreed to give me a chance to catch my leopard alive. I had to make a promise to shoot to kill if the escaped animal became a menace to passengers or crew. There was small likelihood of danger to the passengers, whose section of the vessel was quickly shut up, preventing access to open deck space. The crew could be warned to keep out of the way.

"But remember, Buck" (the captain speaking), "I reserve the right to step in whenever I see fit and order the animal killed. I can't let this leopard chase go on forever. The minute I decide you've had a fair chance to catch it, you'll have to submit to my decision. You know enough about the sea to realize I can't let this sort of thing interfere with efficient operation of my ship. Go ahead. But don't take any unnecessary chances. No leopard is worth it. Good luck."

Before leaving, I asked the captain if he would have instructions sent to the ship's carpenter to repair the broken cage at once. He readily agreed. "I don't know what I'll do with it," I said as I left, "but I'll want a place to put that damned leopard if I do catch him alive."

I returned to my cabin, where Lal had completed his task. I didn't realize until he started questioning me that I had failed to tell him why I had routed him out of bed. The early morning assignment of castrating the revolver cartridges had puzzled him badly. By now he was used to any kind of instructions from me, and he took his orders like a good soldier; but he'd get cross and irritable when he thought I was being secretive. I explained hastily that I had not had a chance to tell him and, pushing him out of the door as I grabbed my rifle, told him that the new leopard was loose.

"*Soo-ur kabutcha!*" [Hindi: "child-of-a-pig"] exclaimed Lal. "Better you shoot him quick, *tuan*, he's bad leopard." Then giving me a sort of disappointed look, he displayed the handful of blank cartridges and asked, "Why you want these no good bullets?"

"Never mind," I said, "just hold on to those blanks. I think I'll have some use for 'em in a little while." A grunt that savored of disgust was his only reply as we hurried along the passageway.

As we made for the iron deck I examined my rifle. It was in fine working order. One of Lal's duties on shipboard was to keep it in good shape, ready for immediate use in just such an emergency as this.

I wanted to get in among those oil barrels and gradually work my way back to the spot where the leopard had taken refuge. How near I should get to the savage beast would depend upon his behavior. But before making any definite decision or plans about taking him alive I had to find out just how his new-found liberty was affecting his morale. If he proved as ferocious loose on the deck as he had been while in the cage, then, of course, he must be shot immediately. While I felt pretty certain that he would be more scared than vicious, my first job was to make sure.

Lal was carrying my revolver, which he had loaded with the blank cartridges. He also had with him, in addition to a further supply of blanks, a round of perfect revolver bullets ready for use.

With Lal at my side I began to crawl in among the barrels. I was prepared to shoot to kill. Lal, aware of this, was delighted. He believed that the animal had sinned grievously and should be punished. The only fit punishment was death.

We crept up closer and closer. I raised my rifle for action, getting a bead on the leopard not more than fifteen feet away. My finger was on the trigger. I had no desire to shoot. But I was prepared to pull the trigger if he gave any signs of springing at me. I crept a few inches closer. All the leopard did was snarl and bare his claws and once or twice make a movement as if he were going to jump up on top of the barrels to get away from me. Everything in his manner indicated that the thought uppermost in his mind was escape. Of course, he would fight unto death if attacked, but my guess was—one plays hunches in my business, there being no rulebook by which to judge animals—that here was a badly worried leopard. In surroundings that were more familiar to him, where he would be surer of himself, he might have forced the fight, lashing out with his vicious claws and ripping open everything in sight with his cruel teeth. But my experience told me that here was an animal that considered himself at a disadvantage.

"We can take him alive, Lal," I whispered. I've never seen Lal's face take on a more disappointed look. The animal had caused much trouble and should be shot before he caused more was the way he felt.

Dragging Lal along by the arm, I crawled out, leaving the leopard where he was, and made for the steps leading from the iron cargo deck up to the ship's main promenade deck, where the officers' mess room was located. I looked the ground over carefully and decided that it would be possible to drive the leopard up the steps and into the mess room.

With Lal's assistance—he still thought the animal should be shot, but that didn't interfere with his speed and sureness as a helper —I hauled the empty cage, now repaired by the ship's carpenter, up the steps to a space near the door of the mess room. Leaving the door open, I had all other means of reaching the room closed.

Then I went after my leopard, revolver in hand. It was loaded with blanks, but I don't mind saying that I wasn't taking any chances. I am not one of those fearless adventurers who snap their fingers, in their memoirs, at any rate, and step right up to the jaws of death while someone, miraculously on the scene with a camera, takes a picture. After all, a leopard is a leopard. These spotted cats have killed many human beings, and I had no desire to be added to the list. My loose leopard, in addition to being worried, was perhaps rather scared (any wild animal, no matter how ferocious normally, is at a disadvantage in a setting that befuddles him), but he was still a leopard, and once he got it into his head that he was fighting for his life, he would become a terror. This is to explain that I wasn't as bold as I seemed when I set forth with my blank-cartridge pistol. I saw to it that Lal was by my side with my loaded rifle, ready to hand it to me any second, or to blaze away himself if there was not sufficient time to hand me the weapon.

Again Lal and I were among the oil barrels facing the enemy. The leopard, at a loss to know what to do, was approximately where we had left him. My mind was made up. There was nothing for me to do but to chase him from the position he had taken up among these barrels, get him to scamper up those steps leading into the mess room, drive him into this chamber, and then slap the open cage against the door and drive him into that.

Lal and I took up a position where I could fire at the leopard at an angle that would drive him out onto the open deck (in the event he was in the mood for being driven). I raised my pistol and blazed away. The fierce spotted cat, in a series of breathtaking leaps—and even if he isn't leaping at you there is something terrifying about those tremendous and seemingly effortless jumps—made for the open deck. Round and round he went, Lal and I in pursuit. After circling the iron deck about half a dozen times I blazed away at the animal three or four times in a row when we were about ten yards from the steps leading to the promenade deck where the officers' mess room was. Instead of scampering up the steps as I hoped he would the animal stopped in his tracks and whirled around. Teeth and claws bared he faced me, ready to spring. I let him quiet down. We stood facing each other this way for a full minute. I could not afford to back away, any more than I could afford to advance. The animal started to relax. His lips began to close over his teeth. His claws were receding. This was a good time to shoot. I let him have another blank, the fire bursting close enough to his eyes to frighten him. He turned and ran. I thought I had him cornered so that he couldn't help colliding with the steps, but he swung wide as he ran and passed my objective. Round he went for two more circuits, making such speed I thought he would lap me. He would have done so in a few more rounds, for by now he was desperate for a means of escape, and he had dropped his halting manner of running. As he completed his second circuit he was not many yards behind me. Swinging round, I advanced and opened fire. The suddenness of my attack was too much for him. At a loss what to do, he swung around and started going in the other direction. As he went around the turn, I heard an agonized shriek. The leopard had almost collided with a Chinese boy carrying two buckets of water. What the boy was doing on deck I didn't know. I thought everyone had been warned to keep off.

The buckets went careening crazily down the deck, the water splashing in all directions. The boy scrambled to his feet, frightened out of his wits. Madly he tore for the bulkhead doorway from which he had recently emerged. The leopard, as scared as the boy, ran uncertainly for the same door, neither of them quite sure what it was all about. When the unexpected takes place in this fashion, the animal is as much at a loss as the human being involved. As he neared the doorway the boy saw a rope hanging from a boom above his head. He grabbed the rope and scrambled up it like a monkey.

I took advantage of the animal's confusion, coming up on him suddenly, as he stood still after a few hesitant movements beneath the boy swinging on the rope. The chambers of my gun refilled with blanks, I blazed away again, and this time succeeded in maneuvering the leopard to a position in front of the steps that led to the deck above. Another series of shots sent him scampering up; and the first stage of my task was over.

In the meantime, the passengers (there were about eighty of them) had awakened, aided by the many shots I had fired. The news of the leopard chase had spread, and the passengers rushed for the glass-enclosed upper deck above the mess room to take in the show, or as much as they could see.

The much-harassed leopard made circuit after circuit of the promenade deck, Lal and I in pursuit. Every other lap or so, he would suddenly swing around and face us, teeth and claws bared as before, ready for action. Again we would stand motionless and give him a chance to quiet down. Once after his teeth and claws relaxed to normal and we thought he was calming down, the cries of passengers startled him, and he poised himself for a leap, his eyes distorted with rage and fear.

"The rifle, Lal!"

Lal was so anxious to place it in my hands he almost threw himself at me in handing it to me. He wanted that leopard killed; there was no doubt about that.

I got a bead on the animal about five or six yards away. My finger on the trigger, I was ready to bang away and catch the enemy in mid-air if he leaped.

I advanced a foot to see how anxious the leopard was for a scrap. He started backing away.

"Give him the pistol, Lal!" I had handed Lal the revolver when I took the rifle from him. Lal blazed away, and again the animal turned and ran.

It was getting to be a tiresome business. I made up my mind to get that leopard, dead or alive, without wasting much more time and energy.

Fortunately my spotted fugitive was tiring too. Weary of the chase, he would hesitate before the open door of the mess room and scamper round the deck again, without much assurance, not quite certain whether he had anything to lose by going in. Finally seeing that there was no other place to go, he entered. I banged the door shut, and the second stage of the job was finished.

Lal and I, after a few moments of well-earned rest, removed the bars from one end of the repaired and reinforced cage and shoved it smack against the door frame, first hastily opening the mess room door. We took the precaution of blocking in the open space above the cage.

So far, so good. This was progress.

With a group of husky sailors holding the cage firmly against the door I decided on the next move.

Going into a hallway from the other side of the deck opening into the mess room, I lowered a dumb-waiter window (through which the mess boy on duty passed food when a meal was being served) and, with a long bamboo pole, tried to prod the leopard into the box.

My spotted foe would snarl his opinion of these tactics, two or three times grabbing the end of the pole between his teeth and biting off a piece. He'd spit out the bamboo and look up at me in a rage, all the bitterness in his heart reflected in his cruel glare.

After fifteen or twenty minutes of this he decided to mock what he must have considered a feeble effort to get him into the cage. Another leopard, under the same circumstances, might have scampered in. This one expressed his contempt for my methods by stretching out on the floor and ignoring me after he was convinced there was nothing to fear from that pole, which he had already chewed to pieces. Perhaps he was taking advantage of a lull in the battle to get a rest. At any rate, he made it clear that it would take more than a bamboo pole to get him inside that cage.

The stubborn beast was beginning to annoy me. It was time to show him who was boss. I sent Lal to my cabin for my lasso. Then I had one of the sailors bring me a long piece of ship's rope, which I securely tied to the end of the lasso. Next I filled my revolver with honest-to-goodness lead-nosed bullets. Then, gun in belt and lasso in hand, I started climbing through the dumb-waiter window.

I heard one of the petty officers yelling: "What's the matter, man? Are you crazy?"

I was too busy to answer. As a matter of fact, I was quite sane. I was doing the only thing that could be done with the facilities at hand to get that mulish leopard into his cage.

Before swinging over the window I threw the end of the rope through the bars of the cage to the sailors outside. "When I tell you fellows to pull," I instructed, "pull for all you're worth."

The mess room was about seven feet wide and fifteen or sixteen feet long. A stationary dining table with clamped-down chairs practically filled the room, leaving just enough space between the chairs and the wall for the officers to pass along to their places at the table. It was an easy step from the dumb-waiter window onto the table. With the loop end of the lasso in my hand ready for action I advanced slowly toward the leopard, which was crouched down by the foot of the table at the other end of the small room.

As I made my cautious approach (advancing only a few feet), the animal let out a throaty snarl, one of those ugly low ones that give you the creeps till you get used to hearing them, and suddenly reared up with his forepaws on the other end of the table.

Again I resorted to the simple expedient that has saved me from being clawed any number of times. Standing motionless, I gave the animal a chance to calm down. This he did, slipping his paws off the table and edging back to where he was when I entered. The only sound that came from him was a faint growl, suggestive of muttering, making it seem as if the creature was talking to himself. Now that the animal was fairly quiet I started once more for his end of the room, working my way across the table toward him in tiny steps.

He lay there cringing, his teeth bared. His snarl this time was more of a wail, and I felt sure that I had him on the run. It was ticklish business, but I was making headway. Only a person who has had long experience in handling animals can get the feel of a weakening enemy in a situation of this kind. Reducing the thing to simple terms, I was making it clear to this beast who was running the show. It is purely a mental proposition, the same psychology that allows experienced trainers to tame the jungle's wildest beasts.

Nevertheless, I don't mind adding that I was comforted by my loaded revolver and the nearness of an open window.

I kept steadily working up to where the leopard was crouching, getting my rope ready as I advanced. With a quick movement as I neared the other end of the table I sent a loop around the animal's neck, taking up the noose's slack in a flash as I yelled, "Pull!" with every ounce of lung power I possessed.

The men responded beautifully, giving a yank that started the roped leopard sliding toward the door. As he was dragged along he let out a series of spine-chilling snarls, struggling to dig into the floor with his claws and, when he saw this availed him nothing, striking out with his paws in a desperate effort to get a grip on a table leg or one of the stationary chairs he was being tugged past.

With a final yank, the men pulled the growling and struggling beast till they could drag him no further. In order to get the animal into the cage he would have to be pulled around a corner of the door jamb, as he was at right angles to the cage opening toward which he was being dragged. A trial tug, to see if this miracle could be accomplished, availed nothing. What we really hoped for was that at this stage of the game the beast would see he was licked and scamper into the cage himself. But he had braced his back against the chair nearest the door, and he couldn't be budged. All that the men could do now was to keep him wedged in by holding the rope taut, which they did. It was impossible for the animal to move backward, and it was equally impossible for the men at the rope to drag him forward another inch.

For several seconds we remained deadlocked, the animal making a perfect bedlam of the mess room with his cries of rage. The rope around his neck was uncomfortably tight, much tighter than I wanted it to be, but there was no other way to hold him, and he gave voice to the murder in his heart in as terrible a solo as I've ever heard from a cornered animal.

Hastily I reviewed in my mind possible ways of getting that leopard the rest of the distance to the cage, his head now being only about a foot from the opening.

I shouted my simple plan to the men outside. "And when I swing him round," was my final command, "pull like hell."

Then I proceeded to put my scheme into effect, the only course that could possibly save the situation. It was a risky business, for an infuriated leopard is a menace, even when partly a prisoner.

Jumping off the table I quickly grabbed the animal by a kicking back leg and squared him around so that the men could pull him straight through the door. Considering that it was my first experience at swinging a leopard around a bend by a back leg, I did a good job. The men at the rope did an even better job. The second I surprised the animal with my attack from the rear, which placed him directly in front of the open cage he had been so stubbornly resisting, they gave a tremendous yank that sent the spotted mule—only this cat was more obstinate than a mule—catapulting headlong through the opening as though he were on the wrong end of a tug-of-war, with an army of elephants working the other end of the rope.

All I heard from the leopard was a strangled gasp as he went whizzing through the opening into the cage. Lal, who was now on top of the box, did a speedy job of dropping the bars that made the animal a prisoner again. With two sailors to assist him in the operation, it was over in a jiffy.

As I mopped the perspiration off my forehead, thinking that my task was over, I was alarmed by the labored breathing that came from the cage. Running around and peering inside, I saw that the animal was choking. For some strange reason that I never could fathom, the slipknot around his neck had not loosened when the sailors at my order slackened their hold on the rope.

Something had to be done immediately. I grabbed the end of the rope and sent the slack twirling through the bars, hoping this would result in slacking the noose. It didn't.

Here was an animal threatened by strangulation. To me, an animal dying is as painful a sight as human death, and I meant to save that pesky leopard's life, even if I got clawed up in the process.

Again I rallied my sailors. I commanded them to grab the end of the rope and jerk the animal forward to the bars.

I got out a heavy pocketknife I always carry. The agonized breathing of the choking beast rattled me as much as anything ever had, and I found myself fumbling with the knife in my feverish efforts to open up the longest blade, with a razor-sharp cutting edge of over four inches. I got the blade open as the men dragged the animal to the bars with a powerful pull. All I saw in front of me was a couple of hundred pounds of tortured leopard as I reached in and slipped the knife under the rope, quickly cutting it through.

Ironically enough, now that this animal was caged, I was in more danger in my dealings with him than at any time since I set out to capture him. I took my chances when I stuck my hand into the cage to slit that noose, but this was as nothing compared to the danger I was in during the fraction of a second that elapsed between the time I restored him to normal breathing with a slash of my knife and the withdrawal of my hand. He seemed to come alive again instantaneously, making a terrible lunge for me, one paw just reaching my right shoulder and ripping my leather jacket wide open. Fortunately I ducked as I frantically backed away or else that vicious paw would have dug down into my shoulder and held me fast while the other paw reaching out through the iron bars got in its deadly work at my throat.

Five weeks later the troublesome creature, considerably tamed though not exactly what you'd call docile, wound up at the Lincoln Park Zoo in Chicago.

CHAPTER XI

KING COBRA

"We want a king cobra, a big one."

Several times I had heard those words from Dr. Ditmars of the New York Zoological Park. For a long time I had been on the lookout for a specimen that would fill the bill but without success. The task of bringing back what was wanted by the man who is considered America's most eminent reptile authority was as worthwhile an assignment as I could ask for, made doubly so by the fact that I looked upon Dr. Ditmars as one who took a friendly interest in my operations.

The difficulties involved in landing a king cobra are many. Most of the Asian traders and trappers who supply me with specimens of other kinds, including dangerous animals and reptiles, have a fear of cobras that makes the disquiet that all other jungle terrors arouse in them seem mild by comparison. Usually when a sizeable king cobra is available for purchase it is the result of an accident or a freakish set of circumstances, there being no regular trade in these reptiles that there is, say, in tigers and leopards.

The reason for this is that of all the creatures that dwell in the jungles of Asia it is the most vicious, being the only one that will attack without provocation. Nowhere in the world is there an animal or reptile that can quite match its unfailing determination to wipe out anything that crosses its path. This lust to kill invests the king cobra with a quality of fiendishness that puts it in a class by itself, almost making of it a jungle synonym for death.

One is always thinking of it in terms of loss of life. I find myself recalling a hundred and one instances of its destructiveness. I think of the many natives, within my own experience, who have succumbed to it, of animals that suffered the same fate. I can't get out of my mind, for instance, the picture of a water buffalo, a fine robust specimen weighing about fifteen hundred pounds, that, walking through a rice *padi*, had the misfortune to step too close to a ridge where a six-foot king cobra lay coiled up. The uncompromising reptile struck, and the buffalo was dead in less than an hour. Then there is a whole series of memories of bullocks and other work animals wiped out by cobras, of the many planters I've known whose dogs suffered the horrible death that follows when His Royal Highness, King Cobra, gets his fangs into play.

It is not a more terrible venom that makes the king cobra the most dangerous of reptiles. In fact, I believe that the poisonous secretions of the Russell's viper of India and the green mamba of Africa are deadlier. The king cobra, however, is a much bigger snake, and its poison sacs contain considerably more venom. Then there is another point to consider. The ordinary poisonous reptile makes a quick strike and injects what venom it can in a fraction of a second. When the king cobra strikes it holds its victim fast in its jaws until it has completely emptied its poison sacs. The result is an injection from which recovery is impossible, the system being too saturated with the killing fluid. No other snake injects so much poison, and no other snake does so thorough a job of destroying its victim. Swiftly and agonizingly death comes, no more certain or painful death having ever been visited upon man or beast.

Nine times out of ten the mere smell of a human being will send a tiger scurrying off into the jungle. The same is true of the leopard. Even the savage sladung (wild jungle buffalo), considered by many the most formidable of all animals, has no desire to pit himself against man unless wounded or cornered. The presence of mankind is the signal for a hasty retreat. The sudden appearance of a native child has been known to stampede a whole herd of wild elephants. The cobra alone refuses to admit that man is anything to worry about. Cross his path anywhere at any time, and he'll raise two or three feet of his body off the ground, stretch out his hood, and go for you. There is a kind of horrible glamour about the unwillingness of this king of reptiles to make his peace with anyone or anything. He's a fighter always. Bump into him, and be prepared to defend yourself.

The only king cobras in this country when Dr. Ditmars was prodding me to locate a colossal one for him were specimens four and five feet long. I had had opportunities to pick up such cobras, but they did not interest me. I was on the lookout for one that measured at least nine or ten feet. Nothing less would have satisfied the reptile curator of the Bronx Zoo. I hoped to do even better than that, though I hadn't the faintest idea how I was going to do it.

I had brought back many of the spectacled cobras of India and the black cobras of the Malay Archipelago, but I had yet to enter the United States with a king cobra. I wanted a specimen that would make zoologists throw their hats into the air, there being nothing more depressing to me than the spectacle of a scientist who can get only mildly excited about a specimen I shove under his nose. Give me joyfully dancing zoologists every time.

Wherever I went on the collecting trips that kept me bouncing all over the map of Asia I looked around to see if there wasn't a chance of picking up the kind of king cobra that was wanted in New York. If there was anything I could do to put a reptile in the Bronx Zoo that would make even one spectator forget himself sufficiently to shout, "Lookit the size of that damned thing!" I wanted to do it.

For some time my efforts were unrewarded. Traders kept showing me king cobras that looked like shoestrings till I almost decided that the species was going back.

Then one day I had a stroke of luck. I was up on the northeastern border of Johore looking over some tigers. At the height of the bargaining—just as I was saying that while these were good tigers I could not agree with the trader who was giving me a line of high-pressure sales talk that they were the finest pair ever caught—an old Malay Sakai [native], looking like an octogenarian, came by with a box on his head. He spewed up a lot of sentences in a Malay dialect that was a bit beyond me. Only two of his many words meant anything to me, *ular*, which means "snake," and *ringgit*, which means "dollars." Two words out of about two hundred isn't much of a percentage, but they told me all I needed to know. If I would part with some of my dollars I could have the snake that this Sakai was carrying on his head.

The offer of a snake wasn't any cause for excitement. Most reptiles made me yawn. I had looked at so many for weeks that meant absolutely nothing to me that when I asked the old man to take the box off his head and let me have a look at the contents, I was merely operating on the principle that there's no harm in looking.

It didn't take me long to see that the Sakai had something remarkable to offer, the largest king cobra I had ever seen. In fact, it later proved to be the biggest in the world. The record had been held for years by a specimen twelve feet six inches long, preserved in alcohol in the Raffles Museum at Singapore. It developed that the monster I found myself looking at that day in northern Johore was almost a foot longer. Four years later my record was broken by a fourteen-foot specimen that was killed on a rubber estate near Ipoh. This amazing reptile was mounted and is also on exhibit today in the Raffles Museum.

I was overjoyed. So was Ali, who accompanied me on this trip. But we saved our handsprings till later. Show too much pleasure over a specimen a native offers you for sale, and you let yourself in for hours of trying to convince the wretch that he's mistaken in his suddenly acquired belief that what he is selling is the most precious thing in the world.

I asked the Sakai how much he wanted. *"Sepuluh ringgit"* ["Ten dollars, Straits money"] came the reply.

I gave him the ten dollars, and the giant king cobra was mine.

The old man interested me. His being a Sakai was enough to accomplish that, for there is no stranger people anywhere in the world than these descendants of the aboriginal possessors of the Malay Peninsula. They hardly ever come out of the jungle, where they live with a classic unconcern about such benefits of civilization as clothes. Among the mature men and women, there are those who conceal their procreative parts; but the younger generation spurn such concealments, perhaps causing the old folks to say there were no such goings-on when *they* were young men and women. Serene in their nakedness, it doesn't occur to them to think of the need for clothes any more than such thoughts would enter the heads of the birds and beasts around them.

To the Malays, the Sakais are a lost people, barbarous and unenlightened, which shows that even in jungle country there is a class system. This is understandable, of course; for the Malays are a civilized lot compared with the primitive Sakais.

The Malays are not above trading with the Sakais, but their method of dealing with these wild tribesmen tells the whole story of the superiority they feel. If a Sakai has anything to offer he is told to deposit it at an appointed place and withdraw. The Malay trader then places alongside the Sakai's offering the merchandise he is willing to give in exchange. They bargain back and forth with at least twenty feet separating them until the deal is closed.

In fairness to the Malays it is necessary to point out that they shun the Sakais not merely because they consider them inferior people but also for the practical reason that most of these jungle folk suffer from skin diseases. They are forever scratching themselves, industriously working their fingers over the queer, shiny, sometimes scaly, skin that is so common among them. But if a Malay trader hears that a tribe of Sakais has something to offer that can be converted into profits he loses no time in heading for their camp.

I was curious to hear from the old Sakai how he had come by the tremendous cobra he had sold me. One of the Asian jungle's strangest products, he stood before me hugging his ten Straits dollars to his chest, pleased with his bargain and smiling that I might get a good look at the hideous black stumps that once were teeth. A sack of bones, he looked half starved, though this was no indication that he was. For at least fifty of the seventy or more years of his life (he might have been eighty, for all anyone could tell) he probably had had that same emaciated look. There are freakish examples of longevity everywhere in Asia, old men who all their lives look as if they can't possibly live another minute and who succeed in outliving by many years thousands of their huskier-looking brethren.

The old man was all dressed up, and I couldn't help wondering how many years he had owned these habiliments he had donned for his appearance in the village where we met. On those rare occasions when a Sakai ventures out of his camp it is necessary for him to put on some clothes, or else the Malays will not permit him to enter their villages. The old man's gala attire (darned gala for a Sakai) consisted of a greasy old *sarong* and a dirty rag wrapped turban fashion around his head. With one hand he scratched himself, with the other he continued to hug to his chest his ten dollars.

I asked Ali to get from him the story of how he had come into possession of the king cobra. The old man, accustomed to being shunned, was pleased when he learned that I wanted to hear his story, and he spoke freely, rattling on so rapidly when he became excited that I marveled at Ali's ability to follow him. Never have I heard a weirder jumble of sounds than came from his lips in those overwrought moments. Authentic Malay isn't especially easy to understand; and when you hear a strange version of it, a local dialect spoken by a stimulated old man who is probably getting his first chance to talk in years, the result is unlike anything else that ever reached human ears.

The *tuan* would never regret asking how he (the old Sakai) had acquired that tremendous *ular*. Perhaps the *tuan* would never again hear such a tale. Before he launched into his tale he repeated over and over again, Ali later told me, that I had done well to seek his story. It was as if, Ali said, he was trying to prolong the novelty of having an audience.

One night when the jungle was a bit chill and damp, he and his comrades started a fire. Sakais have a habit of rolling in the warm ashes on such occasions. One of the men was going through these strange gymnastics when he felt something strike him in the chest. Instinctively he reached out and grabbed it, yelling for all he was worth as he did. Curled up in the ashes, some of them half asleep, were other Sakais. When they heard their fellow tribesman cry out they jumped up to see what was wrong. They found him holding an enormous king cobra. It would not have been difficult for him to do this, as the cobra has no formidable power in its body like constrictor snakes. Seeking a warm place the reptile had come into the Sakai camp. Lying directly in the path of the poor devil who was warming himself, it had raised up and struck when he came rolling along to violate the privacy of its resting place.

As the victim kept shrieking away that he had been bitten by an *ular,* one of the Sakais who had scrambled up out of the ashes got a firm hold on the snake behind the head and took it away from his doomed comrade. Only a Sakai would have had the nerve to do that. Among these wild people is found a knowledge of animals and reptiles that is equaled by their courage in dealing with them. Only a Malay, with his capacity for making these queer jungle folk feel like so much dirt, can frighten them.

The man with the snake yelled for a *kris* (dagger). He would cut the creature's head off. Our skinny old man, who had shaken himself out of his slumbers and joined the group, ruled no. He was the chief of the tribe (we hadn't realized that we were in the presence of a tribal leader), and what he said was law. He ordered the snake taken alive. Why kill it when it could be sold to the next Malay trader who came along? In all the time he had lived in the jungle—he was sure it must be close to nine hundred moons—he had never seen so enormous a cobra, and he felt sure it would fetch a good price.

The Sakai who was holding the snake had a very good grip on it. With the old man directing the operations, a long pole and strips of rattan were quickly produced, and the cobra was stretched out and lashed to the pole. Later it was transferred to an old wooden box that a Malay trader had left behind.

Meanwhile the women of the camp were making a grand to-do. One of them, the official healer who, we were told, had many miraculous cures to her credit, was working over the moaning victim. First she tried to suck the devils out of the man's chest, then she made a poultice of herbs and applied it. These measures, the old man assured us, were effective in treating many kinds of bites; but this *ular* was too full of devils. So many of them had been transferred to his unfortunate comrade when the poor chap was bitten that they had no trouble killing him long before daylight set in.

For weeks the Sakais waited for a Malay trader to appear. None came (their visits were irregular), and the old man decided to dress up and take the cobra to the nearest village, feeling sure that he could find a trader who would want to buy the giant *ular*. The box had started to rot, and he was anxious to dispose of his prize before the problem of providing new quarters for it arose.

The first thing I did when I got back to Singapore with my record-breaking king cobra was to order of Hin Mong, my Chinese carpenter, a fine teakwood box with a heavy plate-glass top sliding in a groove. I wanted to get Dr. Ditmars's future boarder into its new box as soon as possible and then go about the business of putting it in good condition. Cobras are hardy rascals, but neglect can harm the toughest of creatures. This one was suffering from too long a stay in that vile-smelling box, a crude affair that couldn't be cleaned, and hardly the right quarters for my thirteen-foot cobra.

When Hin Mong delivered the new box we prepared to transfer the snake by placing the old box over the new and knocking the decaying bottom out of the old. The snake would drop through, and with one quick slide of the plate-glass top I would finish the job of installing him in his new and more comfortable home.

I didn't have Ali with me that day. But I had two Chinese boys and two Malay boys working with me in the compound, which gave me more help than I needed for the simple task to be done. The scene of our operations was a nipa-thatched shed in my compound, enclosed on three sides, open in front, and partly filled with empty tiger cages and other boxes stacked to the roof.

I sent one of the Chinese boys for the old box. With the rear wall of the shed at my back, I was standing beside the new box, which was in readiness for its tenant. As the boy approached he stumbled over some object on the ground, jarring the box sufficiently to cause the rotten bottom to fall out. The snake fell with it, landing on the cement in front of me, belly up.

In a fraction of a second my four boys were frantically scrambling to places of safety. One of the Malay boys, developing a speed that was little short of miraculous, got to the top of the stacked-up tiger cages in record time. If he had been pursued by a whole army of demons he could not have got there more quickly.

I'm not criticizing the boys for running. I was debating whether to do the same thing myself. It was really the sensible thing to do. After all, who wants to fight a cobra? It's all right in case you're interested in the idea of suicide, but if you're as keen about life as I am, there's no strategy equal to running while there's still time when you're in a situation like the one that confronted me as I stood in that blind alley. The piled-up tiger boxes formed a wall on my left, the solid side wall of the shed was at my right, and behind me was the back of the shed.

I hesitated long enough to give the snake a chance to right itself. It reared its head three feet and spread its greenish brown hood. Then it saw me.

Instinctively I jumped backward. There wasn't far to go. Another four or five feet, and I'd hit the back of the shed. As I made my brief retreat the snake struck, missing my leg by only an inch or two.

I was trapped. I suffered more from plain ordinary fright at that moment, and I'm not ashamed to admit it, than at any time in all my career. Through my mind flashed a quick picture of what had happened to the Sakai whom this terrible reptile had bitten. It made me pretty sick.

I flattened myself against the back of the shed, grimly eyeing the killer that lay almost at my feet. The expressionless eyes calmly looking back at me gave me a cold and clammy feeling. I didn't want to die this way. It was not my notion of a decent death. Surely there must be some way out. Desperately I ran my eyes around for something to bring down over the enemy's head. I wasn't particular. Anything would do, anything that could be converted into a club, a stick of wood, a . . .

The cobra was poising itself for a second strike. The hideous head rose slightly and stretched forward a bit. I got the impression of a calculating foe gauging its distance before launching another attack.

I had passed the point where fear was any longer a definite emotion. It had disappeared, along with all other emotions, and all I was aware of was a numbness of mind and body.

Staring hard ahead I poised myself too for a fight to a finish, though just how I was going to fight I didn't know. I had nothing to fight with, nothing with which to fend off the attack.

My hands, with which I had successfully defended myself in the past against animals of many species, including the human, now seemed ridiculous. Hands, without something to wield, aren't much good in a scrap with a cobra. They might be strong enough to strangle two such enemies—and they were—but if my grisly antagonist punctured one of them with his fangs the fight would be over. And he had so many other targets: legs, arms, body.

Mechanically I found myself going through some motions. I don't recall that they were part of a plan. They represented, rather, the final idea of a paralyzed brain, stirred into action by the second assault of the enemy. As the cobra struck, I went through those motions to which I refer. Frantically slipping over my head the white duck coat that I was wearing over a bare skin (quaint custom of the tropics) I held the coat in front of me, and as the snake came on I lunged forward and threw myself upon it. I hit the ground with a bang, the cobra under me. I could feel the wriggling body under mine, and with each wriggle I pressed down harder, hopeful of keeping the reptile so weighted down that it would not be able to do anything with those murderous fangs.

I screamed like a lunatic for those boys of mine. A picture of them roasting in hell flashed through my mind, and it seemed too kind a fate for them.

The cobra continued to squirm and wriggle. With a crazy kind of desperation I kept pressing down with my body, cursing the pavement for not having handles that would enable me to get a grip and bear down harder. Picture a man trying to dig his fingers into a cement floor, and you have a fair idea of how demented I was at that moment.

Part of the snake got loose and kept hitting against my hip. In my unhinged condition I decided that the part that was free was the head, and every time it struck I imagined myself being bitten. Knowing how cobra bite affects the human system, I quickly developed all the symptoms and in the next few minutes managed to die a dozen times.

My shrieks finally accomplished something. One of the Malay boys appeared.

The *tuan* was mistaken. That was the snake's tail that was loose, not his head. Of course, it was the tail. Who said it was the head? The head was under my chest. Couldn't I feel it? Didn't I know the difference between the tail of a snake and its head?

And now that he had reassured me, my hysteria vanished, and I no longer felt the cobra's tail biting me. How I could ever have taken that flapping end for the head I'll never be able to explain, for plainly the head was under my chest. It was as obvious now as if I could see it.

I barked out some orders. The gist of them was that the boy was to slide his hand under my chest and wad the coat around the head. With my weight pressing down on it, the snake was unable to strike. It was a ticklish job, but it was one that could be done. I would slowly raise up and . . .

The boy backed off. He would have none of it. He wanted to help the *tuan* but . . .

I started yelling like mad for one of the other boys. One of the Chinese lads appeared. He was game. And intelligent. As I cautiously raised up a bit, not sufficient to allow the reptile to lift its head high enough for a striking position, he slid his hand underneath me and made a quick grab for the snake behind the head; and as I slowly raised up higher and higher he began the process of tightly twisting the white duck coat over the cobra's mouth, head, and neck until it was helpless.

Less than ten minutes later the king cobra that had almost succeeded in killing me was dropped into his new box. I never ceased to be grateful to the courageous little Chinese boy who came to my rescue when the Malay walked out on me. You'd have thought I was handing him a million dollars when I presented him with the wristwatch I bought for him at de Silva's in Singapore. I also tried to give him some money, but he refused it. The watch was sufficient, he insisted.

When I was ready to start my king cobra on its trip to America I directed one of my helpers to round up a supply of food for it. This meant gathering up some small snakes, for the king cobra, one of the cannibal reptiles, eats nothing but other snakes. He belongs to a species that can go for weeks without food, but when I tested his appetite with a two-foot brown snake he made it disappear so fast it was obvious he was hungry and would be in the mood for eating on board ship.

My assistant had no luck in his quest for small snakes. Few native traders handle them (there being a very limited market for them), and it looked as if the cobra was in for a long fast. I knew I could find plenty of small snakes to feed the villain in America, but I didn't feel like letting him go that long without a meal. I was anxious to deliver this record-breaker in the finest condition possible, and I made up my mind to consult every source in Singapore until I located some snakes for him to bolt.

Failing to find what I wanted, the day before I was due to sail I bought two small pythons from Chop Joo Soon, the Chinese dealer with whom I frequently traded. Each of these reptiles measured about six feet, small enough for pythons but powerful reptiles. Normally I would not have considered such formidable specimens as food for my cobra, but I had no choice. They were better than nothing.

The main thing that worried me about these pythons when I considered them as cobra food was that, being constrictors, they might give the hooded chap more of a squeezing than was good for him before consenting to be food. The cobra, having no constricting powers, would have to confine himself in the skirmish that would ensue to striving for a quick headlock that would enable him to swallow the enemy. This I felt confident he would be able to do. The cobra's poison sacs meant no advantage over the venomless constrictor, for snakes are unaffected by the deadliest poisons of other snakes.

When our ship, the *Granite State,* was well out and all of my specimens were stowed away where they belonged, I decided to give the cobra its first meal. I reached into the box where it lay and grabbed a python by the back of the head. If a twenty foot python had been involved this would have been a dangerous operation, for a constrictor that size is capable of crushing a man to death. The little fellow I was handling possessed no such powers, of course, but he had to be carefully watched just the same. A python about this size once wound himself around my wrist, and by the time I got him unwound he had done so good a job of squeezing that my whole arm felt as if paralysis had suddenly set in.

As I pulled the python out of the box I had a helper (Ali's nephew, who accompanied me) straighten him out and stretch him out taut. I opened the slide door of the king cobra's box and quickly stuck the python's head in, working him in as if I were handling so much heavy rope. I pushed the constrictor in as fast as I could, increasing the opening of the adjustable door as the body grew thicker. (At its thickest point the python was almost as wide as the cobra was at a corresponding point.)

As the python made his forced entrance the cobra spread his hood, raised up a few inches, and prepared to strike. When about a foot of the constrictor was inside the box, the cobra made a sideswipe for him, his jaws gripping the enemy's head at about the midway mark.

When I had worked in about two-thirds of that living rope, the python required no further handling, fairly flying in to get at the thing inside that had that terrible grip on his head. In a series of lightning-fast whirls the python got three coils around the cobra, one around the hood, another about six inches farther down, and a third about six inches below that. Madly shaking his head and squeezing the cobra for all he was worth, the python struggled to break that first vicious hold that had put him at a disadvantage.

The reptiles tumbled over and over in a tangled ball, a struggle that would not cease until one of the antagonists was dead. The silent fury of the snakes and the total lack of expression in their artificial-seeming eyes added a note of ghastliness that gave the struggle a kind of unearthly fascination.

I began to grow worried about my cobra. I kept my eyes glued on his jaws, knowing that if they relaxed and let go, it meant that the python was squeezing him to death. Once, after the python had put him through a series of terrific whirls in the course of which those coils tightened like vises that are being clamped closer and closer together, I thought the cobra was going to let go. Quickly I slid back the glass top of the box, and with a heavy stick that I kept in my hand, I made ready to swat the constrictor and break his hold. I had no intention of losing that giant cobra.

The straining and tugging continued, the cobra still retaining that awful headlock. The python seemed to tire from his convulsive struggle to whirl himself free, confining himself for half a minute or so to an attempt to squash the enemy by squeezing hard in those three places around which he lay coiled. As I looked down I noticed that the cobra was cleverly working his head around. Slowly but surely he shifted his jaws until he had improved his side hold to a front hold. (It will be remembered that originally he sideswiped the python, retaining the same grip till now.)

Instead of trying to draw the python to him the cobra was working his jaws over his antagonist's head, until he had it almost entirely in his mouth. This roused the python to a new series of violent whirls, tumbles, twists, and squirms.

The cobra kept drawing his head over the python, and when the constrictor's head started disappearing I slid the glass top back in place, knowing that the fight was over. The python continued furiously struggling, but with each deft forward movement of the cobra's head there was less and less python.

When a whole foot of the constrictor was down the cobra's throat their bodies were as much of a tangle as ever, with the disappearing victim still struggling hard. Even when he was half swallowed, the python continued to fight, squeezing with a fury that would have burst the sides of a less hardy opponent.

There was something horrible about the methodical way in which the cobra kept working his head over the defeated foe, a soundless, steady, unemotional process that seemed the work of a machine rather than the efforts of a living creature. Not a drop of blood was shed, which gave the battle a further note of unreality.

An hour after I had started feeding the cobra, the last bit of the python's tail, wriggling hard, as if to let the world know that he hadn't given up yet, disappeared down the cobra's throat.

Dr. Ditmars was delighted with his giant cobra when it was delivered to the Bronx Zoo three or four weeks later. It was the prize exhibit of the Reptile House there until 1929, when, tired, perhaps, of being stared at or eager to see what the snake hereafter was like, it died. This, however, did not halt its earthly career. Mounted and tagged with the details of its reptilian importance, it may be seen in the American Museum of Natural History.

CHAPTER XII

THE PATSY

Some animals are born lucky. Bad fortune never pursues them. After untroubled lives they depart this world without a wrinkle or a gray hair to show for their presence on Earth. Other animals are forever experiencing tough luck. They just never get the breaks. With luckless feet they instinctively tread on all of Fate's banana peels and, without quite knowing what it's all about, go skidding into Old Man Trouble.

Such an animal was The Patsy, a young female elephant I brought out of Ceylon some years ago. (In the Far East the term *The Patsy* is still widely used to designate the one—man, woman, child, or beast—who is forever getting the worst of it.) No living creature I have handled in my many years as a collector of animals, birds, and reptiles for the zoos and circuses had a run of bad luck comparable to this elephant's.

The fates started plotting against The Patsy when three natives of Ceylon—Sinhalese—set out one day from Kandy for the interior. Harmless-looking natives they were too. Aside from work knives they carried no equipment with them as they stepped into the jungle, and anyone observing them and guessing at their vocation would hardly have written them down as elephant-catchers. Yet that's what they were.

In India, Burma, and Siam the capturing of live elephants is an elaborate process frequently calling for the services of hundreds of men and much equipment. The elephants are rounded up and driven into a *keddah* or corral. In Ceylon, where the natives are content to catch one elephant at a time, the method is much simpler, as witness the performance of the three Sinhalese.

Shortly after stepping into the jungle the trio started plucking *lalang,* a tall, wiry grass. They also cut down jungle creepers, stripping off and retaining the outer peeling and throwing the rest away. As they walked along they busied themselves with the task—a simple one for these experts—of weaving these tough jungle fibers into a rope. On they moved, plucking the raw material and, when it was ready for use, braiding and twisting it in the prescribed Ceylonese manner.

After two or three days, in the course of which they slept in the jungle and lived largely on wild fruits, they had a rope about seventy-five feet long and about two inches in diameter—a rope neat and pliable and of well-nigh incredible strength.

Then the elephant-catchers entered upon the second phase of their job, the business of locating a small herd of wild elephants. This accomplished, they calmly proceeded with the next step, the ticklish task of getting the herd headed toward a narrow, wooded ravine (which these men had found convenient once before in their elephant-catching exploits). In carrying out this part of the assignment the trio from Kandy had to bring all their knowledge of pachyderm reactions into play. Occasionally one of them would sneak around the herd, remaining in view just long enough for the animals to see him and get it through their heads, in case they had any doubts, that they were being pursued.

In a chase such as this, the quarry frequently veers off the course and has to be worked back cautiously to the right direction. This requires a tremendous amount of patience, a quality in which the Sinhalese are not lacking.

Once they had the herd definitely headed for the ravine, two of the men ran around till they stood facing the far side of the gorge toward which the animals were moving. When the beasts were inside the borders of the narrow opening the Sinhalese pair dashed forward till they were directly in front of the herd, jumping up and down, frantically waving their arms, and emitting ear-splitting shouts designed to halt the elephants in their tracks with a suddenness sure to result in a jam.

The person who remains behind in an operation of this kind is the one who is handiest with the rope. He also has to be the nerviest of the three, for his is no feat of long-distance roping. His rope is much too heavy and cumbersome for such work, and, besides, these natives know nothing about lassoing.

As the shouting and arm-waving pair started their crazy dance, the elephants suddenly halted in their flight, rearing up on their hind legs and emitting snorts of dismay. The ravine was now choked with milling, trumpeting elephants struggling to work their way out of the wedge. The man with the rope, the working end of which consisted of a loop, had been waiting for this moment. His job was to slip cautiously in among the panic-stricken herd and get the loop around the upraised leg of one of the churning and jostling pack—an animal in or near the last row that wasn't too massive to handle. Hastily looking over his prospective victims, he selected his elephant—a medium-sized female that was locked between two larger elephants in the rear—and waited for her to lift one of her legs.

The second she did, he slipped the noose around the upraised member and speedily tightened it. Then, without losing any time, he ran back with the rope and worked it several times around the nearest stout tree, one that he had picked out earlier as the likeliest for his purpose.

This done, he shouted to his jumping, gesticulating comrades to notify them that it was no longer necessary to hold the herd at bay. The pair quickly left their posts and rushed to his aid. Simultaneously the elephants in the front rank went tearing straight ahead, releasing the other animals in the ravine, and soon the herd—minus only The Patsy, who was caught—were moving along peacefully through the jungle, browsing again as before the Ceylonese three appeared.

The next move was to take a half-hitch around the tree with the rope to doubly secure The Patsy. Then the animal was worked back till she was flush against the tree, one of the trio jumping up and down and waving his arms as before to accomplish this, his companions readjusting the rope and taking up the slack. When their captive was lashed fast to the tree the natives proceeded with the job of hobbling her front feet with rattan.

Then began the process of taming, which covered a period of two to three weeks, and which I shall not attempt to describe here. It's a story in itself, the details of which are not essential to the present narrative.

The job of taming over, the Sinhalese entered upon the final stage of their task—the business of walking their captive home, a long and arduous proceeding.

I had just arrived in Kandy from Colombo. Kandy is only a short journey from Colombo, and I had made the trip there to see if I could pick up a good-natured, medium-sized elephant capable of being trained to carry children. I had an order for two such elephants.

One of these animals secured (it was in my compound at Katong, outside Singapore), I was now looking for the other. Kandy is the main clearinghouse for elephants in Ceylon.

I learned from the first trader I visited that a young elephant very much like what I wanted had just been brought in from the jungle. For a fee he agreed to accompany me as interpreter to the open field where the animal was being held. Not long afterward I opened negotiations with the three Sinhalese for The Patsy.

They told me how they had captured her, their story varying only slightly from what I had once observed myself on one of these strange equipmentless elephant hunts. The primitive process is standard among the expert elephant-catchers of the Ceylonese jungle.

First I gave The Patsy a thorough examination. She was a good, strong animal and of the right size. Her feet were in good condition, and her legs were straight and sturdy. Her only deficiency was that she was full of ticks. The creases in her trunk and behind the shoulders and ears and the wrinkles on the inner side of the upper legs were alive with these little pests.

I suppose it sounds surprising that as thick-skinned an animal as an elephant can be annoyed by ticks, but it is a fact nonetheless. The skin where the creases and wrinkles form becomes very tender, and these places are the ones sought out by the vermin.

An elephant that has as many ticks as The Patsy (luckless devil) is bound to be fretful and fidgety. The pestiferous insects make her uncomfortable, and as a result the job of transporting her becomes very difficult. I know of few things more trying than the task of traveling with a restless elephant for any real distance.

I told the three Sinhalese that before I would consider buying their elephant (they were very anxious to sell) they would have to remove the ticks. The spokesman laughed and assured me that ticks on an elephant weren't anything to worry about. Most elephants had them. Surely the gentleman must be having his first experience with elephants if he did not know that. I didn't trouble to tell him how many dozens of elephants I had handled. I concentrated on getting the interpreter to convey to him that no elephant with ticks had ever entered my compound and that I had no intention of setting a precedent.

Seeing that I meant business, the spokesman promised to have the ticks removed by the following day.

The next day I met the three Sinhalese at the appointed hour. They were jabbering away excitedly when I arrived. The Patsy was snorting and stamping around as if in considerable discomfort, rubbing against a tree by way of scratching herself. I could see at a glance that her skin was badly inflamed in several places.

I soon learned that in deticking the animal the Sinhalese had used too strong a solution of a powerful disinfectant used extensively in the East. They had employed a mixture strong enough to remove the hide along with the ticks.

The damage done was not serious, but the searing liquid had given The Patsy a severe burning, and she was in considerable pain. That elephant simply had no luck.

I bought The Patsy for two thousand rupees ($720), hoping a change of ownership would change her luck. Three or four days later the entire outer surface of her skin started peeling off, a process involving more pain and discomfort. All over her body and legs and trunk, patches of peeling skin were curled up ready to drop off. She was pretty much in the predicament of a person who has suffered a severe sunburn.

When the rolls of burned skin finally separated themselves from the under surface of the thick hide, they left the animal a little lighter in color. For about a week she was sore all over.

I got The Patsy back to Colombo without mishap. There I found that one of the Blue Funnel boats was due to leave for Calcutta the next day; so I engaged passage for myself, a Sinhalese assistant, and my livestock. But when the boat came in she had a heavy load of deck cargo, and the captain refused to add my freight to it, mainly on account of the elephant, which would take too much room, he said.

This was a tough break all around—but mainly for The Patsy. After an overnight train and ferry crossing from Colombo to the India side, we would entrain at Talaimannar. The trip by rail from there to Calcutta involves three days of the hottest, most uncomfortable riding imaginable, during which time The Patsy would be tied up, one hind leg and one front leg lashed to the sides of an all-metal freight car made sizzling hot during the day by the tropical sun. Had we been able to go by boat the elephant would have had far more comfortable quarters and easier riding. (Lucky indeed is the man or beast who can escape a trip on one of these perpetually jolting Indian trains, run by engineers who seem to enjoy throwing on their brakes with all possible suddenness.) The Patsy was in for all manner of jouncing and jarring.

We finally entrained. A Sinhalese boy whom I had hired for the trip to Calcutta remained in the freight car with The Patsy. I rode in one of the passenger coaches forward. (In India, mixed trains carrying both freight and passenger cars are quite common.)

The Patsy got an even worse jolting than I had anticipated. Before we had traveled more than a few hours her knees were badly bruised, and her sides were sore. It's no fun to be constantly thrown against the walls of a sheet-iron car.

As we headed into the monsoons, our troubles had hardly begun. These tremendous Indian rains regularly do a terrific amount of damage. As we plowed along through flooded areas I couldn't help wondering how long it would be before we should have to stop. Creeks, ponds, and rivers along our route were overflowing, and we were due to be marooned if the storm continued.

The bad news came when we were about five miles outside of the ancient city of Madura, our next important stop. A serious washout had made further travel impossible. The railway officials had already arrived on the scene. Arrangements were made to take passengers to Madura by boats. Nothing could be done about freight. I was told that it would be twelve days before the railway company could undertake to get the elephant and my crates and cages containing birds and small animals to Madura. That meant only one thing: I would have to get them to Madura myself. A twelve-day wait would have wrecked my schedule, which involved an early return to America with my present collection and the hundreds of other specimens of all kinds that I had in Calcutta and Singapore.

First I rounded up some of the native boatmen who swarmed around the train with their dugouts (stout native canoes, each dug out of the solid trunk of a tree) and sturdy rafts. I arranged with the more dependable-looking of the raftsmen to carry my bird and animal cages to the point nearest Madura that was reachable in these craft. Then I rounded up a gang of coolies and got them started building a gangplank. I had made up my mind to swim The Patsy across the flooded area—the only thing I could do unless I chose to be stranded with my live freight for almost two weeks—and the gangplank was to be used in walking the elephant out of the car (there being no station platform available).

The Patsy, having no doubt read or heard about the dangers of "walking the plank," became very balky for a normally good-natured and responsible young lady. The newness of her surroundings bewildered her, and it was a tough job to get her to venture out onto the wooden incline, but I finally accomplished my purpose.

At last we had the luckless animal on the ground beside the train. The next move was to drive her into the waters of the flooded area straight ahead. This I achieved after more than an hour of coaxing, prodding, and what not, in the course of which I had some anxious moments, for The Patsy was plainly frightened, and an elephant is never so full of dangerous possibilities as when in the clutches of fear.

I had hired six of the dugouts, with three men in each boat, to move along beside the swimming elephant and keep her headed in the right direction. I rode in one of them and directed the operations. We had good luck at the start. For a hundred yards or so The Patsy kept to the course laid down for her.

Then the much-harassed lady decided to swim downstream instead of straight across, which, on account of the current we were bucking, was much tougher going. Swimming strongly, she drew away from us, but we finally caught up with her by paddling like fury. We swung her around in the right direction after she had covered a needless quarter of a mile and kept her to the course without further trouble until we touched land a little more than a mile across from the point where we started.

From here it was a three-mile trek to Madura. With coolies shouldering my cages and crates and with the Sinhalese boy leading the elephant, we got under way. No stranger caravan ever traversed this dismal stretch to the Madura railroad station. Half the time we were ankle deep in mud, and there were points where we had to slop through water over our knees with our precious cargo. More than once the men faltered, and I would spur them on.

We finally reached Madura and got my freight loaded on a train that had been assembled by the railway officials to take care of the passengers who were being brought from the stranded train. It was the same sort of nondescript local, made up of passenger and freight cars.

When my crates and cages were in place, The Patsy was installed in an iron car as before and lashed front and back. Again she was thoroughly uncomfortable as we started jolting our way to Calcutta. It was an unbearably hot trip, and the elephant—now definitely the unluckiest animal I had ever handled—suffered frightfully from the heat. The best I could do for her was to have her Sinhalese attendant douse her with cold water at every station. This helped, but it hardly afforded sufficient relief.

When after three days of the toughest kind of riding we pulled into Calcutta, I experienced as prodigious a feeling of relief as I've ever known.

At Calcutta I picked up Lal Bahudar, my number one Hindu assistant. We combined my Ceylon collection with the Calcutta collection that Lal had been supervising and got them all to Singapore without mishap—which surprised me no little since that ill-starred lady, The Patsy, was among those present.

At Singapore I made arrangements by cable to meet the *President Cleveland* at Hong Kong. I was desirous of shipping on this boat because of its fine skipper, Captain George Yardley. Another good person on board was the mate, Bill Morris. These old friends would load my stock properly, find good locations for it on the ship, and take care of me in every way.

I arranged to go from Singapore to Hong Kong with my combined collection on the *Lake Falk*, a cargo boat known as a "feeder." Its function was to pick up freight at various ports and take it to Hong Kong for shipment via trans-Pacific liners and freighters to America. Lal accompanied me on the trip and did a characteristically good job of helping me look after my animals.

My principal problem now was the slowness of the *Lake Falk*. She was proceeding at only eight knots, which meant that there was a chance of my missing the *President Cleveland*. This would have cost me no end of inconvenience.

I got into wireless communication with the *President Cleveland,* giving Captain Yardley the exact position of the *Lake Falk* and telling him the rate at which we were traveling. Yardley addressed his reply to the captain of the *Falk,* asking that gentleman to put on all possible speed. This the skipper of the "feeder," who was familiar with the situation, agreed to do.

Yardley, in a subsequent wireless, notified me that the latest his ship could be held at Hong Kong would be two o'clock of the afternoon of its scheduled departing time (three days hence). This amounted to holding the vessel a whole hour for me.

The *Lake Falk* pulled into the entrance to Hong Kong Bay at two-fifteen—or fifteen minutes after my deadline. I was on the bridge with my binoculars to see if I could locate the *President Cleveland* at Knowldoon Dock. As we drew closer I spotted her. I could see her lines being taken in, and I could hear her drawing-away whistle.

By this time Captain Yardley had seen us. He signaled to the captain of the *Falk* to pull alongside the *President Cleveland.* As we drew up to the departing steamer she threw out lines both fore and aft, which were lashed to the fore and aft quarters of the *Lake Falk,* making the boats fast together. Then the *President Cleveland* with the *Lake Falk* attached to her started backing out into the stream.

The *Lake Falk* being a small coastwise freighter and the *President Cleveland* being an imposing ocean liner, there was a considerable discrepancy in size. When they were lashed together the deck of the "feeder" was about fifteen feet lower than the *President Cleveland*'s main cargo deck.

The minute the smaller boat was made fast, mate Bill Morris of the *President Cleveland* started shouting orders to his men. The winchmen let down the *President Cleveland*'s booms and lowered the hooks onto the *Falk*'s deck for the first load. In the meantime I had been firing out orders myself with the result that we were ready with a cargo net full of snake boxes and bird cages, which were quickly picked up and hoisted aboard the bigger vessel.

Up forward I heard alternately Bill Morris's deep voice and the shrilling of his whistle as he directed the loading of my animals. Aft, the second mate was roaring instructions to the men loading my supplies—bales of hay, bags of rice, crates of sweet potatoes, cases of canned milk, and quarters of beef (the latter to care for the appetites of my carnivorous animals).

Above the straining of the winches and the creaking of the blocks and tackle could be heard the tremendous rumble of the donkey engines that wound up the cable controlling the hoisting gear on the booms. On the bridge Captain Yardley stood shouting orders to the signal men in the bow. And all the while the *President Cleveland*'s ear-splitting whistle kept screaming a hoarse warning to the hundreds of Chinese sampans, dinghies, and other small craft that clutter up Hong Kong Harbor.

The work went quickly, both boats drawing farther and farther away from the dock as it progressed. Soon we had everything loaded but my carnivores—leopards and tigers—and my two elephants. Lunging at the bars of their cages and roaring their displeasure, the fierce cats were lifted in the air and deftly lowered to the deck of the *President Cleveland*. Next a canvas sling was fastened around the belly of the first elephant—an Indian variety—and she was lifted, swung wide and deposited on the ship's deck beside my other specimens. So many orders were being fired at the Chinese man who was working the forward winch that was loading the animals (the aft winch was handling my supplies) that he seemed a little rattled. I noticed that in handling the first elephant he kept her in midair longer than was necessary before shifting the boom over. The animal, frightened to find itself stock-still about eighteen feet in the air, started kicking around furiously.

I yelled to the faltering winchman to shift from the lifting gear to the gear that does the swinging. I heaved a sigh of relief when he did as instructed and lowered the elephant gently to the deck of the *President Cleveland*.

It was The Patsy's turn next. Quickly we got a belly sling around her, and a few seconds later the winchman was lifting her up. When he had reached the requisite height he seemed to forget what to do next. I shouted to him. So did Bill Morris. "Swing that elephant wider," shrieked the mate. The winchman, perhaps suffering from the terrific strain of loading my vast collection of livestock, fumbled with his levers but accomplished nothing. Overhead The Patsy was kicking around wildly in her lashings and trumpeting like mad. Fully a minute had elapsed, and the flustered Chinese man had not yet swung the boom over. I cupped my hands and roared in order to stir him into action. Bill Morris dashed over to work the winch himself. But before he could do anything the terrified animal had managed to kick herself loose. She slipped out of the canvas sling backwards, turned a complete somersault in midair, and came crashing down eighteen feet to the iron deck of the *Falk,* brushing past and barely missing me.

As The Patsy hit the deck, shrieks and groans came from the hundred or more passengers of the *President Cleveland* who were watching the loading. The elephant lay where she landed, motionless and, to all intents and purposes, dead. The Patsy, the unluckiest of animals, was again running true to form.

I leaned over the prostrate creature looking for signs of life. After about two minutes I noticed one of the eyelids flutter. Then, without warning, The Patsy jumped to her feet and, swaying unsteadily, started running down the deck. Lal and I grabbed her with elephant hooks and led her back. Without further ado we got the sling around her again, and, with another winchman on the job, quickly transferred her to the deck of the *President Cleveland.* The secret of loading an elephant by the air route is to give the animal no time to kick itself loose. The second it is high enough in the air it should be swung wide and lowered.

The Patsy was still pretty shaky, so I resorted to my favorite—and most successful—method of restoring animals that have the willies, only The Patsy, being an elephant, received a more generous treatment. I got a bottle of whisky and poured it into a bucket. Next I added a gallon of water. Then, with a brass force-pump, I worked the resultant highball down the elephant's throat, with Lal assisting me. The Patsy's shakiness disappeared, and she was soon herself again.

Which, to anyone who knows anything about elephants, was little short of a miracle. The only thing that saved The Patsy (her first stroke of good luck, to my knowledge) was the fact that in falling she landed on the fleshy lump over her shoulders. Had she fallen belly first she would have been instantly killed. An elephant's intestines are fastened to its spinal column, and the downward jar of such a fall would have shaken them loose, and there'd have been one pachyderm less on Earth. Had she fallen on her side she'd have cracked several ribs, with probable internal injuries to complicate matters. Had she landed on her back she'd have snapped her spine. So, if she had to fall, The Patsy didn't select the worst way of landing.

A little over a month after the accident, The Patsy wound up at Golden Gate Park in San Francisco, where the goddess of fortune finally smiled upon her. Which is to say that she landed a swell job—one that any elephant would be glad to have. No tough circus career for her, none of the confinement of zoo life. She got a job carrying the children of San Francisco around in a *howdah* that I designed. And she's doing it to this very day—one of the happiest and best-loved elephants in America.

The Patsy, after the most sustained run of bad luck I've ever known an animal to draw, got a break at last.

CHAPTER XIII

KILLER OF KILLERS

I thought I knew something about man-eating tigers until I started hearing about the animal that came to be known as the Killer of Kuali. Never in the history of any Asian country has there been the equal of this animal.

Kuali is a village in the center of the vast rubber-producing district of Johore. At the time the Killer appeared on the scene, I was in Singapore, preparing for some rather elaborate motion pictures of various types of jungle beasts. I was just starting a series of trips out of Singapore to the different parts of the Malay Archipelago where I could find the particular animals I wanted for the screen.

The Singapore newspapers had begun to run frequent items about the depredations of three man-eating tigers, which seemed almost to be competing with each other, although located in different parts of the country. There was the Killer of Kuali, and at the beginning he didn't attract as much attention as another animal that came to be known as the Toungoo Butcher. Third place went to an animal that in our discussions we designated as the Johore Mauler.

At the Raffles Hotel, where I lived in Singapore, the bloody deeds of these man-eaters constituted the principal topic of conversation. In the other hotels and in the various clubs of the town, the topic was the same.

The Johore Mauler got a head start in the statistics, accounting for three natives in a fortnight. Then the Toungoo Butcher came to the front, with four killings. The Killer of Kuali up to this time had slain only two people, but both his killings had been so audacious that he got a good deal of space on the front pages of Singapore's two small newspapers.

Local authorities were actively engaged in efforts to track down and destroy all three animals, but they weren't having much success, and all the amateur tiger-hunters around the Singapore bars had a busy and happy time telling just how the situation ought to be handled. Fortunately they were far enough away so that they didn't have to back up their suggestions.

There must have been some amateurs right on the spot at Toungoo, however, for one day the Straits *Times* brought this choice morsel from that town: "Expert hunters are preparing to hunt down the worst man-eater Toungoo has ever known with the aid of an armored car. The approach to the plantation where the terror is hiding is fraught with danger, but there is a cart track that will permit the passage of a car, and it has been proposed to improvise an armored car and meet the animal on its own ground. Meanwhile this new jungle assassin, one of the worst on record, has added another victim, an Indian cowherd, who was almost completely devoured."

The day this article appeared, several of the Singapore amateurs seized upon the absurd idea of an armored car for tiger-hunting, and seriously proposed to me that I lead such an expedition against the Killer of Kuali. I thanked them for their suggestion but explained that I was leaving the next day for Sumatra and would therefore be unable to assist in their commendable enterprise.

Obviously such a conveyance would be far too clumsy for use in the tangled brush and heavy jungle where an elusive cat like the Killer would seek refuge. Besides, the Kuali tiger was operating in the neighborhood of an enormous rubber estate run by Bob Gattle, manager of the Kuali Plantations, Ltd. Gattle was much too wise to let so idiotic an enterprise come into his district.

When I returned to Singapore some weeks later there was plenty of news about the man-eaters. The Johore Mauler had been hunted down after killing his sixth victim. The Toungoo Butcher had apparently been driven away from Toungoo—at least nothing had been heard from him for several days. But the Kuali Killer had developed a ferocity that bade fair to beat all records. He had just accounted for his twelfth victim, and the whole district around the Kuali Plantations was terrorized. The newspapers were agitating for the organization of a superexpedition to go after this mad jungle cat and get him at any cost.

All sorts of wild rumors were flying around Singapore, blended with garbled facts and pop-eyed gossip. My steward at the hotel tried to sell me the idea that certain evil spirits had decreed that the Killer of Kuali must have twenty lives before his appetite for human flesh would be appeased. If I doubted his word—and it must have been obvious that I did—he would introduce me to a notable who would soon convince me that I was wrong. This was no less a celebrity than one of the local Hindu fortune-tellers. It was all right for me to doubt a humble hotel employee, but surely I would not challenge the word of one of Singapore's leading mystics. Faced by such compelling logic I could do nothing but nod agreement.

Bob Gattle visits Singapore about once a week. On his next trip in, he looked me up and earnestly sought my advice on the best means of hunting down the animal that was terrifying the whole region in which his company operated.

Gattle wanted me to return to the rubber estate with him the following day to see if I couldn't figure out an effective way of battling this demon. I was unable to accompany him, however, as I was scheduled to leave for Siam the following day and couldn't possibly postpone my mission.

But I went on to say that the advice I would give him if I visited Kuali and looked over the scene of the animal's depredations probably wouldn't differ a bit from what I ventured to suggest as we sat there at the hotel that day.

"I hope there are no more killings," I said, "but if there should be one, you'll have to let the body stay where the tiger left it if you expect to shoot the villain when he returns."

Gattle shook his head. "That's out," he said.

"I know what you're going to tell me," I replied. "It's against the law."

"Exactly so," said Gattle.

"Then you'll have to break the law," I insisted. "There are times when it's got to be done."

"I'd like to," said Gattle, "but it would raise the very devil. You know how superstitious these Chinese people are. I'd never get another day's work out of them if they caught me using a human body as bait."

All the heavy work at Kuali—as in other parts of the Straits country—is done by Straits-born Chinese. If a planter wants to clear off a thousand acres of jungle these are the people he selects for this strenuous assignment. Lighter and more skillful work, like the tapping of rubber trees, is done by the Tamils. The Malays participate very slightly in any of these activities. They live among themselves in settlements of their own, where most of them confine their ambitions to raising enough food to provide for their own needs and those of their dependents. Some of them trade in jungle produce, others specialize in fishing, trapping, or rattan-gathering, and around the plantations they act as *tukang kebun* or gardener.

Gattle went on to remind me of the tremendous respect that the Chinese have for the dead. He could not afford to tamper with this feeling. It would mean antagonizing the men who did all the backbreaking work on his rubber plantation, and that would slow up production and bring down upon him the wrath of the owners.

"So you'd better give me some constructive advice, Buck," he said solemnly.

"No," I said. "You won't take constructive advice. Twelve killings is getting pretty close to a world's record, Bob. You're dealing with an animal that's blessed—or cursed—with the very maximum of brains and cunning. I've told you how you've got to deal with him, and you're too stubborn to take my advice. But I don't believe you'll ever catch your killer till you follow it."

We argued the thing back and forth for an hour or more, but I couldn't budge him. Finally we adjourned to the lobby, where we were joined by one of the town pests, the same amateur hunter who had suggested organizing an armored car expedition. He was feeling a bit humorous for a change, I suppose, because his latest idea was that I should "go out to Gattle's place and drag the tiger back by the tail."

I was in no mood for a kidding match, so I just kept silent and let him ramble on. "You're in the business of collecting live animals, aren't you?" he asked. "Well, Bob Gattle will let you keep the tiger if you capture it. Think of the money you could make exhibiting the world's most terrible man-killer!"

I shrugged my shoulders and managed somehow to get away from him. Gattle and I went on to the hotel entrance, where I bade him good-bye, after promising that I would visit his plantation on my return from Siam.

"We actually might try trapping the animal," I suggested. "There's an outside chance that we would succeed. But you'll have to get over your stubborn idea about the bait. This killer is fussy, and he won't be interested in goats or other small animals. He wants human flesh."

An interesting fact about the Kuali Killer was that not one of Gattle's workers was among the twelve fatalities so far. While the animal's tracks had been discovered several times in various parts of Gattle's estate, all of the killings had taken place in adjacent territory.

Such good fortune was attributed by the superstitious natives to the presence on the estate of a crude Chinese temple. This place of worship was erected by the early Chinese immigrants who went into that section of Johore to start clearing out jungle for the planting of rubber when tigers were even a more dangerous menace than they are today. These pioneer workmen in what was to become one of the world's richest rubber districts wanted an altar where they could go to implore their Joss God[†] to protect them from the ever-present striped terror, and the temple was built in the center of the heavy jungle then in the process of being cleared. It still stands—now surrounded by cultivated rubber—as a monument to the fears and superstitions of the early settlers from the Celestial Empire. Owing to the fact that it was erected solely because of fear of tigers, and originally used exclusively to beseech the gods for protection against these marauders, it has always been known as Tiger Temple. It has a remarkable reputation to this very day among Malays and Tamils, in addition to the Chinese who conceived it, for living up to its purpose.

Tiger Temple is a square building made of hand-hewn jungle planks, with a high gable roof thatched with rice straw. The structure has no floor, but to compensate for this lack it stands on a slight elevation in the ground that makes easy drainage possible when it rains.

The temple consists of one room, in the center of which stands a Chinese hand-carved table with a receptacle for burning joss sticks. Against the wall there is a wooden Chinese altar, studded with porcelain figures representing various gods. Here are the perpetually burning candles, their flickering light giving the worshiper a foretaste of the eternal light that shall be his in the hereafter.

[†]   A joss is a Chinese house idol or cult image.

The temple is presided over by an aged Chinese priest, who on account of his garb seems more like a wrestler than a holy man. Naked from the waist up, he looks as if ready to take on all comers, catch-as-catch-can. This priest has officiated at the temple for more years than anyone can remember, maintaining the establishment with the money he collects at the altar for the joss sticks and the prayer papers that the worshipers burn as part of the observance of the religion.

The prevailing belief around Kuali is that any Chinese person or other local resident who regularly burns joss at this altar—and who in so doing displays the proper fervor toward the gods—is immune from attack by tigers.

As the depredations of the Killer grew worse, the receipts at the Tiger Temple grew larger and larger, until the old priest was doing a land-office business and had to hire a servant to assist him in his sales of joss sticks and prayer papers.

On one occasion when the Killer's tracks were found, they formed a complete circle around the little plot of ground where the Tiger Temple stood. This somehow served to confirm the native belief that the temple could confer an absolute immunity. I always suspected that the old priest might have created some counterfeit tiger footprints, just for the sake of helping business along, but maybe I'm just a natural-born skeptic. Or—in fairness to myself—perhaps I was taking too seriously the hints of a Singapore friend who claimed to know the holy man better than any one in the district.

At any rate, the Killer's footprints were found frequently and plentifully all around the Kuali district. They were unmistakable, owing to the fact that the inside toe of the animal's left hind foot was gone, probably lost in some jungle battle, leaving only three pads. This three-toed imprint had become a symbol of death, and wherever it was found it struck terror in the hearts of the natives. So, while there had been no deaths among Gattle's coolies, a pervasive unrest had come over them, and some of them contrived to spend more time in the temple than they did at their work.

While I was in Siam I received a letter from Gattle informing me that the insatiable Killer of Kuali had accounted for eight more lives. This gave the tiger a record of twenty deaths and established him unquestionably as the worst man-eater the world had ever known. There was a reported case of an Indian tiger that was supposed to have slain sixteen people, though I had not been able to satisfy myself that the figure was accurate. But never had I heard anything to approach the wholesale butchery achieved by the demon of Kuali.

The government, Gattle informed me, had raised its original reward for the killing of the animal from $150 to $250, which is real money to the average native. While this had spurred them on in their campaign against the enemy, they were meeting with no success. Gattle wound up by begging me to remember that I had promised to visit him on my return to Singapore. Perhaps if I looked the ground over, he suggested, some means of exterminating this epoch-making death-dealer would occur to me.

I still felt that my original advice to Gattle was all I had to offer, but I made up my mind to visit Kuali as soon as I could and see whether anything could be done. On my return to Singapore I had hardly set foot on the dock when I began getting further news. The Killer had added eight or nine more victims to his tragic score, and the Johore government had increased its reward to $750, an almost fabulous sum in those parts; in fact, any native who could earn it would be a Croesus. As a consequence, many natives from distant points had been flocking to Kuali to take up tiger-hunting as a regular business. But most of them, apparently, had been so frightened by the stories they heard that they had abandoned their new profession promptly and had hastened to the Tiger Temple to purchase immunity from the affluent priest.

Not a night passed without the three-toed trademark of the Killer being found somewhere in the surrounding district. Two of Gattle's employees were among the latest toll of victims, but the natives insisted that the two were agnostics who had not kept up their regular dues in joss sticks and prayer papers.

I had several urgent business matters in Singapore, and it was three days before I could arrange my affairs so as to make the trip to Kuali, which is about sixty miles from Singapore. Gattle seemed to have aged since I had seen him. "It's getting on my nerves—and then some," he admitted as we sat down in his living room for a discussion of the situation.

Gattle called in his Tamil "shooter," a young man named Johoral whom he regarded as the most intelligent and dependable of his native workers. A "shooter," I might say parenthetically, is a sort of watchman on a rubber plantation whose principal duty is to keep moving about the estate all night and scare off the deer that are in the habit of feasting on the young rubber trees. He walks up and down the lanes between the long rows of rubber trees letting out weird cries and frequently shooting into the air to keep these antlered poachers on the move, at the same time maintaining a sharp lookout for tigers. In his cap he wears an acetylene lamp that throws a beam of light to give him his bearings and help him to locate the game.

Johoral was one of the few "shooters" in the Kuali district who had stuck to their jobs night after night despite the fact that there was a killer loose. Johoral actually seemed to relish the idea of an encounter with the jungle assassin. He had made up his mind to get that $750 reward if such a thing was humanly possible.

Johoral was an upstanding young man, and I liked him from the minute he started talking, at Gattle's suggestion, giving me the complete details of each of the recent killings. He hadn't missed a single significant point, and I hardly needed to ask him a question when he concluded.

He was sure that the Killer did not touch any other food than human flesh. Three or four domestic animals had been killed around Kuali during the past few weeks, but Johoral had investigated each case and was satisfied that the man-eater had not been responsible. This confirmed my feeling that it would be no use trying to lure the striped murderer with goats or lambs.

I renewed my pleading with Gattle to leave out a dead body, and Johoral listened solemnly to my argument. I had learned from questioning him that what remained of the latest victim, the twenty-ninth, had not yet been buried, and I begged Gattle to have this body taken back to the spot where it had been found. There two or three crack shots could set up a day-and-night vigil.

"The chances of getting the Killer will be at least fair," I urged. "There is always the possibility, of course, that he will get wise to the fact he is being watched and beat a retreat. But there is also a good chance of his being drunk with his success in battling man. And if he comes, the rifle-bearers can pump him full of lead."

"Buck," said Gattle, shaking his head, "once more I'm tempted to take your advice, but I'm afraid to. Don't forget that the Chinese were responsible for the passage of the law that makes it a crime to use a human body as bait. If we run counter to their respect for the dead, which goes beyond that of any other race in the world, we'll have trouble. I don't want a delegation of them going down to the capital at Johore Bahru with a complaint to the sultan that we're breaking his laws."

"All right," I said with a sigh of resignation, "have it your way. What can I do to help?"

"You said something weeks ago about building traps," was Gattle's reply. "The natives have set out a few, but I doubt if they've studied the movements of that tiger enough to know just where the traps should be placed. How'd you like to look the ground over and make some suggestions?"

I agreed, not too enthusiastically.

"Thanks," said Gattle. "Johoral will go out with you, and later on I'll join you. He's the only person around here who really knows just where that three-toed calling-card has turned up on this plantation, and he can be of real help to you."

Johoral and I set out for a point where Gattle's plantation borders on the jungle, and here—in terms of the animal's past maneuvers, as related to me by Johoral—we selected two sites for traps. Our task might have been simplified had the tiger been accustomed to using any regular path or game trail in crossing or entering Gattle's estate. For then we could have dug a pit, camouflaging the opening with leaves and branches, at a location where the animal could be counted upon to tumble into the hole the next time he came our way. But this fiend of the Kuali jungles seemed to have no regularity whatsoever about his habits or movements, as tigers usually have. He was as likely to turn up in one corner of the estate as another, though his tracks showed he did at frequent intervals visit that section of the plantation that bordered immediately upon the uncleared jungle.

Johoral had superintended the building of tiger traps before, and it was unnecessary to give him much advice in the matter of construction. I suggested a few improvements on the type of trap he had in mind. We had started back when Gattle came up to join us and expressed his appreciation.

"Glad to help you out, Bob," I said. "But don't depend too much on those traps. This doesn't sound like a tiger that can be trapped."

I returned to Singapore late that evening, pretty much discouraged by Gattle's obstinacy about what I felt was the only possible way of dealing with this particular demon. I was even sorry that I had consented to select sites for a couple of traps because I was sure they would accomplish nothing.

I was too busy for the next day or two to think much about the Killer. The third day one of my English friends, who had been out to Kuali for lunch, brought tidings of the fiendish beast's latest accomplishment.

Two Chinese woodchoppers had been working within ten yards of each other in the jungle a short distance from the spot that I had selected for Johoral's traps. Without warning the Killer appeared out of the tall grass and with a mighty lunge reached one of the choppers. A single slap of the paw sufficed to send the terrified Chinese man sprawling. A few seconds later the man-eater, its jaws gripping its victim's head, was making off through the jungle while the other woodchopper, paralyzed with fear, stood rooted in his tracks. Ironically enough the victim's screams could be heard from inside the tiger's jaws while his friend could make no sound come from his throat. Not that it would have done any good had he been able to yell, for there was no help near at hand.

Johoral and a number of armed natives had taken up the trail a short time after the woodchopper was carried off. All they managed to do was to determine that this was another job by the Killer of Kuali, since the telltale three-toed footprint was there. They did not succeed in locating the body of its victim, and the indications were that it had been dragged three or four miles into the jungle and there devoured.

The fact that this killing had taken place almost within a stone's throw of my traps showed me how foolish it had been to waste any time trying to trap this crafty animal. I was sorry I had ever let Gattle persuade me to take any part in the attempt to trap him. The result had been merely to give Gattle a false feeling that something was being done, and another life had been lost.

I determined that I would see Gattle as soon as he came to town again and renew my argument on behalf of the only way I could see of ending the Killer's career—luring him with a human body. Law or no law, things were getting desperate.

Gattle didn't come to town that week, but there was more news from the Killer. One of the shooters from an estate just south of Gattle's had been standing near the edge of the jungle waiting for a coolie to bring his supper. Dusk was setting in when he heard the coolie greeting him with a characteristic "Yoo-hoo!" from a point about 150 yards off. It is customary in jungle country for people to make it known that they are approaching as soon as they are within earshot.

The shooter responded with a welcoming shout of his own. The coolie replied. The shooter greeted him again. Again the coolie shouted "yoo-hoo," and this time he was so close that the shooter could hear him coming through the heavy brush that bordered the narrow path along which he was walking.

Then suddenly there was silence. The footsteps ceased. The shooter loosed another "yoo-hoo!" but there was no reply. Again he yelled. Silence once more.

The shooter became worried. He started beating around in the brush in search of the supper-bearer but failed to find him. He began to realize something was wrong and decided to make a dash for the coolie lines and get help. It was growing too dark to investigate much of an area single-handed.

He returned a few minutes later with a crowd of natives, five or six of them bearing lanterns. All were alarmed over the strange disappearance of the man who had set out with a pan of rice curry for his friend.

A member of the party tripped over something in the semidarkness and let out a shriek. He had stumbled over the dead body of the food-bearer. A few feet away lay the dish that had contained the curry, its contents scattered everywhere.

The Killer, perhaps crawling up quietly on its belly in the sly manner of the species when about to make a surprise attack, had lunged so swiftly and surely that its victim didn't have a chance to yell for help. This time the Killer had taken his victim within fifty or sixty feet of a professional hunter who was lying in wait for him.

The body was taken back for burial. It was the least mutilated of the Killer's string. The throat had been ripped open, and the animal had lapped up the hot blood that poured out. One of the cheeks and part of the shoulder had been torn off and devoured. Aside from this the body was intact. A careful tracing of the animal's tracks again revealed the three-toed symbol.

A few days later I left Singapore on a business errand and spent the night at Senai, about sixteen miles from Johore Bahru. Imagine my surprise, while I was eating dinner, to look up and see Johoral standing before me in a respectful salute. He had followed me all the way from Singapore, he said gravely, to seek my advice about the Killer.

Conditions were getting worse at Kuali, he told me. The natives were in such a state of panic that anything might happen. There had been another victim the night before. A Tamil woman and her twelve-year-old son had been on their way to the village from their home on one of the rubber estates. The youngster had the horrible experience of seeing the animal attack his mother and drag her off screaming into the jungle.

The Killer's total of deaths was now well beyond thirty. Even Bob Gattle no longer felt safe, Johoral declared. A day or two before, as he was returning from a party at a nearby estate with a neighbor and his wife, Gattle's car broke down at three o'clock in the morning. Only with considerable difficulty was Gattle able to get his *syce* (driver, literally Indian groom or stable attendant) to climb out and have a look at the motor to see what was wrong. The *syce* was perfectly frank in stating that he feared an attack by the Killer of Kuali. He pointed out that they were within two hundred yards of the spot where one of the animal's victims was found.

When the *syce* made this announcement the woman in the car turned on poor Gattle and hysterically accused him of exposing them to danger. They were two miles from their destination, but the woman, assuming command, insisted that they remain where they were until daybreak. The automobile was a touring car. The side curtains were located, and the marooned group curtained themselves in. On the whole, it was the most sensible thing they could have done, for at least they managed to keep out of sight. To walk those two miles at night would have been foolhardy.

Before the advent of the Killer, Johoral pointed out, the group would not have dreamed of penning themselves up in that fashion. They would have taken the walk without giving it a second thought.

Johoral wanted my advice as to the best means of tracking down the Killer. The traps, he said, had proved futile.

I found myself getting a bit provoked. "How many times do you people want me to tell you that you'll have to leave a body out before you can hope to get that man-eater?"

Again I heard the same old story about the law that prohibited such a proceeding.

"To hell with that law!" I exploded. "The longer you observe it the more deaths you'll have!"

Then I started talking earnestly to Johoral. In addition to being extremely likable he was a fearless lad, and I couldn't help being fond of him. Nothing would have pleased me better than to see him win the government's $750 reward.

"Do you want that money?" I asked.

His eyes glistened. "Yes, *tuan*," he said eagerly.

"Well, then, do as I tell you. I hope there'll be no more victims. But I'm afraid that's expecting too much. Keep your eyes wide open for any bodies that may be found. Try to get some other shooters to join you in a secret agreement not to report the next killing. Of course, that may not be possible, but see what you can do. If you can manage to leave out a body long enough, there's more than an even chance that the man-eater will return to it. That's the only advice I can give you. If you don't want to try it, please don't bother me with your problem any more."

Johoral seemed to get some of my own fervor. "I shall try, *tuan*," he said simply but feelingly and went on his way.

About three weeks later I came back to Singapore, arriving about daybreak. I was reading my newspaper at the breakfast table when my eye lit on a headline that immediately captured my attention. The man-eater of Kuali—the Killer of Killers—was dead. He had been killed by a shooter named Johoral. The dispatch was typical of most British colonial journalism; there were very few details.

I was too interested to wait for the town gossips to fill out the picture. I hired a car and drove out to Kuali. And what a kidding Gattle gave me when I arrived.

"You and your traps!" he exclaimed. "Why, the Killer never went anywhere near them. It took my man Johoral to figure out a way of meeting the situation. Wait. I'll send for him. He'll tell you how he did it."

A few minutes later Johoral appeared. He was wearing a new silk *sarong* and looked every inch the winner of the richest reward of its kind the government had ever offered. Gravely he began the story of his triumph. It was all very simple, he said. He had heard one day that a Malay rattan-cutter was missing. Mysteriously missing. Yes, *tuan,* the matter called for investigation.

Johoral knew something about the chap. This Malay was in the habit of visiting a girl—his unofficial wife who lived in the coolie lines. To get there he used a path along the edge of a ravine. Johoral decided to look for him near the path. He did—and came upon the amazing sight of the Killer eating the man's body. Johoral raised his rifle and let the tiger have it. And that was all there was to it.

Gattle was delighted with Johoral. "You and your traps!" he said to me once more, completely forgetting that I had never expressed any faith in the darned things. "It took a native to save the day."

Gattle dismissed Johoral, and we took a drink. I didn't have much to say. There was something a little fishy about Johoral's story, but I didn't tell Gattle so. Presently I excused myself and went for a little walk. I sought out Johoral for a private conference.

"Now, you liar," I greeted him, "tell me how you got the Killer."

First looking around cautiously to make sure no one was listening, Johoral told his story.

"It was like this, *tuan,*" he said frankly. "One day I happened to notice a rattan-cutter rushing toward the coolie lines screaming for help. I ran to meet him. He had been out cutting rattan with another Malay. While they were working, a tiger suddenly appeared and made off with his friend.

"I swore the rattan-cutter to secrecy. He was not to say a word to anyone about his friend's fate. I agreed to pay him for keeping his mouth shut.

"Then I set out to find the body. With the rattan-cutter as a guide, I found it in three hours. It had been dragged a mile from the place of the killing.

"I felt that the gods were on my side at last, for the dead man had no relatives in the district to make a fuss over his disappearance. Also he was a Malay, which made things easier." (The Chinese had caused the passage of the law that made it a crime to use a human body for bait. If the dead man had been Chinese, Johoral's risk would have been much more marked, for the Chinese have a way of investigating such matters and making trouble.)

"I climbed a tree," Johoral went on. "I had my rifle ready, hour after hour. I did not close my eyes the whole night. Just at dawn, the Killer came to finish his eating. I shot once, twice, three times. The Killer was dead."

Then Johoral tried to get me to accept part of the reward money. Needless to say, I would have none of it.

Johoral insisted, however, on giving me a present. I still wear occasionally the pair of Malay slippers he secretly gave me the next day as I was leaving.

The official record of the Killer of Kuali—thirty-five deaths— will, I hope, never be equaled.

CHAPTER XIV

A BEAR IN TIME

The star clown of the animal world is a honey bear that has been raised as a pet. Tame monkeys know plenty about the art of clowning, especially the little rhesus fellows from India, but honey bears are their superiors in the field of plain and fancy comedy. Call the lion the king of beasts, and I'll probably pick an argument with you; but name the honey bear as court jester, and you'll find me in perfect accord.

The honey bear is the smallest member of the bear family—a coal-black ball of fur that as a new cub resembles in size and shape a chow puppy. Full grown, he is about one-third the size of our American black bear.

There are several animals that are erroneously known as honey bears, among them the kinkajou of South America, the Himalayan panda, and the Australian koala bear. None of these are true bears, the last-named being the only one that is even remotely related to the bear family. The true honey bear is to be found only in the Malay Peninsula, Sumatra, Borneo, and adjacent islands. And as I've said, he is the star comedian in the animal world.

The prize clown of all the honey bears I've handled—and I've brought many of them to this country—was a lovable little rogue who came to be known as Toto. A visitor to my compound insisted that the animal was so like the famous circus clown of that name[†] that no other sobriquet would do. The name stuck.

[†] Toto the Clown, stage name of Almando Novello (1888–1938), performed in vaudeville as well as in the circus. He was a favorite of royalty, including Germany's Kaiser Wilhelm II and Great Britain's King George V.

I picked up Toto on one of my visits to Perak in the Malay Peninsula. He came out of a leaf-lined hole under the roots of a tall jungle tree, where he had evidently been left by his mother. I was attracted to his hiding place by a sound of plaintive whimpering. Walking over to where he lay, I found myself confronted by the most wistful-looking bear cub I'd ever seen. As I lifted him up I couldn't help noticing how thin he was. And how weak.

He had been so long in need of food that I hardly thought I could save him. It was an even-money bet that this emaciated youngster would not survive the long fast that he had already endured. But if I left him where he was he would soon either starve to death or be devoured by some beast on the prowl. There was something so touchingly affectionate in his manner that I decided to take him along and try to bring him back to health.

My guess was that his mother had gone to scout for food two or three days before and had never returned. Many a honey bear that sets out in search of the dainties this species lives on—principally wild honey, birds' eggs, and jungle fruits—winds up inside a tiger, leopard, or python.

The little waif cuddled contentedly against me as I picked him up. He was glad to be out of the dugout where he had lain so helplessly. I put him into my knapsack and carried him back to my headquarters in Ipoh, where I was assembling a collection of animals for shipment to my compound at Katong, a few miles outside Singapore. There I laid him tenderly on a shelf and opened a can of sweetened condensed milk, which I thinned with warm water to the consistency of ordinary milk. This I placed in a saucer beside him, but he was too weak to stand and lap it up with his long tongue in the ordinary way. So I put the milk into a nippled bottle and let him lie on his side while he took his first meal in several days. I have never seen milk disappear more rapidly. It was plain that he was famished. I was afraid he would choke to death in his efforts to make up for lost time, and I took the bottle away from him every few minutes so that his stomach could accustom itself to the novelty of food.

A week later the cub was normal, and when I arrived at Katong he was in as good condition as any of the animals I had brought from Perak. His listlessness had left him, and he had added several ounces of weight. If there was any doubt in my mind as to whether he was now well, it was removed by the perpetual inquisitiveness he displayed over every little event and happening in the world around him.

Most of the humor connected with the antics of a honey bear cub has its roots in an insatiable curiosity. He pokes his nose everywhere and investigates everything. In this respect he is different from other animal clowns. The humor of the monkey, for instance, is due to the fact that he is the prince of mimics. His fun-making is largely confined to his habit of imitating humans. The honey bear's antics are not imitative, but his own, and there is no limit to the amount of mischief that his endless curiosity gets him into. Whatever is going on around him is something for him to investigate. He is as tireless as a senatorial committee.

Toto was so tame and so completely attached to me that I saw no need to keep him confined all the time. An animal is always better off when allowed to roam the grounds at will. Then he can get all the sunshine and exercise he needs. But, of course, freedom can be given only to very tame specimens. Toto had five or six companions in freedom, among them a baby orangutan and a cassowary, an ostrich-like bird. These "trusties," of course, were put back in their cages at night.

Toto proved a never-failing source of entertainment, amusement, and interest from the very day he arrived at Katong, where I lived in a sprawling bungalow built on concrete pillars rising three feet from the ground.

Every morning, as soon as he was out of his cage, he would make a tour of inspection of the house, inside and outside. Having satisfied himself as to everything within, he would go down underneath, first looking over the pillars carefully, tapping them with his paws, as if to see that they still had the proper solidity. Then he would run around each pillar, perhaps suspicious that some foe might be lurking there. Eventually he would become fascinated by the cracks of light coming through the floor above him. The bungalow had the characteristic native floors, laid so that there is a space between boards about three-eighths of an inch wide. This provides ventilation and facilitates sweeping.

One morning I noticed him down there at sweeping time. In the room above, Ah Kee, the *tukang* (janitor, laborer), was wielding a broom, as attested by the dust that came flying down, filling Toto's eyes and nose and furry coat. Impatiently he pawed it out of his eyes and sneezed it from his nose. But he stood his ground, looking up with a questioning frown as he studied the situation.

I went back to the compound and returned a half-hour later. There was Toto in the center of the living room, shaking himself and distributing a cloud of the dust that he had collected down below. Angrily Ah Kee picked up the little mischief-maker and administered a spanking, which resulted only in sending new clouds of dust flying in all directions. The more he spanked the dusty offender, the more work he made for himself. Finally the outraged *tukang* took the little rogue by the scruff of the neck and sent him flying onto the lawn.

I had an errand down by the road, so I merely grinned appreciatively at Ah Kee's anger and went my way across the lawn to my destination. Toto righted himself and came running toward me, seeking sympathy. He had a comical, galloping gait, moving over the ground in a series of ungainly bounces and lopes. This was typical of his species, but I've never seen a honey bear travel with quite the mirth-provoking awkwardness that characterized Toto's movements. When he got into a real hurry, he would usually place his weight wrongly and go over head-first, heels over teapot, in a furry heap. Frequently he would convulse visitors by running toward me so eagerly when I waved a milk-filled nursing bottle at him that he not only went tumbling head over heels, but also turned a series of complete, uncalculated somersaults in the process.

He used to climb up on me whenever I sat down anywhere, investigating the contents of the pockets of my khaki coat. Usually they contained a pair or two of pliers and a monkey wrench or some similar treasure. Toto always gave them a thorough study. Unable to dislodge them, he would lick them with his long tongue to see what they tasted like.

If he had nothing else to do, he would follow me down to the animal sheds. He had brains enough to keep a safe distance away from any of the cages where he might encounter any personal danger. He made many friends among the animals, particularly among the birds. The Shama thrushes always attracted him, and he soon discovered ways of stealing little morsels of food from the cages occupied by some of the larger birds. His little thefts were done so whimsically and good naturedly that even the victims didn't seem to mind a bit.

One afternoon I saw him go galloping across the lawn. An hour later he was discovered in a hammock under a tree, where the *tukang kebun* (our native gardener) and his wife kept their eighteen-month-old baby. Toto had climbed up into the hammock, made friends with the baby, and finally both of them had gone to sleep, the child's arm around Toto's neck. Bear and baby had plainly hit it off. But the scandalized *tukang kebun* didn't think much of the friendship, and when he discovered what had happened he sent Toto bouncing out of the hammock on his furry little bottom.

I learned a few days later, however, that the *tukang kebun*'s wife took an entirely different view of the matter. The baby had taken a shine to Toto and spent the next day or two crying for its playmate. The mother thought the baby was right, and behind her husband's back she continued on numerous occasions to bring Toto over to the baby's hammock.

With visitors Toto was the most popular animal on the premises, even though he played many pranks on them. With the servants he grew more and more unpopular. To placate the irate domestics I had Toto tied up for two solid days, but the cub languished so visibly under this punishment that I didn't have the heart to keep it up.

His first act on regaining his freedom was to get into my room, pull back the covers of my bed, and get underneath. Ah Kee spanked the suspicious-looking mound with a slipper, the resultant squeals confirming his worst suspicions. Again the *tukang* gave Toto the bum's rush. That evening, when the humorless Chinese man voiced his bitter complaint over the occurrence, I began to wonder how much of an asset the little rogue was. After all, it was essential to keep the servants happy.

But one day Toto removed all doubts from my mind.

It all came about this way: I was in the Raffles Hotel in Singapore one evening when I was greeted by an acquaintance, a solemn young man who worked as an assistant in the American consul's office. I have so many friends in the consular service that it is impossible for me to think of this branch of the government except in the kindliest light; but I could never bring myself to like this particular chap (who ought to have a name, so let's call him Kinkley).

I did not relish the meeting, for Kinkley was the club bore. If he once caught your ear, he would talk interminably and monotonously on his favorite subject—himself. I had no desire to hear again about the memoirs he was writing. In fact, it had never seemed right to me that a young man, whose only experience had been a few years of pouncing on consular invoices with a rubber stamp, should annoy the world by writing a volume about it.

I wouldn't deny anyone the right to pen his memoirs. It's one of the world's most popular pastimes. But I take violent exception to the fiend who produces a sheaf of his dull reminiscences and starts reading them aloud, uninvited. That was one of Kinkley's failings.

After we had swapped greetings, the diplomat-author remarked, "I hear you've moved to Katong, Buck. You've got the right idea. I'd like to get away from Singapore myself."

"Why don't you?" I said, not knowing what I was letting myself in for.

"That's just what I'm getting at. Your new place in Katong is too roomy for you. I'd like to have a look at it. If it's the right sort, I might be willing to share it with you."

I groaned inwardly. My first impulse was to protest that I needed every inch of room in the house. But that wouldn't do, for it was generally known that I was looking for someone to share my place with me. Although Kinkley would be about the last person in Singapore I would want for a tenant, I mustn't be rude with him. After all, he had always been very helpful to me in making out my consular invoices on shipments to America and in assisting me to get passports for my native attendants.

The diplomat-author pressed his point, and before I knew it I had promised to show him the house in Katong. One Saturday afternoon, after I had received many reminders of my indiscreet promise, I consented to meet Kinkley and take him out to Katong to show him the house. That much I would do. But once there I would find some way to set him against the place.

Shortly after we arrived, Kinkley looked over the house and grounds, ecstatically announcing that my home was ideal for him. Just the place to finish his book, he observed, as he deposited on the front porch a bulky briefcase containing the first few hundred pages of his manuscript, which he planned to read to me later in the day.

I plugged away at my job of discouraging this tiresome enthusiast. As a starter, I pictured the danger of living near a compound full of wild animals. I mentioned that I frequently kept tigers and leopards in cages under the house. I was sure that the noises that the animals made at night would wreck his sleep. He waved these objections aside without difficulty. He craved the "experience" of life so close to these animals —it would make an interesting chapter for his book. As for sleeping, he was a heavy sleeper and would not be bothered at all by any noises the animals might make.

I tried another tack. Did he realize that it was practically impossible to get satisfactory servants in Katong? Mine were terrible, I warned him, barely keeping a straight face in the process. That was nothing, he assured me. He would bring his own servant.

Weren't there some other means of dampening his enthusiasm? Surely there must be some way. Another idea came to me. Did he know that I was in the habit of coming and going at the weirdest hours, that this unfortunate habit was part and parcel of the business I was in?

That was perfectly all right, he declared blandly. He was sure I would not disturb him.

We made our way off the porch onto the spacious lawn. He was jaunty, I depressed. As we stood there, Kinkley, facing the animal sheds, piped up buoyantly, "I suppose that's where you keep your animals."

I nodded. As he spoke, I could see Toto shuffling up the front steps of the house. I watched him as he reached the porch and began scrutinizing Kinkley's briefcase. A sudden hope sprang up in my breast as Toto moved over to investigate this new plaything he had found. Kinkley's back was toward the porch as he made some patronizing remarks about my animals.

I watched Toto poke at the diplomat's briefcase with one paw and then the other. If I could get Kinkley away for half an hour, Toto might do something to annoy him out of wanting to live here.

I suggested that we look over the animals, and he assented. As we passed out of sight, I noted that Toto had dealt the briefcase a couple of extra wallops with his paw and then, convinced that it was now dead, started lugging it off toward the porch stairs.

Feeling that Toto could be depended upon now to do something that would seriously annoy the boring Mr. Kinkley, I spent a leisurely half-hour showing him all the animals in the compound, elaborately explaining the antecedents and eccentricities of each. All the time I was praying silently that the roguish little Toto would not be deflected from the plaything he had found but rather would stick to it until he had done enough damage to that briefcase to make the diplomat-author feel that my home at Katong was no place for him to live. I was sure that Toto was in good form, for only a short time before Ah Kee had caught him rummaging through the linen closet, where he had already pulled from the shelves dozens of sheets, pillowcases, and napkins.

Toto did not disappoint me. In fact, he so far outdid my wildest expectations that I could only gasp as Kinkley and I returned, arm in arm, from our half-hour in the compound. As we rounded the corner of the house, the broad front lawn caught my eye. It looked as if a sudden snowstorm had visited it. The entire length and breadth of it, between the wire fences on either side, was white with sheets of paper that the gentle afternoon breezes were blowing hither and yon with gleeful abandon. Flower beds and bushes were decorated with paper. And in the center of everything was Toto, still scurrying about, chasing little bits of fluttering foolscap or creating miniature whirlwinds of paper as he somersaulted gaily here and there amidst the devastation he had wrought. The remains of the briefcase lay in the gravel path, its leather flap showing an irregular design where Toto's white teeth had tested its desirability as food.

Kinkley paused in the middle of a long sentence about the pleasure that was in store for me when he began reading me the recently completed chapters of his memoirs, dealing with the climate and natural history of Aden and Addis-Ababa.

His mouth suddenly flew open as if he were preparing to swallow a football. Blood rushed to his head until his face went through all the gradations of color from his normal pink to a flaming red and a violent purple. His hands flew up over his head like those of a drowning man clutching spasmodically at the air for support.

"My book! My book!" he finally gasped, still too stunned to move from the place where he stood.

There was a long pause while Kinkley choked, seeking for breath.

"Somebody's going to answer for this!" he said fiercely, as he began picking up the nearest sheets of his life's work.

I routed out Ah Kee and sent him to fetch all the servants, including the *tukang kebun* and Ali, my number one animal expert. Soon we were all busy gathering up the pages of Kinkley's masterpiece. I had contrived to smuggle Toto into the arms of the *tukang kebun*'s wife, with instructions to let him play with the baby in some out-of-the-way place for a while.

I can still hear Kinkley's agonized falsetto as he directed the rescue of his masterpiece. Incoherent sentences reached my ears in which I caught threats of reprisal . . . hints that the United States government would hear of the outrage . . . bitter references to my carelessness in permitting vandalistic creatures to roam at large . . . all the indications that Mr. Kinkley was nettled.

It was a shame, I replied. I always felt badly when a strange briefcase got itself all chewed up on my premises, especially one full of memoirs. But visitors to an animal collector's headquarters should take care not to leave valuables lying around. The owner always did so at his own risk.

Kinkley thought that over for a time, while we all continued to pick up the scribbled foolscap pages from bush and shrub.

"Well," he said finally, with splendid repression, "this settles any chance you ever had, Buck, of getting me to live with you out here."

I glanced up at him. "I'm sorry," I said. "But, of course, I understand, and I won't insist."

To seem properly indignant about what had taken place, I denounced the unknown animal who had done this deed—Kinkley apparently had not seen Toto—and I pretended to be in a rage as I commanded the uncomprehending *tukang kebun* in English (of which he understood not a word) to find and punish the fiendish brute.

Kinkley collected every sheet and fragment of paper, thrusting them into the tattered remains of his briefcase. Then he excused himself from staying to dinner, explaining that he must return to his rooms at once and spend the evening and night in arranging his manuscript and ascertaining whether any of it was missing.

Toto sat in Kinkley's chair at dinner that night and had a special meal of sweet biscuits and bonbons. He had saved not only the day, but also the night. For I had had gloomy forebodings of spending the hours after dinner listening to Kinkley, manuscript in hand, reading his precious memoirs to me until the wee small hours.

Toto's place of honor in the household was preserved until I left on my next trip to America. Then I gave him to an old friend of mine in Manila, an American who had a particular hate for Kinkley.

He had developed a touching fondness for the little bear the first time he heard the story of Toto's service to humanity in the matter of Kinkley's memoirs. The gay little mischief-maker is still a member of his household.

CHAPTER XV

SPITTING COBRA

We talked it over one day on the famous veranda of the Raffles Hotel in Singapore—Joe Winter and I. It was an appropriate place. For the veranda of the Raffles is the social capital of Singapore, and Singapore is the center of everything in the Federated Malay States and Straits Settlements.

Joe Winter was the manager of a rubber plantation fifty miles north of Singapore. I had recently made a minor contribution to it—an Airedale I had brought from America—and Joe was almost embarrassingly grateful. Every planter likes to have at least one good dog on his place. The type of dog available in Johore is a mongrel, so Joe welcomed the gift of the smart and lovable "Bunkie," to which he soon became attached. Dog and master were inseparable, and my friend, placing too high a valuation on my gift, never could do enough for me.

Joe, over a gin sling, was accusing me of being unsociable or unbusinesslike. Or both. He was pointing out that several weeks had elapsed since I had visited him at the plantation. His company, he said, had recently made a deal with a contractor who specialized in clearing off heavy jungle, and even now eighty choppers were at work removing the tall trees and thick brush.

"Come up with your men for a week, Frank, and if you don't get some wonderful animals, it's your own fault."

A collector of wild animals doesn't have to be told how lucky he is to have a chance to mop up in the wake of woodchoppers working in dense jungle, full of wildlife. Accompanied by a group of natives skilled in the catching of animals, he can reap a real harvest.

This particular stretch of Johore wilderness was packed with animals that I wanted. It was the home of the raffalii, the most beautiful of the squirrels, an animal whose head and hindquarters are a velvety black, its forequarters a snowy white, and its belly a bright red. Here also were to be found the white-handed and silvery gibbon, the binturong (popularly known as the bear cat), the honey bear, the brush-tail porcupine, the red-crested green wood partridge, the python, the yellow-banded mangrove snake, the black cobra (known as the spitting cobra), and other animals.

I had standing orders for all these. Of the species mentioned I was particularly anxious to secure at least one good specimen of the spitting cobra, a dreaded demon known throughout the East as the implacable foe of all living creatures. Give it a chance, and your reward for meeting this gruesome reptile will be twin jets of a deadly amber-colored poison squirted at your eyes. The snake always shoots at its victim's eyes, and its aim is accurate at any range up to about four feet.

India and Malaya are full of conflicting stories as to what happens to you if this poison hits your eyes. There are those who tell you that temporary blindness sets in, resulting in a serious and permanent impairment of vision. Others would have it that this impairment is only temporary. Still others will tell you that if there is the tiniest scratch near your eyes when the horrible fluid hits them, death is your portion; and there are those uncompromising chaps who claim that, scratch or no scratch, you die.

During my many years as a collector I had sifted these various stories and had become pretty well convinced that the poison of the spitting cobra was not essentially different from that of the other species. If it gained entrance to the bloodstream, it would kill, and the slightest scratch or opening in the skin would ensure its deadly penetration. But if there was no scratch or abrasion, it acted merely as an irritant, which probably would be painful to any delicate surface like the eye, but whose ill effects would eventually pass off.

The spitting cobras I had brought back to America had fortunately never given me any test of my theories. And my plan was to keep on handling them so cautiously that I would go through life without knowing firsthand just what does happen when a black cobra aims for your eyes and hits his target. I don't mind saying that I take no unnecessary risks with these or any other creatures.

I accepted Joe Winter's invitation and went to his place a few days later with Ali and two other expert Malay animal handlers.

The morning after my arrival I took a walk with Joe, who was accompanied by his ever-present Airedale, to the stretch of jungle where the choppers were working. Ali joined us as we entered the clearing.

Suddenly the wandering Bunkie, who had stopped beside a felled tree, started barking furiously. It didn't take me long to know what it was all about. In the shadow of the fallen timber I could see a black cobra's head raised six inches off the ground, with hood spread.

Frantically Joe yelled to the dog in an effort to call him off. The reckless Bunkie remained where he was, toying with destruction. In his excitement he probably didn't hear Joe's voice or was too fascinated by the creature in front of him to respond. Joe picked up a heavy stick and made for the log.

"Keep away from that snake!" I shouted.

Joe had hardly completed his first stride when Bunkie started backing away whiningly. Shaking his head queerly he emitted as plaintive a howl as I've ever heard from an animal in distress. He was rubbing one eye with his right paw, then the other with his left.

"Cobra spit!" shrieked Ali. "Cobra spit!"

The dog was now running around in circles, his howling dying down to an agonized whimper. As he swung round aimlessly he hit a heavy branch and toppled over, righting himself with the halting movements of the sightless. The animal was unquestionably blinded.

The snake had spat its twin streams of poison. That was plain—though none of us had been close enough to see the thin lines of amber fluid shoot through the air on their way to their target. Having delivered its blow, the cobra had glided back under the log. It would be another day before his poison sacs would refill sufficiently to enable him to spit again, but there was nothing to prevent his striking in the regulation manner. And it meant death if he managed to sink his fangs.

"He's ruined my dog, the slimy—!" Joe yelled. "And I'm going to bash his head in!"

He called over some nearby choppers. "Roll that log back!" he commanded.

"Don't!" I countermanded, waving the men away.

Turning on me angrily, Joe cried, "What do you mean by—"

He didn't trouble to finish his sentence. If the men wouldn't roll the log back—and it was obvious that they had no desire to get so close to the snake—he would kill the reptile where it lay, partly visible under the log. Advancing close enough to strike, he took a fresh grip on the heavy stick in his hand and raised it over his head. I seized him by the arm and wrenched the stick away.

Eyes blazing, Joe demanded to know what I meant by protecting the grisly thing that had blinded his dog.

"Leave the snake to me, Joe," I said. "I know how to handle these brutes. You look after the dog. Maybe you can save him if you act quickly."

I pointed to Ali, who was bending over the suffering Bunkie but very carefully avoiding any contact with the dog's poison-smeared face or paws. Joe went over and knelt down beside him. I tossed him a pair of heavy gloves that I had in my belt.

"Put on the gloves, Joe," I said. "Then you can get hold of his paws and keep them away from his face. If he scratches himself, he's done for, you know."

Joe thrust his hands into the gloves, then held the dog's forepaws in one hand, while with the other he tried to wipe off the venomous fluid with his handkerchief.

Ali came to my side, awaiting instructions. I told him to get one of the coolies to fetch a dip net.

I had determined that I would capture the snake alive. It was as fine a spitting cobra as I had ever seen.

I ordered the coolies to roll the log away, but none of them was willing to approach the snake's lair. So I got a long stick and then rolled the log over an inch or two with my foot.

This was enough to disturb the cobra, and I caught a glimpse of his wriggling body. I poked at him with the stick and in a minute or two found it a comparatively simple matter to scoop up his head in the net. Another poke, and his whole body was inside. Once in a net of this kind, with the top closed, a snake is helpless. I have carried reptiles for miles through the jungle in this fashion without giving any more thought to them than if I had so many feet of rope.

I handed the laden net to Ali, with instructions to take the black captive to the supply hut and dump him into a wooden box with a lid of half-inch mesh wire.

When we had reached the house, Joe stood by, tears in his eyes, as I prepared a wash of boric acid, another of warm soapsuds, and a third of soothing olive oil. He held his beloved pet while I carefully washed out the animal's eyes with soft pieces of absorbent cotton.

Poor Bunkie was suffering terribly, and my washes did not appear to do anything but aggravate his pain. I kept up my careful applications for nearly an hour. The dog's agonized whimpering gradually grew less, but the twitching of his limbs showed me that he was still in torture. Then suddenly, at the end of an hour, his muscles grew rigid. I recognized the symptoms. The venom had somehow got into his system, and I knew that nothing could save him.

He was dead almost before I could tell it. Joe stood up, trembling with grief. I pulled the gloves off his hands and tossed them into a little heap with those I had been wearing and the soft sponges of cotton I had used, directing a servant to burn them all in the kitchen stove.

Joe and I went inside. He did not say a word—just went over to the sideboard and dashed off a half tumbler of neat cognac. I did the same. Then Joe excused himself and went to his room, where he remained all day.

I stayed another week at Joe's place, and he seemed to have become a little more reconciled to the loss of Bunkie. I promised myself that on my next trip I would bring back to him the finest Airedale I could find in America.

Ali and the other men reaped a profitable harvest in the jungle. By the end of our stay they had captured seven honey bear cubs, three binturongs, twenty-six raffalii, three brush-tail porcupines, four ordinary Malay porcupines, one eighteen-foot python, three smaller pythons, three white-handed gibbons, thirty red-crested green wood partridges, and two pied hornbills.

I carried the entire collection in two of Joe's motor trucks to my compound at Katong. The new specimens, added to those already on hand, made quite a zoo, the entire contents of which would soon be on its way to America.

Joe came into Singapore with me and went to the Raffles Hotel, where I promised to meet him for dinner.

Toward the end of the afternoon, all the new arrivals were placed where they belonged, and I went on my first tour of inspection before leaving for my dinner appointment. I started with the main shed. It was necessary to check up on the efforts of even as reliable a number one man as Ali. The best assistant needs supervision in work such as mine.

First I found myself passing a group of cages containing one hundred Malaccan cockatoos, the biggest of the white cockatoos—so called, although they have a pinkish tinge. I looked to see whether they had been supplied with grain, fruit, and water. Everything was okay here, and I walked on to the cages that housed the honey bear cubs. Finding that these little fellows were plentifully supplied with their rice-and-milk mixture, I moved on to a vicious orangutan in an adjoining cage.

My primary concern was that the ape should have plenty of clean, fresh straw for his bed and a blanket. He knew just how to spread the straw out on the floor of his cage; and on cool nights he rolled himself up in the blanket like any other lover of comfort. I made an inspection at a safe distance, for this ill-natured ape had a habit of reaching out through the bars, and I had no desire to be embraced by him. Ali had done his job well here, so I moved on to the next specimen.

This was the spitting cobra that had caused all the trouble at Joe Winter's plantation. So that it would be where it could do the least amount of damage—and where it could be conveniently handled—its box had been placed in the corner of a deep table-high shelf adjoining the orang's cage. It would have facilitated matters from the standpoint of safety if a board could have been kept over the top of the box. But this would have shut out all light, and the reptile would not have thrived. This phase of my problem would be solved as soon as Hin Mong, my efficient but slow-moving Chinese carpenter in Singapore, delivered the glass-top snake box I had ordered.

Needless to say, I exercised all the caution at my command in making my inspection of this treacherous reptile. Here I had my first moment of annoyance, for when I pulled the box forward from the depths of the shelf and gave the contents a hasty glance I saw that Ali had failed to place a drinking can inside. A sardine tin is used for this purpose. It is placed in the box by the simple process of opening the wire top at one corner and working the can through the opening.

At Johore we had watered this rascal by merely dumping a bucket of water into his box, the method I usually use with reptiles en route. That's one way of giving a snake a drink. Also a bath. Effective but sloppy. Entirely different rules applied in my compound, which was as carefully conducted as a well-managed zoo. Here each snake had its own drinking tin, which when empty was refilled by means of a watering can with a long spout that could be thrust through the wire netting on top of the box, or through an opening at the side in the case of a glass-top box.

Ali had received instructions to equip the spitting cobra's box with a water tin. Perhaps the job was one he had no desire to tackle after seeing what the snake had done to Joe Winter's dog.

I decided to do the job myself. My first move was to get the burlap sacking that I always keep near a box of this kind. Next I secured the empty sardine tin that I would stuff under the wire as soon as I pried it open. Carefully spreading the burlap over the wire, I went to work with a pair of pliers. I moved the sacking back an inch or so to get at one of the staples, and I remember the hissing of the creature inside as I did it. What happened next I'll never be sure of. I recall a hairy arm reaching out from the orang's cage in an effort to reach the burlap. I yelled at the ape in an effort to scare him off. The next thing I knew my eyes were suddenly burning, as if they had been doused with vitriol. I was blinded. The cobra had spat his venom into my eyes.

As long as I live I shall not forget the strange and awful sensation I experienced when I suddenly found myself sightless. Never was I more thoroughly scared—and I'm not ashamed to admit it.

Yet my first thought was not of myself, but of the cobra. Had it already escaped from the box? If not, would it find the opening I had left in the corner and get out shortly? Almost automatically I went through the motions of sealing up the hole in the netting. Frantically feeling my way I yanked the sack back over the box and pushed a wad of the burlap into the opening. The cobra's hissing informed me that it was still inside. How could I keep that burlap in place, how could I weight it down so that the snake could not work its way out? I remembered a brick that had been lying on the floor, and I reached down, fumbling for it. Finally I located it by the simple process of stumbling against it.

After I deposited the brick on top of the burlap, my next move was to find my way out of the shed without getting anywhere near the orang's cage. My eyes burned horribly as I tried to calculate my steps and my direction. I could hear the orang sucking in wind and grunting, the animal's favorite method of expressing anger, but without my eyesight I was not sure how close I was to him.

My hands kept raising themselves toward my eyes in an almost overwhelming desire to scratch and rub, and it was only by a concentration of will power that I was able to keep them down, realizing that my only hope of safety lay in not giving the poison a chance to penetrate the skin.

In the course of that tortured journey from the snake's box to the open air a dozen eternities seemed to elapse. All the time I was in the clutch of a terrible fear—the fear of death or permanent blindness. The picture that arose in my mind was of Joe Winter's moaning Airedale after he had been struck by cobra poison and of his quick death.

I walked on, each step seeming to take a year as I picked my way along that miserable floor. Finally, after more time seemed to pass than I had put in altogether on the Earth, I could hear the squawking of the cockatoos, and I knew I was nearing the door. Once there, I yelled for Ali. No answer. I yelled again, and I'm sure the cry must have burst most of the eardrums in Katong.

My eyes burned with a new intensity as I came out into the sunlight and stood there waiting for Ali to appear. It was the worst pain I had ever suffered. Again I concentrated my will in an effort to keep my hands from going up to rub my eyes.

Finally I heard Ali's bare feet shuffling on the pathway and the question, *"Apa ini, tuan, apa ini?"* ["What's the matter, sir, what's the matter?"]

I quickly told him. Ali set up a characteristic wailing. I would never see again, he said.

Then he noticed my hands go up to protect my eyes from the burning sun. This galvanized him into action. He did not propose to let me scratch myself. He grasped my hands and held them firmly down at my waist.

"Take hold of my arm," I ordered, "and get me to the house." I described a boric acid bottle in my medicine chest and sent him for it. He mixed it with warm water, and I began bathing my eyes, applying the solution with sponges of soft cotton. The only result was to intensify the pain, but I was sure I could wash away a good deal of the poison from the surface of the skin. So I kept at it, meanwhile sending Ali to a shop in Katong village where there was a telephone.

His orders were to call up Joe Winter at the Raffles Hotel in Singapore, tell him what had happened, and ask him to bring out a doctor.

Half an hour later Joe and the doctor arrived in an automobile. The doctor applied a drug of some kind, followed by cold bandages.

The doctor's medicine gradually eased the pain. I sat there with heavy wet compresses over my eyes while the doctor changed them every minute or two.

My thoughts were busy analyzing my symptoms. I was watching for some indication that the poison had entered my system. I wondered just how it would first manifest itself. Presently a cramped foot acted numb, and I felt sure that this was the sign I awaited. Then the numbness passed, and I breathed a sigh of relief. I felt an itching sensation along my spine, and I wondered if this could be the beginning of the end. Then my head began to ache with a pounding throb, and again I was sure that the poison was at work.

At the end of three hours of mental and physical torture my blinded eyes began to distinguish faintly the lights of the room, as the doctor changed the dressings. Another hour, and I began to see hazily. But the terrific pain continued.

Joe remained by my side all night long, fortifying himself from time to time with long drinks of Scotch. The doctor, who had gone home about midnight, returned in the morning. My eyes were as bloodshot as if I had been out on a ten years' drunk. But I could see. The doctor examined me carefully and pronounced me cured.

Zoologists with whom I discussed the matter afterward agreed that the most significant detail of my story of Joe's dog was that which had to do with the animal's frantic scratching of his eyes after the cobra had spat at him. The Airedale's death was undoubtedly the result of his scratching.

Perhaps Ali's holding of my hands during those few moments of intense agony down by the animal shed saved my life. Had I scratched my eyes after the cobra shot his venom, death might have resulted.

Let me say in conclusion that after a week I was seeing as well as ever. And today I can see well enough to lasso a crane on the wing.

But that is another story [see page 62].

CHAPTER XVI

ANIMAL MAGIC

My idea of the strangest book that could possibly be written would be one dealing exclusively with Asian superstitions. One of the queerest chapters would be the one devoted to the various superstitions that prevail regarding animals.

There is, to begin with, the belief among the Chinese that the gallbladder of the tiger contains a panacea for all ills. There is no ailment, no matter how severe, that cannot be cured by the bitter gall—dried and taken internally—of the jungle's striped cat. Diseases of the heart and lungs, so the legends go, disappear as soon as a little supply of tiger gall appears on the scene. He who possesses this magic substance instantaneously becomes a lucky man, a favorite of the gods. Realizing the futility of trying to vanquish one so richly endowed, the demons of ill health move out of the body of the blessed one and take up their abode in a frame that will offer less resistance.

This superstition about the curative powers of tiger gall once proved costly to me, under circumstances that eventually managed to get fairly exciting.

Practically all boats plying Far Eastern waters have Chinese stewards and crews; so it wasn't surprising that, on a trip I was making some years ago between Singapore and Hong Kong (on a British freighter that carried a small passenger list), there should be considerable interest on the part of the help in the news that one of my tigers was sick. This animal was not well when I came on board, but I figured that a thorough worming would be good for what ailed it. The treatment left the tiger alarmingly weak, and it began to look as if the animal were developing serious complications. In fact, I had never before seen a husky full-grown tiger go to pieces in just this fashion.

My sick tiger kept getting worse and worse, and it began to look as if there wasn't much chance of saving him. It soon became apparent to the Chinese crew members that Lal (who accompanied me on the trip) and I were using heroic measures to keep the animal alive, and there was naturally much excitement among the stewards and the crew.

The stewards were Hinan men, and the deck crew were Cantonese. I hadn't been on board that boat very long when it became plain to me that the Hinan stewards and the Cantonese crew hated each other. Enmities between different groups of Chinese people are a very ordinary phenomenon, and I saw nothing in the situation to get excited about.

Both the Cantonese and the Hinans were helping me in my work. The Cantonese assisted me in loading and placing my specimens, shifting cages when I thought that necessary, rigging up awnings over cages, etc. The Hinan men helped me in such matters as boiling the immense quantities of rice I needed for my birds and small animals. There was other food for my specimens that had to be cooked, and these men always responded cheerfully.

Once it became known to all the help on board that my tiger was not expected to live, I got more service than ever. The Cantonese and the Hinans, in other words, were in competition with each other for the remains. Each faction wanted to emerge with the gallbladder that meant so much good health to the lucky possessors.

One day the Cantonese bosun came to me, and after standing first on one foot and then on the other, told me he understood that my sick tiger was dying and that he would appreciate receiving the body. He volunteered to present me with the animal's skin if I would permit him to keep the body and remove the gallbladder. I promised to think the matter over and let him know. In fact, I showed real restraint, for I didn't like the idea of the fellow feverishly waiting for my tiger to die.

Shortly after this visit from the Cantonese bosun I received a call from the Hinanese chief steward, who, after bowing his way up to me in a series of near-somersaults, hemmed and hawed and finally reached the subject of my dying tiger. He, of course, also wanted the gallbladder. Somehow he didn't offend me nearly so much as the other applicant. He seemed to realize I felt badly over the prospect of losing the animal, and once I thought he was on the point of tears. Maybe all this proves is that Hinan men are better actors than Cantonese; yet, on the whole, I liked him better than the too hard-shelled Cantonese bosun.

Despite which I made no promises. I told this representative of the Hinan interests that perhaps we'd better wait for the tiger to die before disposing of his remains.

The morning after my visits from the Canton and Hinan emissaries my tiger decided to pass out of the picture. I couldn't help feeling that it was a shame to lose him, especially after risking my neck, as I had, to get him out of the pit, in which I had trapped him, into a cage.

Lal and I yanked my tiger corpse out of his cage and deposited him on one of the hatches. Word of the death had not yet got out. As I stood there staring at the body and thinking what a pity it was that this animal had to die, the Hinan steward came along with some food supplies for my birds and small animals.

His eyes popped as he took a look at the dead jungle cat. Before he had a chance to say anything, I said, "Get your men out and have them skin the tiger. Give me the skin, and you can keep the gall."

Had this Hinanese man just been handed a million dollars he could not have been more demonstrative. I thought he would kiss me. The situation, I felt, called for a drink. I went off to get it.

When I returned, about twenty minutes later, a strange sight greeted my eyes. The Hinan chief steward and two of his men, knives in hand, were preparing to start skinning the tiger. The Cantonese bosun was giving them a hot argument. I had promised the animal to him, he was saying, and he meant to have it. He was the rightful owner of that tiger's gallbladder, and he had no intention of letting anyone take it away from him.

At this juncture Lal intervened. "Which of these Chinese men did you give it to, *tuan?*" he asked, adding that if I didn't quickly decide I'd see a Chinese man skinned instead of a tiger.

I told the bosun he was mistaken, that I had not promised him the tiger. The roughneck bosun had the nerve to call me a liar, at the same time giving one of the Hinan men the elbow and knocking him over.

I was tempted then and there to pry that bosun loose from his front teeth. But it's bad business to hit a member of a ship's crew, and, by an epoch-making feat of restraint, I didn't strike a blow. I confined myself to the comparatively ladylike business of grabbing the rascal by the back of the neck and sending him spinning a few feet—not more than a dozen at the outside. He banged his head against the rail and wasn't even knocked out, which shows that an animal collector can be gentle when he wants to be.

Fortunately the mate (an Englishman like all the officers) had taken in the altercation from the bridge. He was on the scene in time to cuff the bosun around a bit when I had finished massaging him.

After this occurrence there were some puzzling developments. I naturally expected that bosun to break all known nonservice records, first, because the other faction had acquired the dead tiger and, second, because I had manhandled him. Instead he was all smiles the following day. I didn't get it at all. He couldn't do enough for me. Didn't I want this cage moved here and that cage moved there?

The morning before we got into Hong Kong—four days after the other occurrence, I found the finest and healthiest tiger in my collection in a state of convulsions. Frothing at the mouth and shaking violently with each spasm that seized him, he lay stretched out in his cage, a pitiful sight. He was unquestionably dying the death of an animal that has been poisoned. He showed all the signs.

I was boiling mad. Someone had poisoned that animal, and I meant to find out who it was.

It was only natural that I should find myself suspecting the bosun. His exaggerated politeness ever since the death of the first animal was enough to make anyone suspicious. It looked like a crude effort to conceal something.

Shortly after the dying tiger went into his final convulsions, the bosun, all solicitude, appeared on the scene. It was too bad I had lost another tiger, he told me. Such a fine one too. But the animal was dead, and he hoped I would not mind his asking me for the body. The chief steward now had a tiger's gallbladder and he, the bosun, would like to have one too. Could he take possession of the body?

I didn't answer his question. Instead I asked one—a very pointed one. What I wanted to know was whether he had access to the ship's rat poison.

As the bosun started stammering out a reply, Lal, who had been watering and feeding my birds, appeared on the scene. *"Tuan,"* said Lal, "I saw this man near animal cages early this morning. I think he put bad medicine in tiger box."

"Are you sure this is the man?" I asked.

Lal then said that there had been some doubt in his mind earlier in the morning—or he would have told me then—but now he was sure this was the man he had seen.

"I kill you!" the bosun cried, giving Lal a look that tallied with his threat.

Turning to Lal I instructed him to find the chief steward and bring him at once. The bosun and I stood glaring at each other as Lal left to carry out my orders.

A few minutes later Lal returned with the boss of the Hinans. "Want another tiger gall?" I asked him. All smiles, he nodded his head till I thought it would come off.

"All right," I said, "take this tiger and skin it."

During my conversation with the steward the bosun was going through some movements that I didn't exactly like, but I said nothing. He was beckoning angrily to Lal and pointing meaningfully to his sheath knife.

When I finished talking to the Hinan man, I addressed the bosun—with my fist. I clipped him right on the chin and sent him spinning across the deck. As I have said, it is bad business to strike a member of a ship's crew—but I knew I could show plenty of provocation. The mate later thanked me for hitting the skunk.

So it goes. Because a Chinese bosun wanted the magic key to permanent good health—a tiger's gallbladder—I lost an animal.

The Chinese are almost as sold on the leopard's gallbladder as they are on that of the tiger, the principal difference being that the leopard is supposed to bring luck on a smaller scale. As in the case of the tiger, this good fortune has to do mainly with matters of health, part of the theory being that if one is well and strong it is possible to achieve almost anything.

One day a lame, emaciated Chinese man hobbled into my compound at Katong and announced that he wanted a job. He had made the journey on foot all the way from Singapore, which is eight miles away. He had heard from Chop Joo Soon, a Chinese animal trader in Singapore, that I was looking for a *tukang* (laborer), and he presented himself as an applicant for the job. He was obviously incapable of doing the hard work he would be called upon to do in the position he sought. I was forced to turn him down, telling why only when he pleaded for an explanation. I gave him a few coins and arranged with a native *gharry walla* (hack driver) to get him back to Singapore. The poor devil would never have lasted out the return trip on foot.

A few days later I had occasion to call on Chop Joo Soon. I was surprised to find the lame would-be *tukang* in the shop. He explained that he had heard from Soon that I was expected and had taken the liberty to call on me. He humbly begged leave to apply for the job again, earnestly informing me that he had hit upon a means of overcoming disabilities. A friend of his, he eagerly explained, had told him where he could secure some powdered leopard gall at a price he could meet. A few years before he had tried to purchase some of this wonder-working substance, but he had not been able to meet the exorbitant price asked. Now he knew where he could get some cheap, and his problem was solved. So was mine, if I still wanted a *tukang*.

I was forced to pretend that I had filled the vacancy. He never would have understood my lack of faith in powdered leopard gall.

I recall an even weirder example of how superstition works in the Far East.

On one of my trips I wound up in Zamboanga, which is the American military headquarters for Mindanao. Some soldiers of the Philippine constabulary were being sent up to Cotabato Province to quell a disturbance there. The officer in command was a friend of mine, and he suggested that I accompany him. Always eager for a new experience when it doesn't interfere with my animal-collecting activities, I accepted the invitation. When we arrived at the town of Parang in a small trading boat commandeered for the trip, we found that the two factions that had quarreled were now in accord but that it was necessary for my friend and his command to make the short trip inland to the scene of the trouble and stay a few days. A thorough investigation had to be made so that a full report could be filed on the killings that had taken place.

I found myself growing interested in the old Moro *dato* of the district, who had a twenty-five-foot python that he kept as a pet. Some of the world's biggest specimens came from this part of the universe.

The longest python skin on exhibit anywhere is the one, originally from this same province, on display at the Bureau of Science in Manila. It is thirty-three feet long. (In the process of mounting, it must have stretched, its real length probably having been about thirty feet.)

Like all Moros, who are the principal inhabitants of Mindanao, the headman was a Mohammedan. But it is a far cry from the Near Eastern centers of the Islam faith to these remote islanders who, many generations ago, were converted by Mohammedan missionaries into "true believers." It is not surprising then that they sometimes mix their Mohammedanism with a little paganism. In the case of the old *dato* this confusion of Allah's guidance took the form of animal worship. The man's love for his immense snake was touching. He explained to me that many years back, when it was only about half its present length and he could safely let it roam the premises, this python had cleared his place of rats. (The Moro language is pretty much like Malay, which I can speak fairly well. Whenever I got stuck I had one of the soldiers act as interpreter.)

The old fellow believed implicitly that his snake was a divine messenger and that while he retained this emissary from a strange heaven, as he tried to explain to me, no bad fortune could befall him.

About noon of the day we were due to leave there was much excitement in the village when it became known that the *dato*'s python had escaped. One of the old man's *carabaos* (water buffaloes) had been browsing in an enclosure adjoining the cage where the python was kept. The animal had got its huge horns caught in the bamboo uprights of the cage, and, in yanking himself loose, had left an opening large enough to permit the reptile to glide out.

The old man stopped his wailing long enough to explain that normally the python (which he referred to as "my god") would not have taken advantage of the opportunity to escape. But the creature was hungry. "I had been looking for a stray dog to feed him," explained the old man. "But I could not find one. I did not want to feed him one of my goats unless I had to." The python, it seems, had not eaten for several weeks and was now ready for a meal. (These reptiles usually eat once every six to eight weeks, depending on their condition. I have known them to go without food for several months without any ill effects.)

My officer friend liked the old man and assigned some of his soldiers to help the members of the household in their search for the missing python. I joined the searching party too, rightly expecting it to prove an interesting experience.

The headman did all he could to spur us on in our search, frantically crying at regular intervals, "My god is gone from me! Now I shall have no more good fortune!"

We combed quite a stretch of woods (not real jungle) near the old fellow's dwelling, without any success. Then, as the officer was beginning to wonder how much longer he could allow his soldiers to participate in the hunt, one of his men yelled that he had located the fugitive. We ran over and found the python coiled up under some heavy brush.

When the soldiers indicated that they did not want to get too close, the old man, now happy and smiling, said, "He knows me and will not harm anyone." I helped him pull the heavy snake (the creature weighed over three hundred pounds) clear of the dark brush while the soldiers stood by ready to shoot in the event of a mishap. We might have been tugging away at so many yards of heavy ship's rope for all the response there was. As soon as we got a good look at the python it was obvious to all of us, from the huge bulge it showed, that it had just eaten. That, of course, accounted for its sluggishness. It would be nine days before this creature would digest its meal and be active again.

Interested to know what the snake had devoured, I ran my hands over the bulge. I could feel a round knobby something that suggested a human head! Working both hands feverishly a little below this point, I found myself tracing the outline of human shoulders. There was no longer any doubt in my mind. There was a human body inside that reptile, probably that of a child.

When I communicated my belief to the old man he showed no concern, his joy over the finding of his "god" representing his one and only emotion.

After we had dragged the snake back to the house and returned him to his cage, which was quickly repaired (although it would be several days before the creature could slip through that opening again), the old headman called a meeting of his family, which consisted of six wives and twenty-one children. Even the offspring who were working in the rice fields were called in for the check-up, the meeting taking place beside the python's cage.

It developed that Taqua, the only son of Tata Kena (I recall the names distinctly) was missing. As Tata Kena was his "number one" wife, her boy was his favorite child. When the headman officially decided that his pet son was no more I expected him to set up a terrific wailing. Instead he entered the cage and, stroking the sluggish python where the boy's head bulged out, said, "My Taqua will sure go to heaven; he is inside god." With this he consoled the weeping Tata Kena, even rebuking her for failing to share his view of the matter.

As a prelude to my next story about superstitions regarding animals, let me say that finding servants in the Far East is about as difficult as locating icebergs at the North Pole. When it comes to locating first-class help, however, this does not apply. One must look the field over as carefully in Asia as anywhere else. Honesty, cleanliness, willingness to work, and a capacity for getting along with the other help are the servantly attributes I found most important in running the house that adjoined my compound at Katong. I prided myself on having a crew that, miraculously enough, conformed rather closely to those specifications.

One day, after things had run along serenely for some time, I discovered to my surprise that a feud had developed between the cook and one of the houseboys. I never could find out what it was all about, but it didn't take exalted powers of observation to see that the situation was getting worse.

It was a feud with an amusing angle in that the houseboy, who seemed to be the aggressor, was a runt, while the cook (both were Straits-born Chinese) was a fairly husky specimen.

This is no David and Goliath story. Every time the combatants clashed, the runt, as his battered appearance attested, got the worst of it. So did I—for the cook, tiring of other methods of fighting, took to throwing my dishes around.

I could have settled the argument by firing both combatants, but I didn't like the idea of parting with two good servants whom I had trained to my ways.

Sometimes it is best to let a pair of fighting servants adjust their differences. But when Ali reported to me that the cook had just beaten up the houseboy for the fourth time, I decided it was time to intervene.

It was a tough situation to handle for, as Ali had failed to find out what they were fighting about, I knew they'd never tell me.

Had it been the case of a bully—the cook—picking on a shrimp, my course would have been plain. But the cook was no bully. Nor, as Ali repeatedly told me, was he the aggressor.

I decided that the situation called first for a talk with the houseboy who seemed to be starting the fireworks. I would make no further efforts to find out what the scrap was all about. I would simply attempt to show the houseboy the folly of trying to vanquish so formidable an opponent. Failing in that, I would fire him.

I sent for the houseboy and started giving him a heart-to-heart talk. How did he expect to whip an opponent who was so much stronger?

The houseboy's reply was one of the strangest of all the weird examples of Asian superstition with which I have come face to face. Some day, the houseboy told me, he would defeat the cook, for he had on his person a set of tiger's whiskers. Surely I knew that he who possessed so certain a bringer of good luck would eventually conquer all his enemies.

The Straits-born Chinese are firm believers in the magic that lives in the whiskers of the tiger. I have known of cases where the whiskers taken from a dead tiger brought a higher price than the skin.

I finally succeeded in convincing both the cook and the houseboy that the next skirmish would result in their both being discharged; and peace reigned once more in my house at Katong.

Hairs from the tuft of an elephant's tail are also regarded as guarantees of good luck, especially by the Hindus and Malays. To one of these natives an elephant's hair bracelet—a blessed protector in time of trouble—is something to be cherished forever.

They tell a story in Giridih of a young Hindu who, having helped a group of his fellow citizens to dig a pit in which they hoped to catch a tiger that had been sighted in the village, went one evening to inspect the trap and fell in—almost landing on a tiger that lay growling at the bottom of the pit. The Hindu, terrified, crawled to the opposite side of the enclosure's floor. All night, cold with fear, he sat facing the snarling and moaning animal.

The next day a searching party of friends found the youth, unhurt, at the bottom of the pit. They lowered a rope and pulled him out, the tiger making no effort to attack him.

Everyone was puzzled until the young Hindu remembered that he had been wearing his elephant's hair bracelet. That's what had saved him.

The natives killed the tiger before they could learn the truth, though it is doubtful if anything could have changed their belief that the lad had been saved by the bracelet. An English friend of mine, who saw the cat before it was put out of its misery, tells me that undoubtedly the luckless animal had broken its back when it fell.

Usually a tiger lands on its feet, but this was one of those exceptions to the rules. The pit was an unusually deep one, and the animal, in falling, had probably turned a somersault in the darkness and landed on its back.

The "floating" shoulder bone of the leopard—a small boomerang-shaped affair, two and a half to three inches long, and supposed to be a guarantee of good luck—is another interesting symbol of Far Eastern superstition. Hardly a year passes without my running into someone who believes that, with one of these charms on your person, bad fortune can never overtake you. The curious thing about this particular superstition is that it has ceased to be just a bit of native silliness, many white men having taken it up. I know an animal trainer who can't be induced to enter a cage unless he has his leopard bone on his person.

And then there was an Englishman who served as a pilot on the Hooghly River. In his spare time he did a good deal of shooting in the adjacent Sunderbunds. One day, in the lounge of the Great Eastern Hotel in Calcutta, he told me a thrilling story of a wild boar hunt in which his Indian *shikari* had been ripped wide open. (The wild boar of India is a very powerful animal, endowed with tremendous tusks, and is a dangerous antagonist, especially when wounded.) "The boar charged me first," said my friend, "but I managed to get out of his way. Why? Because I had this on me." With which he produced a leopard's shoulder bone. To see if he really had that much faith in the charm I offered to trade him a fine jade ring for it. He flatly refused. "Think I'm crazy?" he said. "I wouldn't part with this for anything," and he meant it too.

Many are the superstitions involving animals and reptiles that one encounters in the East. Some of them are well-nigh incredible. If Mr. Ripley, the believe-it-or-not man, ever runs out of material, I suggest that he delve into Asian superstitions. If he does, he'll find himself blessed with enough new material to keep him going for a long, long time.

CHAPTER XVII

COILED LIGHTNING

More bunk has probably been disseminated about the python than about any other species known to the collector of reptiles and animals.

There is, for instance, a popular fallacy that the python has no constricting powers unless it happens to have its tail wrapped around a tree. This, they tell me, aids the creature in "getting a grip." A man once told me a story (a chap who knows Asia too) about a jungle explorer who, suddenly coming upon a python that had poised itself for an attack, saved his life by dashing for a convenient clearing where there were no trees stout enough to provide the would-be killer with sufficient tail leverage.

The sheer absurdity of this yarn would be more obvious if the reader could see a python coiled around a deer, wild pig, or other animal and watch the huge reptile's muscular contraction as those deadly coils tighten up on the victim, pressing harder and harder until practically every bone in the creature's body is crushed. And while the terrific constricting power of the main part of its body deals destruction, the immense snake's tail, instead of being wrapped around a tree, thrashes and switches about in all directions, pounding the ground until clods are pulverized to dust, leveling every standing blade of grass and bringing down all the shrubbery within reach.

It is very unusual for one of these constrictors to single out a man for attack. A python's natural prey is something it knows at a glance it can swallow. Not many men fall into this category. The man under discussion certainly didn't, for I learned that he weighed 220 pounds.

In the course of years spent as a collector I know of only one case of a python actually swallowing a man. I have investigated a number of rumors involving alleged occurrences of this kind, and time after time the stories proved false. Not until the summer of 1931, eighteen years after I investigated the first rumor of such a fatality, was I able to secure incontrovertible proof of one of these massive constrictors attacking and devouring a man.

It happened this way. While I was in Rangoon word came in from Thaton that one Maung Chit Khine, a Burmese employed as a sub-agent by the firm of Coombes and Company, had mysteriously disappeared while hunting in a nearby jungle. According to the Rangoon *Times,* investigation revealed that the poor devil had been crushed and eaten by an enormous python. Here was something worth looking into. I made up my mind to visit Thaton the first chance I got to see if I could verify the story. If it was true it had real scientific value. It would place in the zoological records the first provable instance of a python devouring a full-grown man. There has been many a case of a python swallowing a child, but nowhere did the records yield an example of the rarity reported in the press and widely discussed that day in the clubs and hotels of Rangoon.

A few weeks later I managed to find the time to make the trip to Thaton, which is about halfway between Rangoon and Moulmein, and I soon learned that the astonishing report was correct. Here are the facts:

Khine and some friends were out hunting deer in a stretch of jungle not many miles from Thaton. When they had penetrated a certain distance they reached a point in the thicket that they considered ideal for their purpose. It was agreed that Khine's companions were to "beat out" the heavy brush and drive the quarry toward the place where he stood, ready to shoot.

The beaters spread out over a fairly large area and began their task. While these activities were in progress a heavy rain began to fall, and the members of the group sought shelter under the nearest trees.

In about twenty minutes the rain ceased, and the beaters spread out again to resume their hunting.

After two or three deer had been driven out of the brush toward their friend and no report from his gun had been heard, the group began to wonder why there was no sign of Khine. There was no reply to their shouts designed to get his exact location (they figured he too had sought shelter and perhaps afterwards had not taken up his original stand), and they grew worried. They promptly ceased the unimportant business of trying to drive out a deer and started looking for their friend. As they combed the brush they kept crying out, but there was no answering shout. Alarmed by now, they sped up the search, feverishly examining every inch of the ground for some sign of their missing comrade.

Not long afterwards one of the searching party frantically called to his fellows to join him. As they came running up he pointed to the ground. Khine's shoes and *sarong!*

They were all puzzled. And more alarmed than ever.

When, a half-minute later, they found Khine's gun on the ground not many yards from the spot where they had found the shoes and *sarong,* they began to fear the worst. They shrieked out their friend's name, but again there was no answer. Maung Chit Khine was definitely among the missing.

Stunned by the weirdness of the situation, they again took up the search for their companion. Not much time had elapsed when a member of the party let out a blood-chilling scream. His friends, who were just behind him (the group had not separated this time) saw at a glance what had caused their comrade to cry out. On the ground, a few feet away, was a huge python. Its tremendous bulge plainly indicated that it had just gorged itself.

It wasn't difficult to guess what had happened. This jungle monster (it later developed that it measured twenty-eight feet) had devoured their friend.

One of the group raised his rifle and was about to pump lead into the giant constrictor.

"No!" shrieked one of his companions. "Suppose a bullet enters the body of our friend inside the python's skin. It would amount to killing him all over again, and we should never be forgiven."

A hardier and less superstitious member of the group raised his rifle and fired. Two other members of the party followed suit. The gargantuan reptile—too sluggish to escape or defend itself—proved easy prey and soon succumbed. In fact, the aroused Burmese almost shot the creature's head off.

There is no keener irony in the whole reptilian realm than what happens to the mighty python after it has made a kill. It becomes as inert as the animal it has swallowed and is practically helpless. Capturing a python after it has eaten simplifies the task of the collector. In my own case I don't mind saying that I have no objection to my work being made easier. Unless there is no way of avoiding it I cannot see the sense of attempting the dangerous task of landing a python when it is in full possession of its faculties. There is nothing to be gained by tampering with coiled lightning.

Nothing stranger has ever been seen in the streets of Thaton—a city that has had its quota of bizarre sights—than the procession that wound up that afternoon in front of Thaton Hospital. The comrades of the vanished Maung Chit Khine—five in number—had slung the dead python over their shoulders and had made the trek with their strange load right to the doors of the institution that ministers to the sick of Thaton and environs. Here the titanic snake was cut open, disclosing the crushed and broken body of Maung Chit Khine. He had been swallowed feet first, the hospital officials reported.

My investigation of this tragic occurrence resulted in my differing on only one major point from the report filed with the local authorities by the friends of the dead subagent. They gave it as their opinion that Khine, when he sought shelter from the rain, was attacked from above—in other words, they contended, the snake had dropped from a limb of the tree whose sanctuary the Burmese had sought when the heavy drops suddenly started to fall. It is my own belief that when the rain started to come down in torrents Khine, making a dash for the nearest tree, ran headlong into the snake, which, thinking it was being attacked, coiled itself around the Burmese, crushed him to death, and then began the process of swallowing by working its head over its victim. Starting with the feet, as officially reported, the enormous constrictor easily dislodged the loosely worn shoes. The *sarong* then came off as the crushing coils of the jungle's deadliest grip clamped themselves more and more tightly around the body of the ill-fated Khine.

This, as I have said earlier, is the only recorded instance of a python swallowing a man. As the slain subagent weighed only 135 pounds there is nothing astonishing about the physical aspect of the story. I know many cases of pythons devouring much bulkier victims, with special reference to the deer family. The amazing angle of Khine's story is that, in terms of the records, man is not the python's natural prey.

To give you a good idea of the swallowing capacity of the python let me tell you another story. I'll preface it with a few facts about the equipment that nature gave the python to make possible its prodigious feats. This sizeable constrictor has a hinged mouth. His lower lip comes out fan-shaped when he unhinges his jaw, making it possible for him to swallow an object more than three times the width of his own head. I have seen many a python that measured six to seven inches across the mouth in repose, and all you have to do to get a graphic idea of what the species can do in the way of swallowing is to multiply this span by three (and a small fraction).

Some years ago when I was in Pelambang, in southern Sumatra, on a collecting trip, a native boy came up to me and told me that a huge python that had just taken his *makanan* (food) was in the jungle some five miles off. My activities are well known in this part of the world, and native tipsters always try to earn a few coins by giving me information about specimens they think I'd be interested in securing.

As I was on the lookout for some good-sized pythons I decided to make the trip to get the snake. The native, who knew just where the snake had been seen, accompanied me as guide. When we arrived we found, to our disappointment, that some Eurasian hunters had reached the scene before us and had shot the python for its skin.

I had the feeling I was in the presence of something unusual as I surveyed that python's bulge. One of the Eurasians told me that the constrictor had devoured a *rusa* (deer). There was nothing strange about this except the size of the deer. Ninety-nine times out of a hundred, when a python swallows a deer in this district, it proves to be one of the smaller species, like the mutjack or the hog-deer. A full-grown buck of these varieties seldom weighs over a hundred pounds, the does averaging from forty to sixty pounds.

It was perfectly obvious from the tremendously swelled-out sides of the dead python that it had swallowed something larger than either a hog-deer or a mutjack. I had the Eurasians cut open the huge snake so that I could take a photograph. I figured that owing to the tremendous bulk of the python's meal the picture would be of interest from a zoological standpoint.

The python was quickly slit open, and I soon beheld something even more unusual than I had hoped for. The snake had swallowed a sambar stag, antlers and all. The sambar stag is the largest of all

Asian deer, and this was a fair-sized representative of the species, weighing about 160 pounds. In making its kill the reptile had first crushed the life out of the animal in characteristic fashion and next had broken the antlers. Then, when the antlers lay back flat on the neck, the snake had swallowed the deer, nose first. I still have that amazing photograph of the stag—its antlers plainly showing—inside the body of the slashed-open python. Editors tell me it is too gruesome to publish, but I have never thought of it in that way. To me the picture is merely one more example of the miraculous side of jungle life.

Ever since this occurrence I had been convinced that the python has the physical equipment to swallow a man, but I did not run into an actual case of it until several years later when I investigated the strange death of poor Maung Chit Khine.

In Kuala Kangsar, Perak, one of the Federated Malay States, they tell a story (which my friends there tell me is authentic) about an Englishwoman, newly arrived in the country, who had a strange experience with a python. This woman was confined to her bed, having given birth to a child a few days before. It was late afternoon, and she lay dozing in bed when, intuitively perhaps, she awoke with a start. A feeling had come over her that someone or something had just entered the room. Looking up, she saw an immense python—a twenty-footer, it later proved to be—gliding into the room through a doorway opening on the veranda and heading straight for the crib in which her baby lay.

Half the snake's body was inside the room when the woman made her first effort to scream. As often happens when people are suddenly confronted by a reptile or an animal that belongs in the killer group, the woman's vocal cords failed her. Petrified with fear, it was as if she had no voice at all.

It was not until the snake started moving up one of the crib's supports that the woman found her voice. She let out a bloodcurdling shriek, and, as she did, the constrictor turned and eyed her coldly. Again the woman screamed.

The *tukang kebun* (gardener), who had been out in front of the house trimming the shrubbery, came running into the room, *parang* [knife] in hand. The Malay was followed by two of the Chinese houseboys.

The gardener arrived as the python, turning his head away from the woman, again centered his attention on the crib. By now the huge snake's head was almost on a level with the top of the crib. In a fraction of a second he would be within striking distance. Putting everything he had behind the blow, the *tukang kebun* swung his *parang* and dealt the constrictor a terrible blow behind the head. By this time the Chinese boys were yanking away at the snake in an effort to drag it out of the room. The python thrashed around furiously, knocking the men in all directions. Meanwhile the *tukang kebun,* having landed one deadly blow that did plenty of damage, kept hacking away until he severed the snake's head. All Malays are skilled knife-wielders, but your average *tukang kebun* can outdo the rest when it comes to handling a *parang*.

This formidable native knife is his principal means of defense as well as his main gardening equipment. He is never without it and in a fight wields it with a skill that is beautiful to behold.

This is one case where cold steel proved itself superior to coiled lightning.

The python, as you have guessed by now, has always fascinated me. Much is now known about the species, but it is surprising how little information there was, until recent years, on the subject of what happens after one of these mammoth snakes devours a sizeable animal and the process of digestion begins.

For years friends in zoos and museums had been asking me to check up on a python after it had made a major kill and give them the facts about the snake's eventual elimination thereof.

It was not until 1926—at least ten years after I had made my first promise to these friends—that I was able to secure the information they wanted.

I was on one of the small Dutch islands south of Singapore. These islands are full of snakes, especially pythons. It is a veritable paradise for the collector of these constrictors.

I had some orders for pythons from zoos, and Ali and I set forth to fill them. One of the snakes we landed was not only a perfect zoo specimen but also ideal for the purpose of the experiment I had promised to conduct. It had just eaten, and from the shape of its prodigious bulge I judged that its meal had consisted of one of the wild boars of the island. It had swallowed its prey so recently that its jaw was still hanging open, the hinges not having yet reset.

We rolled our sluggish catch into a rattan fiber net and hired four natives to shoulder it on carrying poles and take it to our boat. This was a twenty-three-foot snake whose normal weight was 275 to 300 pounds; with the wild boar inside of him he took plenty of carrying.

In addition to this boar-filled specimen, we landed three others —smaller but worthwhile representatives of their interesting species.

When we got back to Singapore I installed my bloated specimen in a vat that had once been used by some Chinese residents for keeping live fish. I inherited this (it measured nine feet by twelve) when I took over the grounds where I built my compound.

I put straw in the bottom of the vat and installed my python in it, covering the top with heavy wire netting. Then I sat back and awaited developments, taking measurements daily with a tape-line to record the decrease in the python's inflated girth.

Each day the snake's bulge grew smaller, and on the ninth day it had its first passage, consisting of general roughage, such as hair, bits of bone, teeth, etc. On the tenth day the constrictor passed the solid meat, which came out in the form of an odorless substance very much like wet talcum powder. This substance, by the way, has medicinal properties. There is a chemical firm in Chicago that buys it from zoos and other sources.

The most interesting part of the whole experiment was that in the roughage that was eliminated prior to the powdery stuff there were four balls of hair, each the size of a tennis ball but much harder. In fact, the spheres were almost as hard as baseballs.

These balls of hair interested me. I was fascinated by their perfect roundness and their almost machine-made appearance.

I got a knife and cut one of the four straight through the center. Embedded so firmly that it had to be dug out, I found a cloven hoof. The hoofs of the Asian wild boar are deadly weapons of almost razor sharpness. In fact, this odd member of the hog family has cut many a snake and small animal to pieces by stamping on it. The cruel cutting edge of these hoofs constitutes a really deadly weapon that has earned the respect of many a jungle creature.

I cut open the other three balls and in each case found a firmly embedded cloven hoof. It was an astonishing experience, for it proved conclusively that nature had made provision for the swallowing of sharp-edged objects by the python. If not for this amazing protection those sharp hoofs would have cut the snake's intestines to pieces.

All of which leads up to the thought that the truth about the python is strange enough. There is no need for stories such as the one I heard on my last trip to the Far East. It had to do with a huge python that was said to have swallowed a water buffalo. The reptile got the whole body down (so the story went), and only the head stuck out because the wide spread of the horns blocked the way. But the python, just to show it could not be stumped, was calmly waiting for the head to rot off. When I tell you that even a medium-sized water buffalo bulks larger than the average bull or horse you will see how ridiculous this yarn is.

In All in a Lifetime *(1941) Frank Buck describes photographing the struggle between a leopard and a python:*
During the filming of *Wild Cargo* I was delighted when a native came running into my northern Johore camp with word that a huge python was coiled beside a jungle trail four miles away.

"Is it a big snake?" I asked.

"Ular besar!" he nodded, indicating an enormous snake with his hands.

"Is it in the open? So I can take pictures of it?"

"Ada, tuan! Ular coil beside clearing on trail!"

That was enough for me. All animals in the jungle more or less use trails through the forest. Some of these trails, the ones that lead to streams and water holes, are almost as well worn as man-made footpaths. Consequently they are much lighter and more open than the surrounding jungle. I knew that if there was a python waiting beside one of these trails, I had an excellent chance of getting a rare picture. The python would be there for only one thing—food. And he would wait there until he got it. Almost any animal that came down the trail would be grist for the gargantuan constrictor's mill. It might be an antelope, a mouse deer, a monkey, or a wild boar. Any of them would make an interesting picture.

I immediately went the four miles by bullock cart and had a look at the Sakai's python. Sure enough, he was coiled up in a light, open spot. I hastily called up my cameras and as quietly as possible placed them behind screens of ferns and creepers.

Then I had a better idea than merely photographing a python eating a normal meal. A few miles away there was a native village that had long been troubled by a black leopard. The animal had killed dogs and goats and once had even attacked a native woodcutter. I knew that if I could possibly get that leopard and python within range of my cameras I might get a rare and unique animal fight, a fight that few people—even those who have lived all their lives in the jungle—have ever seen.

I talked with the villagers about it. They were more than pleased at the prospect of getting rid of the *kucing* (cat) that had been preying on them. They agreed that all the men of the village would form a long line and beat the jungle toward my cameras and the spot where the immense python lay.

All arrangements made with the Malays, I went back to my cameras to wait. This waiting is the hardest and most patience-trying part of making wild animal pictures. I have had cameras masked and screened in one spot for days at a time. For there's no telling when your actors will perform, or how they will perform, and a few seconds of delay in grinding a camera can mean the loss of a long-hoped-for scene.

It seemed hours before anything happened. Every now and then I would peer out through our screen of ferns to see the python coiled by the side of the trail, apparently sleeping. But I knew he was hungry and alert, ready for instant action if a meal came along. I knew too that the python would not attack the leopard, if the leopard came. A python, feeding only once every six or seven weeks, will never without provocation attack any creature except for food, and nothing bigger than he can swallow whole.

I put my faith in a fight in the leopard. For the black leopard is the villain of the jungle. He is as tough as any animal that walks on four feet, and he knows it. He will even go out of his way to pick a quarrel, and usually he will win it, for he can beat anything of his weight that moves. I was confident that if the leopard came, there would be a battle, and a battle royal.

The sun slipped over the rim of the trees, and the light began to fail, and still the leopard had not come. Unless things happened in the next fifteen minutes there would be no picture. And then, off in the jungle to the north, I heard the first sounds of the Malay and Sakai beaters from the village. They were doing a good job, beating through the jungle in a wide circle and raising a young hell of noise with tin pans and clubs on hollow tree trunks. I knew that unless the leopard had holed up in a den, he must be ahead of them.

All at once I saw him, a black face with shiny green eyes at the far side of the clearing. He looked around boldly, missed us behind the screens, and loped into the clearing. In his excitement at the unusual noise behind him, he entirely overlooked the coiled python. He almost stepped on the huge snake, and the snake, no doubt thinking itself attacked, came to instant life.

There was a lightning-like movement in the grass. Like anchor chain running down the side of a ship, that python struck. He caught the leopard by the neck with his huge mouth, and a coil of silver muscle shot into the air and fastened around the black body.

The leopard let out a savage scream that shook the jungle. He tore with his sharp claws at the gigantic snake. He squirmed and fought and flung his body into the air with all his cat strength. But another huge coil of the python slipped over him with the power of an imposing silver wave over a bit of black beach.

The leopard tore at the snake with claws and fangs, just as he had torn at Sakai goats and would have torn at native children. But he was tearing at solid snake muscle now, muscle strong as steel, muscle that bound him, coil after coil, link after link, in a powerful and unbreakable chain of python.

When it was over, the vicious cat lay crushed and still; there was nothing of him visible except a black head and a slim, still tail. His 150-pound body was entirely surrounded by python coils.

I turned excitedly to the cameramen.

"Did you get it all?" I asked.

They nodded, their faces white and their eyes awed. The whole thing had been finished so quickly. Three minutes had seen the death of a black demon that had terrorized a whole village. And three minutes had put "in the can" the most thrilling animal fight ever filmed.

A python also attacked Frank Buck, as he describes in Animals Are Like That! *(1940):*

Once I was forced to kill a python according to the old jungle rule of self-preservation. It happened that I was releasing a *pelandok* (mouse deer) from a native trap. When the tiny animal had scampered back into the forest, I decided to break up the trap. As I reached for it, something struck my arm like a hammer blow. I felt a painfully strong grip on my forearm, and then I saw the head of an immense python.

The jaws were firmly clamped on my arm. Through the intense pain I realized that once he got his coils around my body he could crush out my life in a minute. I called for Ali, who quickly started hacking at the python's neck with his *parang* as a coil of the snake's body went round my arm. The pressure on my arm was tremendous—it seemed that any moment the terrible strain must snap the bone. Somehow, with the superhuman effort men manage under stress, I loosed my revolver from its holster with my free hand. I had to be careful not to shoot into my arm, but I quickly brought up the gun and put three rapid shots into the back of the snake's head. There was a slackening of pressure on my arm; a wave of relief swept through my body as the python slid to the ground and I stood free.

There were twenty-two sharp triangular teeth that came loose from the snake's jaws into my arm. I stood gritting my teeth as these were picked out with tweezers, one by one. My arm and shoulder were miserably sore for more than a week, but the only permanent harm was that I had merely a dead python on my hands—and my business is bringing back live ones.

CHAPTER XVIII

TERRIBLE TUSKS

The most terrific struggle that can take place between any two living creatures is a battle between two full-grown bull elephants.

The jungle has known much combat of this kind, but few people have been privileged to witness it.

Sex is invariably the cause when one of these titanic encounters takes place. A pretender comes along to dispute the sovereignty of the leader of a herd.

The boss elephant of a herd is like a sultan traveling with his harem. He does all the breeding. The herd is made up mainly of females that cater to his sexual needs. The rest of the pack consists of young elephants that have not yet reached maturity. As soon as the young males become potential breeders they are driven out to seek their own herds or to become lone bachelors of the jungle. The leader brooks no competition. Out these young lads go to shift for themselves as soon as they reach the age of puberty.

In other words, in the elephant world the strongest do the breeding. Only those that can fight for their females and win them can participate in the business of reproducing the species—which is the main reason why the race of elephants has retained its virility. When a herd leader no longer can hold his own he is ousted by a younger and stronger elephant that takes over the defeated one's females and sets himself up as chief.

Some time ago I happened to be in Colombo, Ceylon, on business. My next stop was to be in the Behar District of southern India. I planned to make headquarters at a small native village about sixteen miles from the old abandoned British military post at Jalna while engaged in assembling some tigers, leopards, sloth bears, and antelope to fill some orders I had from zoos.

At the time Lal was in Calcutta looking after a collection of animals, birds, and reptiles I had rounded up there. I wired him to turn these specimens over to Atool Achooli, a well-known local animal trader, who could be depended upon to take good care of them. His further instructions were to meet me at the village above Jalna (where we had spent several days a year or so earlier). I would need his aid in landing the animals I sought.

I was about to leave Colombo when I saw an opportunity to pick up some bonnet monkeys, langurs, and other small Ceylon specimens. This delayed me considerably, and I arrived in Jalna several days behind schedule.

Going up to the hamlet where Lal awaited me, I found the gloomiest person I have ever known. It was depressing to look at him. His expression was funereal.

"What's the matter, Lal?" I asked. "Are you sick or sad or what?"

Lal opened up and told all, in the process giving me one of the meanest frustrations I have ever had. For I realized before more than a small part of his story had been unfolded that the fates had conspired to make me miss one of the thrills of a lifetime. I found myself cussing those Ceylon specimens—and I'll tell you why.

About the time I was due to arrive from Colombo, a bamboo-cutter had brought word into the village where Lal was waiting for me that about five miles off in the jungle two bull elephants were fighting it out for the leadership of a herd. A young intruder—full grown and powerful—had come upon a pachyderm pack that was grazing in the district. Without so much as saying hello, the newcomer—an animal weighing between four and five tons and standing about nine feet at the shoulders—tried to mount one of the females. The herd leader, a virile veteran of the jungle that had probably bred that herd for forty or fifty years, resented the intrusion of the young upstart. With a snort and a bellow of rage, and tail straight up in the air in the characteristic manner of his species when attacking, the boss elephant charged the interloper and butted him clear of the female.

And then the fight began. . . .

What made Lal sick was his knowing that for years I had hoped to come upon such a scrap, by far the most epic of all jungle hostilities. Here, by good fortune, the stage was set, and I was late.

The day of my arrival Lal told me the story of that elephant fight once, twice, three times. Then he told it to me all over again. This was two days after the grand duel of tusks was over and the thing was still fresh in his mind.

I had never known Lal to be so talkative. Nothing in the past—and we had been through some thrilling experiences together—had ever loosened his tongue to such an extent. He strained his English vocabulary to its limits, and, when he had taxed it until it could serve him no longer, he sprinkled his narrative with picturesque phrases in his native tongue.

Lal had induced the bamboo-cutter to guide him to within a fair distance of the struggle. With his keen knowledge of animals, Lal knew that he must approach from upwind so that his scent would not be carried to the combatants. As he worked his way toward the scene of the fight it was easy for him to tell that the tussle had been going on for some time, for the brush had been trampled down and mashed into the ground over an area of several hundred square yards. Branches of eight-inch-thick bamboo had been snapped off like matchsticks. Trees had been uprooted and pounded into the earth.

Lal, as soon as he caught sight of the combatants, looked around for an unobtrusive roost that would afford a good view of the struggle. He selected a tree on a rise in the ground. From this elevation he could see everything. Only if the pachyderm gladiators forsook their battleground and disappeared into the jungle would they be lost to view.

As Lal took up his perch in the tree the fighting elephants, forehead to forehead, were struggling for advantage. Neither had yet inflicted a serious injury on the other. Each was bleeding from superficial wounds, but both seemed to regard these as flea bites.

This first look, Lal said, was unimpressive. The animals appeared to be stalling. Barra Sahib—Lal's name for the older animal—seemed to be perfectly confident of the outcome and almost seemed to be resting. (*Barra Sahib* means "the big boss," usually applied in India to the head of a firm or government.) The interloper, whom he designated as Do (meaning "Number Two"), apparently had not given the old herd leader much to worry about.

What amused Lal at the outset was that the females, scattered about in the nearby brush, grazing, seemed to take little or no interest in the fight. Complacently they lumbered about on the fringe of

221

the battleground, munching the various greens—leaves of trees, shrubs of all kinds, bamboo, and other jungle dainties—that they encountered as they moved back and forth. Only now and then did they look up to see what was going on. Either they were accustomed to the sight of their sovereign disposing of an impertinent pretender or they didn't care who won, confident that regardless of the outcome they would have a leader and their physical needs would be ministered to. After all, that and food were all that mattered in the life of an elephant.

After a few minutes of this stalling, Do backed away about fifteen feet and made a charge at his older adversary, futilely trying to sideswipe him with his seven-foot tusks. Barra Sahib's tusks were perhaps a little longer, and heavier at the base, he being the older animal.

(Which is a good time to point out that the tusks of a full-grown elephant constitute the most terrible weapon the jungle knows. The layman has no idea of the potentialities of these weapons, for circus elephants are the pachyderms he is mainly familiar with, and these are practically all females, with no tusks at all or very small ones. Occasionally one sees a bull elephant in the performing ring, but without exception it is an animal whose tusks have been sawed off.)

Barra Sahib easily evaded the attempted sideswipe. The result was a head-on collision that left the animals, forehead to forehead, as they were before.

For almost an hour, Lal said, it was all head work, so to speak, and pushing. Nothing much happened, and he started to wonder whether he had let himself in for a dull show.

Just as it began to dawn upon him that perhaps the fights between bull elephants he had heard of since he was a tot were overrated stories that had become fables, there was some action. The herd leader got off to one side and jabbed Do tellingly—but not seriously —in the shoulder, ripping the flesh wide open. Do set up a tremendous snorting and trumpeting and started to retreat. Barra, seeing his advantage, went after his wounded opponent and tried to get him from behind. After a retreat of about thirty yards Do braced himself and whirled around suddenly, again meeting the sultan of the herd head-on. It was a real collision this time. When two elephants whose combined weight is nine tons or more come together (Lal estimated Do's weight as four and a half tons and Barra's as close to five) the impact is jarring. But elephant skulls are elephant skulls, and concussion of the brain seems to be an unheard-of ailment in the realm of the pachyderm.

Again there was a long spell of pushing and stamping around, with nothing of importance happening. Lal began to think that perhaps those females that kept calmly grazing were right in their unconcern.

The interloper, evidently tired of the indecisive nature of the scrap, decided to give it some finality. He didn't succeed, but he evened things up in the way of shoulder wounds, dealing the herd leader a painful (though unimportant) one. Do, to be specific, dug into his adversary's shoulder, and when he was finished there was a small chunk of the chief's flesh flapping in the sultry breeze.

Barra Sahib decided that this was a challenge that called for a meaningful answer. Lowering his head and veering off to one side, he charged. Do was unable to get out of the way in time. The herd leader got one of the pretender's front legs between his tusks and raised the intruder's forequarters straight up in the air. In the course of this maneuver the overlord of the disputed herd succeeded in making a short rip, crosswise, under his adversary's chest, in back of the front legs.

But Do, on account of his quickness of foot—Lal made a point of telling me that the interloper was a bit the faster of the two—backed away before a fatal injury could be inflicted.

As Do retreated he was unlucky enough to crash into a heavy clump of bamboo. Down he went, snapping the stalks as he fell. This was Barra Sahib's chance to make his kill. In fact, Lal thought it was all over. But again superior speed came to the rescue of the younger animal, and he scrambled to his feet before the herd leader, now puffing, could dig in his murderous tusks and end the scrap.

Do managed to get completely out of the way of the onrushing Barra Sahib, with the result that the old sultan, unable to stop himself, crashed right into a jungle tree straight ahead. He hit it with such force that, though the tree was nearly a foot in diameter, it came right up out of the ground and toppled over.

The herd leader miraculously managed to keep his footing, but he was badly shaken up. He hesitated for a moment, leaving his side exposed. This was not lost on the alert pretender, who made a charge for the expansive target. Again Lal thought the fight was over. But

Barra Sahib, breathing hard, just managed to swing around in time, meeting the enemy head-on as he had several times before.

Almost the same second that the heads of the bulky pachyderms came together there was a tremendous clap of thunder, accompanied by a sharp flash of lightning. Rain started coming down in torrents without any preliminary sprinkle, in the characteristic Far Eastern fashion.

Lal, though the tree afforded a certain amount of protection, was soaked to the skin, for there is nothing half-hearted about these sudden Asian storms. When it decides to rain, it rains, and if you happen to be in the jungle only the most unusual kind of shelter will keep you from becoming thoroughly drenched. But the fight was still on, and it didn't even occur to Lal to beat a retreat. It was a rapidly improving scrap, and his interest in the outcome kept him rooted to his perch.

For the first few minutes of the downpour the elephants remained head to head, the slippery footing making them cautious. Besides, by now they were pretty well spent. Froth ran from their mouths and blood trickled down their shoulders. The rain, seemingly bent on minimizing the struggle's brutalities, washed away the blood as fast as it appeared, and this gore soon mixed with the mud and watery ooze at the feet of the mammoth contestants.

Brow to brow, the animals kept pushing away, neither able to gain an advantage. They skidded and slipped around meaninglessly, unable to accomplish anything in the way of offensive tactics. Neither, it was plain, was much of a "mudder."

The slippery muck finally bested them, and both animals lost their footing. Down they went on their haunches in a spatter of mud and water, their forefeet sticking out in front of them. Each tried to scramble to his feet quickly to make a charge while the other was down. Do, a bit quicker than his older adversary, got to his feet first and was about to charge when he suddenly changed his mind, probably because he didn't like the treacherous footing. He turned and ran, plainly willing to call it a day. Barra Sahib, all used up and chugging like an asthmatic engine, decided to have one more shot at the intruder. He made for Do at a gallop, just managing to catch up with the retreating foe and jab him in the hip with one tusk. The pretender, bleeding freely from his new wound, didn't even turn around. He kept heading for heavy jungle and soon disappeared from view.

Barra Sahib, a not-prepossessing picture of leadership, dragged his heaving frame over to a nearby spot where some of his herd were contentedly browsing.

Lal, drenched and hungry, headed for the village. There he filled his stomach and changed his clothes. He retired early for, being expert in the matter of animals, he knew there was a good possibility of a renewal of the struggle between Barra Sahib and Do. Such fights have been known to last for three whole days, and Lal figured it was at least an even bet that Do, encouraged by his success in holding his own against the enormous old herd leader, would return to repeat his challenge of Barra Sahib's sovereignty. An elephant in quest of mates does not give up easily.

Lal made up his mind, he told me, to be on hand at daybreak near the scene of the battle he had witnessed. The least he could do, he assured me with feeling, was to make an effort to get an accurate close-up of the kind of fight I had always hoped to see.

Needless to say, he was not sure that the animals were going to fight again. The odds favored it, yet there was considerable uncertainty connected with the whole business. If they were going to continue the duel, how could he possibly know when the struggle would be renewed—and where? It seemed fairly safe logic that Barra Sahib, painfully wounded, would not move overnight far from the scene of the original skirmish. Yet move he might—and a small distance for an elephant is likely to prove a long distance for a human being.

The next morning, before dawn, Lal set out for the scene of yesterday's hostilities. As he made his way through the jungle he kept pondering the question of whether or not he would witness a resumption of this epic feud.

He turned these thoughts over and over in his mind, and before he knew it he was approaching the herd's grazing ground. They had shifted their location only slightly. A browsing elephant pack disturbs and cracks the brush in a manner all its own (animal experts recognize these sounds in their sleep), and Lal knew that once again he was nearing that same pachyderm family. No other herd had been reported in the district. Barra Sahib and Co. were having a peaceful breakfast, he told himself, but he quickly changed his mind as he came closer. For suddenly a shrill trumpeting reached his ears, followed by an answering cry of the same sort.

Then, before he realized it, there was a tremendous charge through the brush, and Do passed within sixty yards of him. About seventy-five yards away, Barra Sahib, head lowered, stood waiting to meet the onrushing pretender. Do, coming on with terrific force, swerved to the right in an effort to sideswipe the old herd leader, but the latter, now used to this trick, swung around to avoid the ivory broadside, and the result was another one of those jarring collisions.

Heads lowered, the animals again started pushing each other around. Do, developing a craftiness that had not characterized his earlier efforts, suddenly broke the clinch and tried again for a side thrust, almost succeeding in achieving it. Lal held his breath as the younger elephant, with lightning-fast footwork for so enormous an animal, made a quick pivot and charge. Barra Sahib whirled around frantically and took the blow on his hip instead of his side. The result was a bad flesh wound; and the suddenness with which it was inflicted, plus the force behind the thrust, sent the old herd leader down on his haunches.

Again Lal thought the show was over. It might have been if Do had been quick enough to follow up his advantage. He seemed to gloat over the agonized trumpeting of his painfully injured foe but did nothing for a second or two but stand there and take in the herd chief's misery.

In a flash, Barra Sahib was on his feet. He charged his tormentor, putting behind the broad forehead that served him as a battering ram the stored-up rage of two days of violent battling that had left him with no visible advantage.

The younger elephant varied his tactics again. Instead of meeting the charge or swerving in an effort to effect a sideswipe, he merely sidestepped—and very nimbly too, Lal said—with the result that the foe shot right past him.

Barra Sahib had lowered more than ever and, missing the target he expected to hit, lost his balance and once again went down on his haunches. Knowing that Do would now attack from behind he quickly rose to his feet and swung around to meet the onslaught.

He was not properly planted to meet the shock; in other words, he had not had a chance after regaining his footing to "dig in" and get squared away. Also there had not been time after getting to his feet for him to lower his head sufficiently. The result was that the younger animal, coming on with a tremendous rush, dug one of his huge tusks into the enemy's right shoulder. Deeper and deeper he probed with this deadly ivory weapon, poor Barra Sahib trumpeting madly as the white dagger went in farther and farther.

The herd leader, in his efforts to push the young intruder away with his forehead, made matters only worse, for the more he pushed, the more solidly the tusk became embedded in his flesh. Do was pushing too . . . and Barra Sahib was beginning to give ground. At first he was shoved back only a few feet. Feet soon became yards, and it was only a matter of seconds before the herd leader was backstepping at a lively rate, snorting and gasping as he made his odd retreat.

The relentless Do kept shoving Barra Sahib backward, backward, backward. The older elephant, with the wicked tusk buried in his flesh, was helpless. Twice he tried to make a stand, but he only helped dig the foe's deadly weapon in deeper. So there was nothing to do but to keep on moving backward.

Fifteen yards of this weird struggle brought Barra Sahib's hind legs to the edge of an expansive ditchlike hollow. With a powerful push Do sent the herd leader toppling into this sunken area, his bloody tusk coming out of the flesh and leaving a deep jagged wound as the elder elephant went crashing down.

Then Do poised himself for the kill. Stepping back to give momentum to his charge, he lowered his head and plunged forward.

It took Barra Sahib only a fraction of a second to realize his predicament. His side was fully exposed, and it meant certain death if he didn't get out of the way. He got to his feet just in time to avoid the twin ivory bayonets—one of them a gory warning—that were heading for him. Retreat was better than being pierced by those terrible tusks. Trumpeting a pitiful song of defeat, the deposed herd leader disappeared into the jungle.

The victor followed the vanquished for a few paces, then turned around and in businesslike fashion began rounding up his herd. His first move was to go over to where five females were grazing. These he pushed forward and, having made it plain to this group that he was boss, rounded up the other members of his newly acquired harem and their young.

One of the females dropped back, not sure whether she wanted to follow this new leader. He soon made up her mind for her. This he accomplished by the simple process of lowering his head and giving her a sample of his gift for butting. Over she went. Then she scrambled to her feet and meekly followed her new boss, who proceeded to lead his new-found family off into the thicket.

Lal had witnessed the jungle's quintessential tragedy—the dethroning of an elephant herd leader. Almost without exception such an animal turns rogue, another way of saying that he goes mad. Suddenly deprived of his family, an awful loneliness seizes him. A demented outcast, he views everything and everybody as his enemy, and he tears through the jungle, uprooting trees and destroying whatever happens to be in his path. More than one luckless native has been pounded to a pulp by a rogue elephant.

I know of one case where a rogue practically destroyed a whole native village, knocking down all the nipa-palm huts and uprooting one by one all the trees in a two-acre banana plantation.

What destruction Barra Sahib eventually accomplished after his expulsion, God only knows.

CHAPTER XIX

STRIPED DEMON

Interest in the wild creatures of the jungle has increased tremendously in recent years. People wonder how the animals in the zoos got there, and this culminated in my being commissioned to head a camera expedition designed to show what happens from the moment an animal collector gets an order for a specimen to the time it winds up in a cage where the public may view it.

The scene of my operations was the Malay Archipelago, whose jungles are the densest known to man. Not many people have an accurate idea of what these Asian badlands are like. The public is more familiar with Africa and its open veldt, which present fewer problems, either to the animal collector or to the motion picture director.

The jungle to which I refer is a four-tiered affair. First, there is the tangle of creepers and grassy growths of all kinds underfoot, combining to make walking as uncertain a proposition as it can possibly be, with damp and soggy areas contributing to this uncertainty. The next layer consists of heavy jungle grass that ranges from waist high to neck high, and ferns that often reach over one's head. The tier above this is a ceiling made up of trees, medium in height, interwoven with countless vines, the whole matted together in one thick green mass. Then, finally, there is the jungle roof, consisting of enormous tropical trees whose tops interlace so completely that very little light can seep through to the ground below.

All of which is said to explain my principal problem in setting out to make a motion picture showing animals in their jungle haunts. After I had picked out what I considered an ideal setting for our first shots, my associates on the expedition cried me down in unison. "We can't make pictures in the dark," they chorused. Animals are my business, not movies, and it was natural for me to think in terms of a spot where wildlife was plentiful, rather than sunlight.

A complete change in the plans I had in mind was therefore necessary. The first assignment was to get some good ground shots of a tiger moving through the jungle, these to be used in our picture as a sort of prelude to a series of scenes showing how one of these cats is trapped and brought back to civilization.

Now that the light problem had eliminated the photographing of the tiger in his jungle fastness, I was faced by the task of locating one of these striped cats at some point where camera shots could be taken in open country, in broad daylight. When you realize that it is unusual for a tiger to leave the jungle, except to do some night prowling, you have a pretty fair idea of what a tough assignment this was.

I got word one day that a tiger was making regular raids on the livestock of the natives at the Forty-one Mile Post, a village that many miles north of Johore Bahru. It was obvious from the details of the story that the animal had taken up headquarters somewhere near the edge of the jungle bordering that primitive settlement.

We moved our paraphernalia to this district and set out to find the tiger. I succeeded in locating his tracks at several different points along the jungle's edge, and as a result felt we had a pretty fair chance to get the pictures we wanted. I collected a small array of beaters and started them into the woods where the tracks led us. These men spread out through the brush and worked toward a given point, pounding with sticks against trees or making whatever noise they could to drive the tiger out into the open.

The beaters wormed their way through the dense jungle as far as they could. Their progress proved much slower than I had expected, and at the end of the first day they had got only about one-third of the way through. I might have called them off altogether except that toward evening we caught sight of the tiger, just a fleeting glimpse of him, slinking deeper into the thicket.

So we kept our men on the spot and renewed our beating the next morning. The jungle got thicker and thicker as we proceeded, and eventually on the fourth day, without having seen the animal again, we reached a point where further progress was impossible without the aid of *parangs,* and while I have hacked my way through many a mile of jungle with the aid of one of these swordlike knives, I knew that this was too slow a process when the quarry is a tiger. So I called off the beaters. All we had to show for our trouble was a fine assortment of cuts and scratches, for this section of jungle is crowded with rattan, each joint of which has a hooklike thorn that doesn't care how deeply it digs into your flesh.

Ironically enough, a day after we had gathered up our equipment and left the Forty-one Mile Post to try our luck elsewhere, the tiger came out of his jungle lair in broad daylight and made off with a goat that was tied up within twenty yards of the spot where our cameras had been set up. His daylight raid was one of those exceptions to the rules of tigerdom that doesn't happen very often, and it was our misfortune not to have been on hand when it occurred.

However, we were well on our way to a point south of Muar, which has always been famous tiger country. Here we came on the trail of another raider, a huge tiger that for some time had been raising the devil with the bullocks and other domestic livestock. Our chances in this case looked much brighter than at the Forty-one Mile Post, for it was obvious, both from information given us by the local natives and from the tracks we located, that the animal had quartered itself in a patch of thin jungle, separate from the dense forest that stretches through this territory. I felt confident that our efforts would be rewarded at last.

We failed to get the ground shots we were after, but we got something else of real importance, a picture of the highest scientific interest, that will make several zoologists change beliefs to which they have clung for years.

It all came about in this way. After five days of steady plugging our beaters drove the raider of Muar into a corner adjoining exactly the location we wanted, a grassy jungle plateau with plenty of good light. At one end of the plateau we had planted a camera behind a carefully constructed barricade of logs and leaves. Our beaters came up on three sides and finally got the tiger on the run toward the camera. Elated over this success in "flushing" the cat and heading him in the right direction, they became excited and closed in too fast, adding all sorts of weird cries and shouts to the noises made by pounding with their sticks. The result was that the animal was in a wild panic by the time he came within camera range. When a last chorus of crazy shrieks from the beaters sent the frightened tiger on the run toward the camera, the only refuge he could see was an imposing tree that had a crotch about ten feet from the ground where the two main branches of the tree separated. About five feet above this, there was another sizeable crotch, where the next two thick limbs divided. The camera man, safe behind his barricade, was turning his crank at a merry clip as the tiger rushed toward this tree.

With one spring the agile cat negotiated the first crotch, and then, with an almost effortless leap, he landed in the one higher up. Here, with all the nervousness of an amateur acrobat, he shifted from one foot to the other and back again, glanced up and down in indecision and waited hesitantly for whatever might happen next.

Now this whole performance was contrary to all the scientific lore. Several authoritative naturalists have stubbornly maintained for years that tigers never climb trees. I forgot all about the camera as I watched this exceptional animal, defying all the conventions and regulations. As a matter of fact, I couldn't have been more astonished if he had started to speak English. I even stopped to wonder what on Earth he would do next.

He apparently was wondering the same thing himself. And he was a long time deciding. In fact, he retained his perch for five or six minutes, while our camera ground away, its operator completely unaware that there was anything unusual about a tiger up a tree.

We got some exceptional pictures, but I am afraid they will prove a bit embarrassing to certain naturalists who will be forced to back water on one of their most aggressive theories.

All the film in the camera was used up, and the operator was busy putting on a fresh magazine, when the tiger suddenly decided to move on. In a flash he jumped to the ground and crashed his way past the beaters and off into the heart of the jungle.

We were lucky to get these pictures of a tiger up a tree, but we were up a tree ourselves, for we still didn't have those ground shots—and according to the plan of the picture we needed a lot of them. We had something much rarer—something that may never again be duplicated—yet our original, and more fundamental, task remained to be performed. We simply must have some good pictures of an Asian tiger in his natural element—slinking through jungle glades, appeasing his thirst at a spring or creek, and doing the natural things that a tiger does in his daily jungle existence.

During the next fortnight we made three more attempts at various likely spots, but they all proved fruitless. I finally came to the conclusion that the only way in which we would be successful in getting Mr. Stripes properly into good close-up pictures would be to fence in a section of the jungle where we could control his movements. I reached this conclusion reluctantly, for the task was an enormous one, entailing much time and money. But it was the only way.

Selecting about two acres at the edge of the jungle, where the forest was thin enough to allow the sun to penetrate between the trees, I brought thirty Chinese carpenters up from Singapore and built all around this area a framework of logs and planks sixteen feet high, with a sort of catwalk along the top. Then I made a trip into Singapore and bought corrugated iron sheets, enough to line the entire enclosure. Motor lorries and bullock carts hauled the building materials to our jungle headquarters.

When the work was completed, we had a structure as efficient for its purpose as it was incongruous in its wild jungle surroundings —a solid wall of sheet iron, sixteen feet high, so smooth on the inside that no joint protruded where a tiger could get a foothold to jump or climb over. This fence encircled about two acres of as picturesque jungle as I have ever seen. A small trap door was arranged in one side, so that a cage could be pushed up against the outside, the gate raised by a pulley, and the tiger permitted to walk in and feel perfectly at home in surroundings to which he was accustomed. Any number of cameras could operate from the catwalk on top of the fence.

Within a week we had trapped one of the big cats, about eighteen miles away from our improvised compound. It was a particularly fine specimen, a male measuring nearly ten feet in length from nose to tip of tail, in the very prime of life—just the ideal animal for our purpose. Having photographed the trapping episode and also that of getting the cat out of the trap and hauling him by bullock cart down through the jungle trails to our headquarters, we placed the huge log crate against the trap door, raised the gate, and gave him his restricted freedom.

The center of our enclosure comprised about an acre, more or less, of heavy brush, cane, and creepers as dense and impenetrable as any of the jungle outside. Within the surrounding walled space were the lighter areas, including a good-sized grass plot entirely open to the tropical sun, a small pond, and other settings deemed appropriate picturizing locations. My hunch was that on being released the tiger would make for the heavy brush but that he would soon come out and wander about, drinking water at the pool and showing himself in the lighter places where we could get some splendid pictures of the jungle terror in his natural element.

My long experience with wild animals proved to me years ago that they just won't do what is expected of them, and this cat proved no exception to the rule. He made a beeline from the trap door to the heavy brush, and there he remained throughout the morning. From our perches on top of the wall we hurled missiles into the thicket, shouted, and did everything we could to disturb his feline solitude, all to no avail. At noon I sent Ali to a village three miles distant, where a Chinese man kept a small store for the sale of Chinese firecrackers (essential merchandise wherever there is a colony of Chinese people). Ali came back with a grand assortment of noise-makers, and I threw package after package with fuse lighted into the brush at different points where I thought the tiger might have taken refuge. Even this did not budge him.

Next I tried "smoke pots." These are devices used for years in the making of movies to simulate clouds and fogs. When this device first came into vogue in the picture-making industry, I recognized its value as an accessory to my animal-catching equipment and have used it on many occasions to rout some stubborn animal out of a den or cave. But my efforts to smoke out Mr. Tiger were as unavailing as those preceding them. He was either unaware that anything unusual was going on, or he was bored—or both. The fact that our smoke pots belched forth enough in the way of dark clouds to make a small bit of Johore look like Vesuvius for a few minutes seemed to mean nothing at all to our bashful jungle cat.

By midafternoon, when all efforts to get the tiger out into the open had met with failure, my associates were beginning to show signs of impatience. Transport a director and camera crew, accustomed to Hollywood actors, local topical events, and nothing more hazardous in the way of animal photography than a tame lion on a studio set, into the raw jungle of Malaya, and they are rather lost. They don't know what to expect next, and they are likely to become impatient when they find that you cannot order jungle animals around as you can movie actors or trained studio animals with keepers in attendance. Not that this worried me so much, for I determined at the outset to use the same patience in the making of wild animal pictures that I had always used in the collecting of animals for zoos.

We had already strained our time schedule pretty severely in attempting to get these tiger ground shots. We had been so confident of completing the work on this day that we had made definite arrangements with the native contractor to have his coolies on hand the very next morning to start scrapping our timber and sheet-iron wall. Also we had planned to move on up country just as soon as this work got under way. Postponing these pictures even for a day would mean a considerable amount of inconvenience and expense to everybody concerned.

So I decided that something had to be done and done quickly to get our stubborn animal actor out into the open. It was a situation that called for direct action, and it seemed obvious that the only course open to me was to get down into the enclosure and rout the tiger out myself.

I did not minimize the danger of such an enterprise. If the animal wanted to be nasty, he would have all the best of it in any encounter that might take place in the thick jungle area, for he could be practically on top of me before I would have a chance to defend myself. My intention, of course, was not to have any encounter with the beast, but merely to rout him out of the brush. Yet I must be prepared to defend myself if he should decide to charge me. And defense would not be easy in a place where the vegetation is so impenetrable that a person has to crawl or fight his way through it.

I placed a good deal of confidence in some flares with which our party happened to be equipped. A few days before, I had located a young leopard a few miles north of our temporary headquarters, and we had made some night pictures of the spotted cat, using flares to light up the vicinity in which we had treed him. We had transported a good supply of these brilliant torches with us from America and had taken a box of twenty-five from our base at Singapore up to the Johore camp. Five of the flares had remained unused after making our leopard shots.

These are what are known as two-minute flares—meaning that when you light one it burns steadily for that length of time. The ingredients are a highly powerful chemical mixture that when lighted by a fuse throws out a brilliant light to a radius of sixty or seventy feet, at the same time radiating an intense heat. As a matter of fact, these light-makers generate so much heat that if you bring one of them in contact with a piece of armor plate it will burn right into the hard metal. The flares are about two feet long and two inches in diameter, resembling a roman candle. The outer surface is of heavy cardboard, with a hollow place at the bottom to permit mounting on a pole.

These were the flares that I proposed to take with me into the enclosure. I decided to enter the brush carrying one of them, not so much to light up the dark interior as to protect myself against a possible charge. For if the tiger came at me, his onward rush could be stopped by a thrust toward him of the burning carbide.

On deciding to go into the brush I had asked Ali if he was afraid to go in with me. He replied, as I knew he would, "Wherever you go, *tuan,* I go." So we prepared the flares by cutting five poles, six to eight feet long, and fastening a flare on the end of each pole. Ali took the flares while I buckled on a heavy revolver—a weapon of maximum deadliness in close quarters—and took up my rifle, a .300 Savage loaded with 180-grain soft-nosed bullets. We lowered a long bamboo ladder into the enclosure from the top of the wall, and the two of us climbed down.

I have no desire to exaggerate the risk we were taking. There was a fair chance that it was no risk at all. It was quite possible the tiger would take to his heels the second we got anywhere near him. These wily cats, like all other denizens of the jungle, have an instinct that teaches discretion as the better part of valor. Under ordinary circumstances they will usually avoid too close contact with human beings. But, after all, a tiger is a tiger, and one can never be sure what these incalculable beasts will do. The best tactic, when dealing with them, is always to expect the unexpected.

This was the mental attitude with which Ali and I approached our task. We got down into the enclosure and worked cautiously over to the edge of the thicket, keeping a keen lookout for any movement in the high grass. I had my rifle ready for instantaneous use, although I certainly would not shoot unless it was absolutely necessary. Ali walked behind me, holding the sticks and a box of matches. I would light the first flare. His instructions were to keep his eyes glued on me, and the second my flare began to burn down he was to light another and hand it to me. I had impressed upon him that I did not want to be in the brush for even part of a second without a lighted flare.

I left my rifle leaning against a small tree, and, taking one of the sticks from Ali, I ignited the fuse, and we started into the real thicket. I kept poking the burning flare into the brush in front of me as we went in, first to the right and then to the left, in all directions. But one thing I had not figured on was that the dazzling brilliance of the torch was almost blinding to Ali and me. I could not see a foot ahead of my flare, and I did not like that at all, but I still felt that this burning brand with its intense heat and brilliant light was sufficient protection from a charge.

The first flare began to die down, and Ali lighted a second one and handed it to me. I had no more than started ahead with it when suddenly I heard a tremendous roar and a crashing of brush. The tiger was coming. He was making for me from a point at my left. I stepped back quickly in order to give myself more room in which to manipulate the flare, the idea being to use it as a means of warding off the charge. As I moved backward my right foot caught in a creeper, and I went down, flat on my back. In falling I dropped the pole and made a feverish grab for my revolver, but on account of the awkwardness of my position, I could not seem to get hold of it. The pole fell across my body, the burning end of it still blazing fiercely not three feet from my face. It all happened in an instant. Before I could make a move the tiger was almost on top of me, coming with a tremendous rush. Then suddenly, with a terrifying roar, he jumped—but instead of landing on me, he leaped clear over me and the sputtering torch.

I could see his striped belly as he went over. He had evidently come with a mad lunge through the heavy brush and then all at once, finding himself faced with that flare, had completely lost his head and jumped clear over me without actually knowing what he was doing. He was just as much in a state of panic as I was.

By the time I got to my feet, he had veered off into the heavy brush. That was okay with me. I had somehow got my revolver out of the holster—anyhow it was in my hand when I stood up, but I had no desire to shoot anything but pictures, and just at that moment my main wish was to get out of that brush.

I became conscious of Ali's presence, just behind me. He had witnessed the entire episode, apparently paralyzed with terror. Now he regained his voice and suggested weakly, "We go now, *tuan?*" I almost grinned at the expressive way he said those words. Both the words and the expression matched my feeling exactly. For now that it was all over I remembered to be frightened.

The whole business gave me the willies in retrospect. While it was actually happening I had been too numbed to have any emotions. Now I was scared stiff, and I didn't care who knew it. If ever a tiger had a chance to make a kill, this was the animal. In my helpless state on the ground he could have finished me in a flash. With one slash of his paw he could have ripped open my throat; the rest—the business of tearing me to pieces—would have been only a matter of seconds.

These things all went through my mind as Ali and I started backing out toward the tree where I had left my rifle.

Ali, following instructions, had lit another flare, mine having burned itself out. His hand trembled as he held the match, and his face was full of fear. Ali, let me add, is one of the bravest people who ever worked for me.

As we backed out, Ali held the flare in front while I gripped the revolver. I watched and listened for any movement in the brush ahead of us, for I half expected the animal to charge again before we were out. There was no evidence of him, however, and Ali and I both felt better as soon as we got back to my rifle.

Replacing my revolver in its holster, I picked up the rifle and held it at "ready" while I stopped to consider what our next move should be. It was obvious that this tiger was going to prove a difficult one to handle and that probably several days would be needed to get the ground shots we wanted.

For the time being, I decided, a quick retreat was indicated. Later on we would have to find some way of getting the animal back into a cage. Then we must thin out all the heavy jungle, chopping down much of the brush, so that when Mr. Tiger was put back into the enclosure, there would be no place for him to hide where our camera lenses would not reach him.

I regretted the difficulties this delay would make in our schedule, but obviously there was no other way. For the moment, our immediate necessity was to get out of the enclosure. Probably the striped foe was far over on the other side somewhere by now, and I hoped the cameramen had been able to get at least one or two flashes of him.

I nodded to Ali, indicating the line of retreat that I thought would be simplest. In fifty paces we were out of the heavy jungle, and as our fourth flare burned down I motioned to Ali not to light another, as it would be of no particular assistance. In this short grass, the cat could not attack us without my seeing him coming. I could have a second or two of grace if he decided to come back for more. We were in sight of the barricade now and began to feel ourselves practically out of danger. I relaxed my grip on the rifle and rested it at ease in the crook of my arm. In order to get to where the ladder had been placed, we still had to pass around one corner of the heavy brush, but that didn't worry us. My mind, in fact, was already occupied with the new arrangements that I would have to make in order to keep the expedition here until we could get the postponed pictures.

We arrived at the corner of the heavy brush and were within sight of the bamboo ladder. Then in a flash, without a flicker of warning, the tiger came bursting through a gap in the thicket. He was more like something that had been thrown through the air from a substantial distance than like an animal belonging on the ground.

Automatically I wheeled around to meet the charge, and automatically I lifted my rifle. There was no time to get it to my shoulder. I shot from the waist. By the time my mind reacted to the fact that the tiger was charging and was almost on top of me, my rifle had sped a 180-grain soft-nosed bullet on its way.

He was too close for a miss. The bullet tore its way into the upper left side of the tiger's chest, just as he reared up, with forelegs outstretched, claws spread, reaching for me. The force of the blow stopped him instantly, and he dropped with a shattered shoulder, thrashing in the brush practically at my feet. I jumped back a few steps and finished him off with a shot in the head.

My motion picture assistants all came down into the enclosure, now that the tiger was dead. We took a tape measure and measured the distance from the imprint of my foot in the soft ground, which showed where I stood at the time I fired, to the nearest front paw of the tiger where he lay. It was just twenty-four inches. If that wasn't a close call, I shall never have one.

Natives of Malaya are always overjoyed at the killing of a tiger. These fierce cats are their natural enemies, and they never fail to evince delight at the sight of one being destroyed. So the Malay men were all happy over the tiger's death.

I was not sure how I felt. It was the first tiger I had slain in the course of a long career that has involved my bringing back to this country, alive, over sixty tigers—Royal Bengal, Malayan, and Manchurian, which are now on view in zoos. More than once, in the course of trapping a tiger, I have thought it would be necessary to shoot to save myself or one of my assistants, but I had always managed to avoid pulling the trigger until now.

Late that afternoon we sent a group of choppers into the enclosure and had the brush thinned out so that the afternoon's performance would not have to be repeated.

A few days later another trap that I had put out yielded a fine tiger, and we got all the close-up shots we needed, showing his majesty the tiger walking, breaking into a run, drinking at a pool, and surveying the terrain about him, so we were able to tear down our temporary compound a couple of weeks after the shooting episode and move on up into Seremban, where the next few weeks were spent trapping and photographing black panthers.

Even a tame tiger may be a striped demon, as Frank Buck relates in Animals Are Like That! *(1940):*

An excellent illustration of the undependable nature of the tiger was a heartbreakingly chaotic scene I once witnessed in Manila, in a circus tent. It was not part of the show; it was murder, committed in cold blood, if ever I saw it.

Now, tiger cubs are like kittens. They are cute, playful, appealing. This story concerns one of the cutest, most amusing, and tamest tiger cubs I've ever seen. He was one of a pair that belonged to my friend the sultan of Johore, who one day over drinks in the Raffles Hotel bar in Singapore offered them to me.

At that time the Fillis Circus, which toured the larger cities in the Far East, was playing in Singapore. On the afternoon that I was invited to tea at the sultan's palace at Johore Bahru, Mr. and Mrs. Fillis were also invited. Mrs. Fillis was so completely entranced with the cubs that the sultan wanted to satisfy her womanish longing for the sweet babies, and I agreed that she should have them. The sultan, in generous exchange, having first offered them to me, offered me anything I might want in his entire menagerie.

I'm used to disappointments and unexpected events in this highly adventurous business, so no one connected with the story realized my disappointment at the time. I very much wanted those cubs, although, as I was grateful to the sultan for many other favors, I did not let him know how disappointed I was. At the time I thought it was just part of a run of disappointing luck. Now I see I was wrong. The luck proved to be all with me.

The cubs went to the Fillis Circus, which continued its show dates from Singapore to Kuala Lumpur, Penang, and Ipoh, where suddenly Fillis died. His wife couldn't run the show alone, and bodily it was shipped back to Singapore for auction. Once more I decided to try for the cubs. Once again I was disappointed, as another friend, Stewart Tait, an American showman headquartered in Manila, was most anxious to get them. I couldn't see bidding against him very strongly. The cubs, after all, were now partially trained and promised to be first-rate performers. They were worth much more to him considering this—and if I got them they'd probably end up in an untheatrical life in some zoo anyway. So for the second time I gave them up.

The third time I saw them was three years later in Manila. Now full grown, they were professional performers. And Tait, who remembered I'd wanted them too on that day when his bid took them, invited me over to see the striped marvels. They were powerful beasts now but gentle as kittens. We put our hands through the bars of their cage to scratch their ears as they rolled over and purred like a couple of overgrown house cats.

I was more than ever anxious to see their act, in which they were put through their paces by an attractive Filipino girl whose beauty and skill in their handling made this a top act in the Tait circus.

I joined most enthusiastically in the noisy general applause for the girl and the two tawny beasts—here was beauty and the beast at their top best. The striped stars leaped gracefully to their pedestals, sat beautifully motionless; the girl, slightly in front of them, bowed. Suddenly, without even moving from its pedestal, the tiger on her right reached out and caught the back of the girl's neck in its wide jaws and sank its teeth in, lifting the slight Filipino off the floor. With a quick twist her neck snapped, and Stripes dropped the lifeless body to the floor. It happened in two seconds—before seeing eyes could believe.

You can fancy the panic that followed, an audience two minutes before enthusiastic and admiring, now stricken with unbelievable horror. While there was no danger to them from the perfectly calm Mr. Stripes, they tore toward the exits, causing general strife. A Filipino detective sent a bullet through the again-well-behaved animal's head.

References

Anonymous. "Talk of the Town." *The New Yorker*. September 14, 1946, pp. 19–20.

Anonymous. "Frank Buck Dies." *New York Times*. March 26, 1950, p. 92.

Anonymous. "Edward Anthony, Writer, Dies." *New York Times*. April 18, 1971, p. 40.

Anonymous. "Buck Sued over Jungle Film." *New York Times*. March 3, 1933, p. 13.

Anonymous. "Ferrin Fraser, 65, Writer for Radio." *New York Times*. April 2, 1969, p. 47.

Anonymous. "Carol Weld." *New York Times*. April 1, 1979, p. 34.

Anonymous. *Indonesian Phrase Book and Dictionary*. Berlitz Publishing Company, Oxford, England, 1994.

Encyclopedia Britannica. Chicago, 1986.

Johnson, Helen L., and Johnson, Rossall J. *Indonesian-English English-Indonesian Dictionary*. Hippocrene Books, New York, 1990.

Oey, Thomas, and Hutton, Wendy. *Everyday Malay*. Passport Books, Chicago, 1994.

Silva, Lee A. "Frank Buck: He Brought 'Em Back Alive." *Petersen's Hunting*. August 1987, pp. 80–104.

Sragow, Michael. Review of *King Kong*. *The New Yorker*. August 24, 1998.

Weber, Bruce. "To the Zoo? In the Cold? But of Course." *New York Times*. January 3, 1997, C1.

Wojowasito, S. *Kamus Umum* (General Dictionary). *Indonesia-Inggeris*. Penerbit C.V. Pengarang, Bandung, West Java, Indonesia, 1976.

Some information and newspaper clippings on Frank Buck and Amy Leslie are from the Billy Rose Theater Collection, New York Public Library. The editor wishes to thank Dr. Tony Go for his help in correcting Frank Buck's flawed Malay. A few words in Buck's original text, although perfectly appropriate in 1930, might be considered infelicitous today. These words have been removed from the present edition, and in certain instances synonyms have been substituted.

Index